Russia at the Crossroads

The 26th Congress of the CPSU

*Rand–Columbia Conference
on the 26th Party Congress,
Washington, D.C.
April 23–25, 1981*

*Published under the auspices of
the Rand Corporation
and the Russian Institute, Columbia University*

Russia at the Crossroads

The 26th Congress of the CPSU

Edited by
SEWERYN BIALER and THANE GUSTAFSON

London
GEORGE ALLEN & UNWIN
Boston   Sydney

© The Russian Institute, Columbia University and the
Rand Corporation, 1982
This book is copyright under the Berne Convention.
No reproduction without permission. All rights reserved.

George Allen & Unwin (Publishers) Ltd,
40 Museum Street, London WC1A 1LU, UK

George Allen & Unwin (Publishers) Ltd,
Park Lane, Hemel Hempstead, Herts HP2 4TE, UK

Allen & Unwin Inc.,
9 Winchester Terrace, Winchester, Mass. 01890, USA

George Allen & Unwin Australia Pty Ltd,
8 Napier Street, North Sydney, NSW 2060, Australia

First published in 1982

British Library Cataloguing in Publication Data

Rand-Columbia Conference *(1981: Washington, D.C.)*
  Russia at the crossroads.
1. Soviet Union – Politics and government – 1953–
– Congresses
I. Bialer, Seweryn   II. Gustafson, Thane
947.085′3   DK274
ISBN 0-04-329039-6

Library of Congress Cataloging in Publication Data

Main entry under title:
  Russia at the crossroads.
Includes index.
1. Kommunisticheskaia partiia Sovetskogo Soiuza. S″ezd (26th : 1981 :
Moscow, R.S.F.S.R.)   2. Soviet Union – Economic Policy – 1981
– Congresses.   3. Soviet Union – Politics and government – 1953–
– Congresses.   I. Bialer, Seweryn.   II. Gustafson, Thane.
JN6598.K5   1981b   947.085′3   82-1599
ISBN 0-04-329039-6   AACR2

Set in 11 on 12 point Times by Computape (Pickering) Ltd
and printed in Great Britain
by Mackays of Chatham

Contents

		page	
	List of Contributors		viii
	Introduction *Seweryn Bialer and Thane Gustafson*		1
1	The International and Internal Contexts of the 26th Party Congress *Seweryn Bialer*		7
2	Changes in Soviet Elite Composition *Jerry Hough*		39
3	Reformism, Conservatism, and Leadership Authority at the 26th Party Congress *George Breslauer*		65
4	The 11th Five-Year Plan, 1981–85 *Daniel Bond and Herbert Levine*		87
5	Soviet Agricultural Plans for 1981–85 *Douglas Diamond*		108
6	Soviet Energy Policy: From Big Coal to Big Gas *Thane Gustafson*		121
7	Reform and Technological Innovation in the 11th Five-Year Plan *Nancy Nimitz*		140
8	The 26th Party Congress and Soviet Foreign Policy *Robert Legvold*		156
9	The Soviet Stake in Eastern Europe *Charles Gati*		178
10	The 26th Party Congress Conference: The Soviet Union in a Time of Uncertainty *Richard Coffman and Michael Klecheski*		192
	Index		220

List of Contributors

SEWERYN BIALER: Ruggles Professor of Political Science and Director, Research Institute on International Change, Columbia University

DANIEL BOND: Director, Centrally Planned Economies Projects, Wharton EFA, Inc.

GEORGE BRESLAUER: Associate Professor of Political Science, University of California at Berkeley

RICHARD COFFMAN: Doctoral candidate in the Department of Political Science, Columbia University, specializing in contemporary Soviet politics

DOUGLAS DIAMOND: Research Analyst with the Office of Economic Research, CIA

CHARLES GATI: Professor of Political Science, Union College; Visiting Professor of Political Science and Research Associate, Research Institute on International Change, Columbia University

THANE GUSTAFSON: Research Associate, Social Science Department, Rand Corporation.

JERRY HOUGH: Professor of Political Science, Duke University

MICHAEL KLECHESKI: Doctoral candidate in the Department of Political Science, Columbia University, specializing in contemporary Soviet politics

ROBERT LEGVOLD: Senior Fellow and Director of the Soviet Project, Council on Foreign Relations

HERBERT LEVINE: Professor of Economics, University of Pennsylvania

NANCY NIMITZ: Research Associate, Economics Department, Rand Corporation

Introduction

One natural way to describe the 26th Party Congress and the atmosphere of Soviet politics at the beginning of the 1980s is to use the image, worn as it is, of the ominous calm before the storm. While outside the Kremlin Palace of Congresses the barometer of social and economic indicators slid downward and the horizon rumbled to the west and south, inside the portals the party elite sat in outwardly untroubled serenity. At the moment when the country stood before some of the most difficult problems it has faced since World War II, the Party leaders chose to stage an elaborate nonevent. So familiar were the faces, so well worn the official speeches, that political life seemed unnaturally suspended. This curious calm, and what it may presage for the decade ahead, are the central themes of the present collection of essays on the 26th Party Congress.

The papers on which these chapters are based were initially presented at a conference held in Washington from April 23 through 25, 1981, sponsored jointly by the Rand Corporation and the Russian Institute of Columbia University, under the aegis of the Ford Foundation. The immediate purpose of the conference was to analyze the main developments at the 26th Party Congress of the CPSU, held two months before in Moscow, as well as the Main Guidelines of the 11th Five-Year Plan, which were adopted at the same time. But the conference participants were also asked to use the occasion to review the events of the last five years and to look ahead. As the reader will see, the authors more than fulfilled their mission; and as a result, this collection conveys not only the paradoxes of the present Soviet scene, but also something of the range of Western disagreements about how to intepret them.

The conference participants were of two minds on nearly all of the major questions addressed: Is the 11th Five-Year Plan a realistic response to the economic problems now gathering before the country, or a failure to face reality? Do recent personnel changes in the political elite reflect a tired *fin de règne* or the beginnings of the succession struggle? Are recent reform efforts real or phony? Is the present "bifurcation of détente" a symptom of conservative lack of imagination in foreign policy or striking evidence, on the contrary, that the Soviet leaders are able to see historic opportunities and pursue them? Is the long

Soviet hesitation in Poland a failure of nerve or a sophisticated waiting game showing realism and self-assurance? In the chapters devoted to domestic, economic, and foreign policy, the reader will find a great diversity of opinions. One would not be surprised to learn that a similar diversity divides the Soviet's political elite too, and even the Politburo itself.

When people disagree over specific issues of this kind, they are implicitly raising more fundamental questions. The first of these is whether the recent Soviet difficulties actually presage a crisis, and if so, of what kind. The second question is whether the problems of the 1980s will require measures drastically different from the ones the Soviet regime has used in the past. The third is whether the Soviet leaders are also asking these questions, and if so, whether in their behavior at the 26th Party Congress they were answering them or avoiding them. So striking was the variety of views among the conference participants on these questions that the editors commissioned an additional chapter for inclusion in the collection, devoted to an analysis of the major viewpoints and their implications. The reader will find this essay at the end of the collection.

In contrast, there is one opinion that all the authors share completely: In the Soviet Union of the 1980s, economic and political issues, and domestic and foreign ones, are more intimately connected to one another than at any previous period in Soviet history. Soviet policy-makers face not only the complexity of an advanced, late-industrial economy, but also unprecedented shortages of natural resources, capital, and manpower. Not since the 1920s has the Kremlin had to wrestle with the problem of economic stagnation. Not since the First Five-Year Plan have the Soviet leaders been so dependent on the West for technology and industrial equipment as they will be during the 1980s, especially in energy. And most important of all, the economic strains of the 1980s will bring home to the leaders the full costs of their military programs and the burdens of empire, raising the issue of military spending for the first time since the early 1960s. In coming years domestic politics will be shaped by economic and foreign issues more than ever before.

If this is true, then what are the political consequences, especially for the impending succession? It is not that foreign-policy and economic issues have been irrelevant to succession politics in the past. On the contrary, one need only recall the role of the industrialization debate of the early 1920s, or that of the "war scare" of 1927 in Stalin's rise, or that of consumer goods and peaceful coexistence in Khrushchev's fortunes in the 1950s, to be reminded that economic and foreign-policy issues have figured prominently in past succession struggles. But Western observers have never quite agreed on their relative importance. Many have held the view that policy issues are masks or screens, behind which the real power game is played for the only thing that counts—the control of the party apparatus. Thus after disposing of the Left with the arguments of the Right, Stalin disposed of the Right with the arguments of the Left, manipulating issues like marionettes at the front of the stage while the real action took place in the wings. In the competition for power, this view runs, the "politics of position" counts for a great deal more than the "politics of policy."

But already in the 1960s and 1970s the role of policy issues was considerably different from what it had been under Stalin and Khrushchev. Brezhnev's slow consolidation of power seems to have required considerably more than a seizure of the levers of the apparatus; indeed, to this day we do not know any details about how Brezhnev's control over the "levers of position" is exercised, through whom, or by what unwritten rules. But most Western scholars feel that much of his victory was due to his ability to build a consensus within the Party elite around major policies, particularly in agriculture and defense spending, as well as his success in reassuring the political elite that, if he were allowed to take control of the levers of power, he would use them responsibly and moderately.

When the issues are tough, consensus is especially hard to build, and in the 1980s they will be so urgent and constraining that choices will be especially hard. What are the implications for the succession? Will the next Soviet leader build his position around slow persuasion and attention to consensus, as Brezhnev seems to have done? Will there be open conflict and competition for control of key bureaucratic positions? Will the apparent "routinization" and stabilization of promotion within the party and the government continue, or will there be a return to political clientelism at all levels of the hierarchy, and a renewal of the merry-go-round that we saw under Khrushchev? If the succession struggle comes to a contest between those whose claim is based primarily on policy expertise or new ideas to "get the country moving again," and those whose strength lies in control of personnel in the apparatus, Western analysts would be hard put to say who might win. Every Soviet succession in the past has surprised the West, because it has turned on some unexpected twist in the underlying "laws" of power formation. This time around, can Western analysts do better? Is it possible to move beyond tote-sheet speculation about individual contenders in the succession sweepstakes to a more systematic focus on sources of power?

This question is closely connected to the issues raised by the Conference participants. The sources of power from which the next Soviet leader will fashion his rise will undoubtedly depend a great deal on the external circumstances, that is, on whether the times favor "crisis politics" or "politics as usual," major reforms or incremental tinkering, daring or caution. In other words, one of the most important tasks facing Western analysts in the next few years is to think hard about the *political* implications, both domestic and foreign, of the economic and social problems that we see looming before the Soviet leadership. There was a good deal of self-criticism at the conference over the participants' failure to address these questions more directly than they did; but in fairness to them it should be said that what we are describing here is a long-term agenda for new research and reflection, one for which a careful appraisal of the 26th Party Congress is necessarily only a first step.

One deceptively simple question that requires careful thought is how bad things have to get before one can speak of systemic crisis. Most political systems, after all, face environments that with a little bad luck could easily turn catastrophic. Most politicians and advisers divide their time between fearing the worst and hoping for the best, all the while trying to steer a course that assumes a world somewhere in between. Most of them manage to cope. Unless we are willing to assume that the Soviet political system has lost all capacity to respond effectively to changes around it—a failing that the Brezhnev regime, slow-moving as it has been, does not demonstrate—we must expect that the Soviet leaders will begin by experimenting with "coping policies," of which the currently more relaxed policy toward private plots may be a forerunner. Another example of a relatively easy-to-adopt coping policy would be a partial legalization of the "second economy" in light consumer goods, for which there is ample precedent in the New Economic Policy of the 1920s; this might enable the military leaders to maintain current levels of military spending. Such a legalization need not be official; it would be enough to issue a quiet order to relax prosecution for "economic crimes," and private enterprise would take care of the rest.

What these examples suggest, in answer to the question raised above, is that what distinguishes "stringent times" from "systemic crisis" is less the overall performance statistics than what the regime does about them to *keep its basic sources of stability from eroding*. In the end, that is a political rather than a strictly economic question, and there is not necessarily a direct, linear connection between the two, but rather a complex linkage. Throughout its history the Soviet regime has shown itself resourceful at maintaining, and when necessary reinforcing, the sources of its political stability and power, even in much more difficult times than the country faces today. So far, the Brezhnev regime has lived in—by Soviet standards—unusually benign times. Its only domestic crisis has been in agriculture, and it has managed to deal with it (more or less successfully) chiefly by throwing large sums of money at it, perhaps as much as $800 billion in the last fifteen years, but otherwise by approaching the problems of the countryside in much the traditional ways. In the 1980s capital and other resources will be too short to deal with other problems in the same "extensive" way. The resourcefulness of Brezhnev's successors will be tested as Brezhnev's was not.

Consequently, foremost on the agenda for future work is careful thought about the effects of economic difficulties on the Soviet regime's sources of stability and on power formation within the political elite. Here the major question is how the economic and social difficulties of the 1980s will affect the roles and powers of the Party apparatus. For two generations the party has owed much of its power and legitimacy to the fact that, through brokerage and bargaining at all levels, it offsets the worst side-effects of the command economy. Thanks partly to the party's daily and ubiquitous intervention, supply bottlenecks are alleviated and the most important targets are given priority. For two generations this system has worked quite successfully, on the whole, and the Party's role enjoys widespread legitimacy. But if the leaders are unable to get the economy moving again, what will become of that most important of all sources of political stability?

The same point holds as we try to foresee how the Soviet Union's domestic difficulties may constrain its foreign policies. In the past the Soviet regime has been quite successful at insulating its foreign policies from its domestic ones; indeed, maintaining such insulation has been an objective in itself, which explains much of Soviet behavior in foreign trade and commercial relations with the West in the second half of the 1970s. Still, there are limits to the price the Soviets can pay to maintain this insulation. To take just one example, in the last two decades the Soviets have been able to derive major diplomatic advantages from timely sales of oil to third-world countries such as Brazil and India, to say nothing of regular support to client states such as Cuba and Vietnam. If Soviet oil output declines drastically, the cost of this support will rise, perhaps to the point of forcing the Soviets to terminate it altogether. That is an example of the "burden of empire" that the Soviet Union may find more difficult to carry in years to come. But what do we know about the connections between internal oil needs and its availability to support Soviet foreign policy? Is it possible to be more precise than we have been so far?

The danger facing us as students of Soviet affairs in years ahead is that we will be tempted to make dramatic predictions about the effects of the Soviets' mounting internal problems; and as we are already seeing, those predictions will be quickly picked up by Western policy-makers and integrated into Western diplomatic strategy. Yet without a better idea of the connections between causes and effects, between economic growth and military budgets, between military budgets and consumption levels, between consumption levels and political stability, between stability and foreign policy—connections that are as much political as anything—we will be doing little more than crying wolf. But that is the subject of another conference and of another book.

The editors would like to take this opportunity to thank the many people whose valuable contributions made this conference and book possible. First, we are especially grateful to Dr. Abraham Becker, who more than anyone else was responsible for turning the conference from an idea into reality. The Ford Foundation, which provided financial support, made the entire effort possible. In addition, we would like to express appreciation to the commentators and discussants who contributed their thoughts and criticism, providing valuable guidance to the authors as they revised their papers for publication: Arnold Horelick, Grey Hodnett, Myron Rush, Joseph Berliner, Peter Solomon, Abram Bergson, Gale Johnson, Robert Campbell, Gertrude Schroeder, Loren Graham, Edward Hewett, William Hyland, Harry Gelman, and Ross Johnson. We are particularly grateful for the highly informative and stimulating panel discussion led by Benjamin Lambeth, Fritz Ermarth, Richard Pipes, and Marshall Shulman. Lastly, the conference could not have been conducted so successfully without the able and devoted help of the staffs of the Rand Corporation and the Columbia University Research Institute on International Change, especially Molly Coleman, Richard Coffman, Michael Klecheski, Guido Ianiero, and MarJean Knokey.

Seweryn Bialer
Thane Gustafson

1

The International and Internal Contexts of the 26th Party Congress

Seweryn Bialer

The Brezhnev era is coming to an end. In all probability, the 26th Party Congress will prove to be the last one at which Leonid Il'ich and his aged cronies successfully defend their positions of power. Memories of similar predictions about the 25th Party Congress alert us to the need for caution in predicting such an imminent departure. Yet our expectations of the approaching end of the Brezhnev era are based not only on the passing of the Brezhnev generation, which must finally occur. Equally significant are the rapid changes that are taking place in the domestic and international conditions and circumstances which shaped the character of the past decade and a half. Thus, even if Brezhnev and his contemporaries were to remain in power for another year or two, dramatic changes in the international and internal environment of the Soviet Union since the time when Brezhnev was at the height of his rule will deeply influence the perceptions, behavior, and policies of the Soviet regime.

While the 26th Party Congress has shown some recognition of the changing international and domestic environment, its attempts to grapple with the resulting issues have been minimal. The CPSU will not have this luxury much longer. In this paper, I would like to discuss the changing circumstances under which the 26th Party Congress convened and to identify the problems and opportunities which the Soviet leadership should have faced and which it will have to face in the near and medium-range future.

The Brezhnev era, particularly from 1965 to approximately 1976, will probably go down in history as the most successful period of Soviet international and domestic development.

Internationally, the Soviet Union fulfilled its major postwar dream—achieving strategic parity with the United States and becoming a truly global power. It was a period when Soviet rule over its empire was legitimized internationally, and when the Brezhnev Doctrine was developed to secure continuation of that empire by any means. Although unable to regulate its relations with China, the Soviet Union was able to take advantage of that country's cataclysmic internal strife by deploying stragetic tactical and conventional forces on its eastern border, thereby changing the military geography of the area and insuring against any surprises from the other Communist giant. It was a period of increased influence in the international arena for the Soviet Union, and, at the same time, of economic and political decline for its chief adversary, the United States. The Soviet Union was able to translate its newly won power and recognition into a new relationship with the Western alliance—particularly the United States—which was called détente and which constituted a promising cornerstone of Soviet long-range strategy. Détente promised economic benefits, but most of all an expansion of Soviet global influence without the danger of confrontation with the United States and its allies; it also promised a further swing in the balance of global influence and power in favor of the Soviet Union.

Domestically, this was a period of great stability of leadership and politics in the Soviet Union, where a system based on elite accommodation, compromise and bargaining fostered a tranquil political climate. It was a period when the Soviet leadership was able to deal successfully with an unprecedented escalation of dissent among elements of the intelligentsia, and to assure a relatively high degree of political and social stability. On the economic front, the Soviet leadership, for the first time in its history, was able to pursue successfully and simultaneously a policy of guns, butter and growth. It was a period when the Soviet regime was able to avoid any significant degree of systemic crisis within its social and political system.

During the mid-1970s, however, these domestic and international developmental trends were reversed, with the previously favorable situation beginning to unravel by the end of the decade. Thus, when the 26th Party Congress convened it faced a number of unfavorable developments which could turn dangerous in the near and medium-range future.

If I had to select a motto to describe the Soviet Union as it enters the 1980s, it would be the saying of a European statesman in the interwar period: "Russia is never as strong as she looks,

Russia is never as weak as she looks." Indeed, Soviet developments are paradoxical, marked by the following weaknesses and strengths, assets and liabilities:

- Today, the Soviet Union is more powerful than it ever was, and yet it is more insecure than it has been during the last ten to fifteen years. It is this curious mixture of insecurity and power that lends a special flavor to Soviet foreign policy and international behavior.
- The Soviet Union has become a global power feared by friend and foe alike, partly because of the successes of its model of rule and development. This model, however, is increasingly considered less relevant by both Marxists and non-Marxists, and the Soviet socioeconomic and political system is held in greater contempt than ever.
- The Soviet Union's expansion is at the peak of its historical evolution, but in Poland, its own imperial backyard, the Soviet Union faces the greatest challenge of its postwar history. The Soviet Union retains its control of an extensive internal and external empire in which its political and military dominance is still strongly pronounced. Yet it has ceased to draw economic benefits from that empire, and must even support the empire economically. A curious situation has thus developed in which the East European standard of living is and will continue to be higher than that in the Soviet Union, and in which the Uzbek peasant lives far better than his Russian counterpart. Moreover, the economic viability of the East European empire depends to a large extent on economic help from and intercourse with Western adversaries of the Soviet Union.
- Although Soviet foreign policy in the Brezhnev era has realized significant gains in international influence, at the same time it has encountered major failures and significant reverses. Such an ambiguous balance of gains and losses leaves the Soviets with undiminished appetites, but also with a sense of deep frustration.
- During the 1960s and 1970s, the Soviet Union built its foreign policy on the cornerstone of competitive accommodation with the West, particularly with the United States. But as it enters the 1980s, this cornerstone has begun to erode; the Soviet Union now faces the greatest challenge of the last twenty years to its global ambitions.
- During the past two decades, the Soviet Union experienced the best economic, political and social period in its history, and

its population enjoyed the fastest growth in its standard of living. But in the 1980s the Soviet Union faces probably the worst period in its post-Stalin history, typified by the onset of a health crisis unprecedented in the twentieth century among industrialized countries.

The 26th Party Congress convened, then, under these paradoxical conditions. The Soviet Union enters the 1980s at least partly conscious of these paradoxes and the resulting dilemmas, but lacking a long-range vision about how to resolve them.

The international situation confronting the Soviet Union is full of uncertainties which have cast its foreign policy, developed during the early 1970s and pursued throughout the decade, into disarray. While Soviet foreign policy requires more than simple adjustment, there is as yet no sign of a necessary basic rethinking of the course to be followed.

What were the major premises on which Soviet foreign policy of the 1970s was constructed?

1 The Soviets assumed that despite several zigzags in U.S. policy, détente with the United States would remain irreversible. It was further assumed that America's pre-Vietnam assertiveness could not be restored and that, under the pressures of the changing military balance, the inward-directed mood of American public opinion and the demands from America's European allies—particularly West Germany—Soviet competition with the United States would remain controlled, with elements of cooperation retained.
2 They assumed that the tilt toward the Soviet Union in the military balance established in the 1970s would continue. The Soviets expected that, while particular adjustments in the military balance might be attempted by the West, there would be no new effort by the United States to regain strategic superiority and that significant attempts to redress the European theater balance would be successfully resisted by America's allies.
3 They assumed that they would be able to translate their newly won military status into power and influence in those areas of the world which are outside of the great powers' recognized spheres of influence without risking confrontation with the United States or its allies.
4 The Soviets assumed that they would continue to exploit targets of opportunity presented by the turmoil in the less

developed countries. They regarded no area of the world to be off-limits to the spread of their influence.
5   They assumed that the balance in Europe would be frozen on both sides, and that while no major changes in Soviet influence in Western Europe could be expected, no major dangers to the stability of the Soviet East European empire would develop.
6   The Soviet Union expected to be able to bear indefinitely the burden of both its expanding role as a global power and its empire without inducing severe economic constraints at home, without violating the existing economic system of planning and management, and without endangering the social and political stability of its home base.
7   They assumed that their expansionist policies would preclude neither the expansion of economic cooperation with the West nor the influx of advanced foreign technology and credits to the Soviet Eastern bloc and the Soviet homeland itself.

The Soviet Union is facing today a United States that has largely left behind its post-Vietnam and post-Watergate doubts and uncertainties. It is facing a new administration whose policies toward the Soviet Union and the world may be a major departure from those of its predecessors in their assertiveness in the international arena and their willingness to steer a collision course with the Soviet Union where vital interests are concerned. There is a high probability of a change in the direction of the balance of military power from that which prevailed in the 1970s, and the Soviet Union may be compelled to undertake a new large-scale arms race with the West at a time when it can ill afford the necessary increased expenditures. The Soviet Union confronts a China which is no longer pursuing a self-destructive course of permanent revolution, but is concentrating on modernization and seeking a virtual alliance with the United States, Japan, and NATO. These problems are complicated by a situation in Afghanistan more troublesome than the Soviets had expected. Even more dangerous is the situation in Poland, the pivotal country in the Soviet empire. The Polish situation has incalculable implications for the future of both the Soviet empire and the Soviet Union itself, regardless of what course of action is adopted.

Presently, Soviet foreign policy is in disarray. Because the foreign policy concepts which the Soviets developed in the early 1970s have collapsed, there is an imperative need to adjust policy to the new international realities. Even more crucial is the need to replace the 1970s version of détente with the United States with a new policy which will guide the Soviet quest for security and expansion without confrontation.

Why did détente between the Soviet Union and the United States collapse? One can assign blame for this development to both sides, and provide an impressive list of the legitimate grievances of each country. However, something more important than specific errors and grievances lies at the heart of the problem. Fundamentally, the collapse of détente is rooted in the basic incompatibility between the concepts of détente held by both sides, and in the basic divergence of expectations regarding the effects that détente should have.

The Americans assumed that they could moderate both Soviet arms spending and Soviet behavior through the creation of a web of arms control and cultural, political and economic relations. The Soviets understood détente as the final recognition by the United States of the Soviet Union's achievement of strategic parity. Furthermore, the Soviets assumed that this military parity could be translated into global political parity with the United States. More specifically, they believed that while détente required a freeze on existing spheres of influence in Europe, it left the Soviet Union the right to expand in an unrestricted manner, even through the use of its own or proxy military forces, into those areas of the world outside the superpowers' spheres of influence which they considered open to unlimited competition. It was these two basically different concepts of détente that accounted for the mutual lack of consciousness of how one's own actions affect those of the other. By the end of the 1970s, these differences led to the irreconcilable gap between what each side expected from détente and what it actually achieved. The Soviet Union recognized that the United States did not share the Soviet image of détente as providing an authorization for expansion into areas of opportunity without risk of confrontations and other attendant dangers. It thus became clear to the Soviets that they could not rely on détente to preserve the evolution of a trend in the balance of military power which favored the Soviet side. The United States, in turn, recognized that if détente did not curtail Soviet military spending and limit Soviet expansionist drives in the third world, then it made little sense to continue with it.

Except in the most narrow sense, the détente policies of both the United States and the Soviet Union have failed to influence significantly the international behavior of the other as originally anticipated. The American failure to influence Soviet behavior has left unanswered the questions of whether the original policy premises were wrong and whether Soviet international behavior can be influenced by American policy. In light of détente's failure, one is tempted to say that these premises were wrong and that Soviet foreign policy is expansionist and not susceptible to influence through a sophisticated combination of incentives and disincentives. Yet such a view has a serious flaw. It does not take into consideration the fact that the arsenal of incentives and disincentives at American disposal in the 1970s was extremely limited and ineffectually used. Most important was the waning of both American power and the willingness to use it against the Soviets. It is a simple but essential truth that incentives for moderating Soviet behavior will not be effective in the absence of the high probability of the employment of powerful disincentives. Yet the United States never even made a serious attempt to apply those incentives at its command. On the American side, the fallacy of détente lay in the implied belief that one could get something from the Soviets for nothing. Moreover, it is at least questionable whether the American social situation, national character and political process can sustain any policy that seeks to strike a balance between competition and cooperation, without creating an atmosphere of either national disarmament or national belligerence. While the United States is able to fight its foes, and often is able to cooperate with its friends, it has a difficult time simultaneously cooperating and competing with its foes. Because the Soviets do not encounter this difficulty, their air of implied innocence regarding the failure of détente with the United States may be more real, and more genuinely felt, than we are inclined to think.

The American election and the assumption of the presidency by Ronald Reagan and his team open a new chapter in Soviet-American relations. Although we know that the general mood of public and political opinion in the United States moved clearly in an anti-Soviet direction, and that the new president has strong views about the alleged weaknesses of the Carter administration in resisting Soviet expansionism, we have only a very dim outline of what President Reagan's policies toward the Soviet Union might be. Certainly, the new president and Congress will increase the effort to strengthen America's defenses and its ability to conduct an interventionist policy. Yet, within these parameters, at least two basic variants of the evolving Soviet-American relationship are possible.

According to the first, more optimistic variant, a state of "soft détente" can be achieved in U.S.-Soviet relations. A thaw can set in while America increases its military spending, SALT negotiations resume and proceed to a point where a possible interim agreement may be reached. Such an agreement may, for example, keep in place the restrictions imposed by the protocols of the nonratifiable SALT II agreement, while long-range negotiations on SALT III are taking place. The Theater Nuclear Forces (TNF) and MBFR negotiations, with the participation of Europe, continue. The momentum of the last years of the Carter administration which brought China and America closer together slows down, and America reassesses its military relations with China, particularly the question of deliveries of militarily significant technology and even military equipment to China. In the economic field, more constructive, businesslike relations are established. America becomes once again a major partner in trade and credit relations with the USSR, but only if the Soviets do not engage in new expansionist adventures. The Afghan issue, where I see almost no chance of Soviet withdrawal or of neutralization of Soviet influence, nevertheless is no longer a hindrance to the improvement of relations with the United States—President Reagan's rhetoric notwithstanding. At this moment, as President Reagan concludes his first hundred days in office, this first variant in the development of the U.S.-Soviet relationship seems unlikely, but it is not impossible. The Soviets, who know that a 1972-style détente cannot be restored, would still prefer the resumption of a "regulated" relationship with the United States to prevent the unnecessary and frightening threat of conflict and confrontation.

The second variant, which we would call pessimistic but probably closer to reality, assumes that a freeze in U.S.-Soviet relations continues and probably deepens. Tensions between the United States and the Soviet Union increase as the United States begins to rearm. The SALT process is abandoned in practice, if not in words, and the Soviets renounce SALT II restrictions. The grain embargo is reimposed and trade restrictions kept in place. The Soviet Union responds to American rearmament by increasing its own military spending. The stiffening American resolve to resist Soviet expansionism in the third world, along with the inevitable appearance of new targets for such expansionism, heightens the danger of confrontation. Despite President Reagan's sympathies with Taiwan, his administration maintains the momentum of broadening military relations with the People's Republic of China, a process which results in a military alliance.

Four variables crucially influence which of the two variants, or their combination, will evolve in U.S.-Soviet relations. The first concerns the situation in Afghanistan. The second, which concerns Western Europe's position between the superpowers, is a critical and potentially moderating variable. The third concerns developments in the Persian Gulf area and the possible eruption of crises there which would involve the Soviet Union and which would be extremely difficult to control. The fourth key variable concerns the situation in Poland and the eventual Soviet response.

The Soviet Union is entering the 1980s with an unresolved problem in Afghanistan. There has been much dispute in the West regarding the meaning of the Soviet Afghan adventure, particularly the question of whether it was a defensive or offensive move. Much of this dialogue is misconceived because it confuses the problem of Soviet intentions in invading Afghanistan with the problem of the consequences of that invasion. It is probably right to assume that the Soviet invasion was a defensive measure, intended to prevent the disintegration of a semi-satellite regime, avoid the creation of another fundamentalist Muslim republic on the Soviet border, and minimize the growing Soviet sense of encirclement by unfriendly states. But the consequences of the invasion were largely offensive in nature: the Soviet Union changed the balance of military power in the vital Persian Gulf region. Moreover, the lack of restraint displayed in the invasion intimidated many third-world countries, particularly Pakistan. The Soviet Union has thus projected the image of a determined and arrogant world power whom the weak should try to accommodate in the absence of protection from the United States and its allies. This intimidating effect in the third-world is much more important in its repercussions than the anti-Soviet feeling evoked in the United Nations and among the Muslim countries. The Afghan adventure remains a low-risk operation for the Soviets, who can bear its direct costs indefinitely, unless the United States escalates those costs dramatically by massive deliveries of antitank and antihelicopter weapons to the Afghani rebels—a course of action which for many reasons remains highly unlikely. One cannot foresee a solution to the Afghan problem that will enable the Soviet Union both to preserve the security of its southern border and to withdraw its troops without losing face. For the Americans the Soviet presence in Afghanistan will continue to constitute a major obstacle to the redirection of East-West relations toward greater accommodation and more regulated competition.

The second crucial variable affecting Soviet-American relations is Western Europe's response to the invasion of Afghanistan. In contrast to U.S.-Soviet relations, Soviet relations with Western Europe—particularly the Federal Republic of Germany—were salvaged from the collapse of détente. In all probability this relationship is replacing détente with the United States as the cornerstone of Soviet foreign policy. For the Soviets, recent developments in the Western alliance and the state of East-West relations provide a silver lining for the adventure in Afghanistan. The Reagan administration has inherited an alliance with Western Europe which is at the lowest ebb in its existence. More than anything else, it was the Afghan crisis which caused a major deterioration in U.S.–West European relations. The Americans and the West Europeans perceived Soviet actions in Afghanistan differently and disagreed about the strategy which should have been pursued towards the Soviet Union after the invasion.

The West Europeans looked upon the invasion of Afghanistan as an isolated, regional crisis and attributed Soviet behavior primarily to defensive motives. The United States saw in the Afghan crisis a continuation of Soviet global expansionist aspirations. Indeed, the crisis in Afghanistan forced the United States to adopt policies which contributed to the deterioration of détente with the Soviet Union. The West Europeans, on the other hand, reacted purely on the diplomatic level and were unwilling to sacrifice détente with the Soviet Union, particularly in the economic arena, to express their displeasure with Soviet behavior in Afghanistan. Equally important, American pressure on the West Europeans to take stronger action increased international tensions and, if anything, unified the West Europeans in their resolve to preserve their détente with the Soviet Union. For the first time in memory, an aggressive Soviet action did not bring the Western allies closer together but rather widened the gulf between them.

For the Soviet Union this split in the Western alliance was the unexpected silver lining of the Afghan adventure because it encouraged a bifurcation of the process of détente. The Soviet Union is attempting to uncouple its deteriorating relations with the United States from its détente with Europe. This desire to exploit the fissures in the Western alliance constitutes a cornerstone of post-Afghanistan Soviet foreign policy.

The resolution of the issue of Theater Nuclear Forces (TNF)

in Europe will constitute a major indicator of the depth of the split in the alliance. For the American side, TNF deployment, dictated by the unfavorable balance of power in the European theater, is a much more important priority than the new arms limitation talks, and indeed is a precondition for new arms limitation talks. For the West Europeans, TNF is tied very closely to arms limitation talks, particularly to the ratification of the SALT II treaty. The resolution of these issues will reflect the degree of congruence between American and West European current conceptions of the alliance's priorities.

At a time when Soviet relations with the United States are at a low ebb and when the Americans and the Chinese are progressing toward an alliance, maintenance of détente with Europe will break the Soviet Union's sense of isolation and encirclement. Furthermore, such a West European–centered détente promises the following additional benefits and opportunities for the Soviets:

- In the absence of economic relations with the United States, it would secure for the Soviet Union the flow of credits and high technology so important for its economic development, particularly the expansion of its energy resources.
- By exploiting the pacifistic and antinuclear trends that have become so prominent among European leftists and youth, it would place major, possibly even insurmountable obstacles in the path of the deployment of new U.S.-controlled theater nuclear weapons in Europe and slow the upgrading of NATO conventional forces.
- Soviet détente with Europe may disrupt the American game plan of "arm first, talk later" and push the reluctant American administration towards the resumption of arms limitation talks before it is ready.
- It may further reduce the willingness of West European allies to play a more active global role, particularly in strengthening Western power positions in the Persian Gulf, a policy which the American administration is pushing on already reluctant allies.
- It may isolate the United States in a new cold war, which would differ from the cold war of the 1950s not only because it would be conducted in a context of strategic parity, but also because it would be undertaken without the wholehearted support of America's West European allies.
- Given the mood of the Reagan administration and of American public opinion, Soviet détente with Europe may

foster within the United States a strong anti-European climate and perhaps even weaken the American security commitment to Europe.
- Finally, the maintenance of Soviet détente with Europe may weaken American resolve to conduct its relations with the Soviet Union from a position of strength.
- Ultimately, the Soviets hope that the United States will be forced to follow in the footsteps of the Europeans and restore détente, but this prospect does not seem very likely.

The third crucial variable in the development of Soviet-American relations is the pattern of events—including the possibility of Soviet involvement—in the Persian Gulf area. The Iran-Iraq war threatens to destabilize the balance of power within the Arab world. The dangers of such destabilization are magnified by the very real possibility of Iran's internal political disintegration, or of its movement to the left. The Iran-Iraq war has created a situation in which the Soviet Union has nothing to lose and can win some of its major objectives. A straightforward Soviet invasion of Iran is not likely, but there is a real threat of Soviet involvement in Iran's internal strife. One can expect, at least for the moment, that the Soviet Union will pursue somewhat less politically belligerent, militant policies. However, one should not expect conspicuous self-abnegation. If Iran begins to disintegrate, or there is an increase in the leftist influence already present in some regions, the temptation for the Soviet Union to pick up the pieces through intervention in Iran's internal affairs may be irresistible. Such a policy would set the United States and the Soviet Union on a course of confrontation because it would involve the core interests of both the United States and Western Europe.

The fourth variable affecting Soviet relations with the West will be the Soviet decision concerning the situation in Poland, a decision which cannot be avoided much longer. By a quirk of history, this small nation in the center of Europe has now become a determining factor in shaping the relations between the giants of the world. The events in Poland have evolved rapidly since August 1980 and possess immeasurable historical significance. They signify the breakdown of the Communist regime, both from below and from above, in a country that constitutes the key strategic and political link in the chain of Soviet imperial possessions. We sometimes speak about the development of a free trade-union movement in Poland, but what has happened in Poland goes much beyond that. What exists in Poland today is a three-party system: the Communist party, the Solidarity movement, and the Catholic Church.

The leadership of the Communist party is deeply split and is challenged from below by a process of reform similar to that in the Communist party of Czechoslovakia in 1968. Lacking discipline and control of its own membership, the party is deeply estranged from its past and uncertain about the viability of its present system. The Solidarity movement constitutes a national party of working people and intelligentsia whose main base lies in the industrial trade unions. Although thoroughly disorganized and lacking clear central leadership, it has made an enormous impact by successfully applying to the regime in Poland the "salami" tactics used by the Communists when they gained power in Eastern Europe after World War II. Conscious of its power and extremely hesitant to compromise, the Solidarity movement reflects the euphoria of the Polish nation, which for the first time in 35 years is tasting real freedom and wants more of it, and is unwilling to think about the fact that Poland's geopolitical situation makes such freedom impossible. The third party, the Catholic Church, will continue to carry the greatest moral authority in Poland, as it always has. Well organized and disciplined, its main function is to mediate relations between the Communist party and Solidarity.

The situation in Poland until recently differed very significantly from the situations in Czechoslovakia in 1968 and Hungary in 1956, both of which resulted in Soviet invasions. Whereas the Soviets had had to deal with renegade Czech and Hungarian Communist regimes which had abandoned the "true" road of socialism, the Polish Communist Party, despite internal divisions among hard-liners, moderates, and reformers, still represented a traditional Communist regime that had simply lost control of its population. Thus, the Soviets have objected not to the lack of orthodoxy and loyalty of the Polish party and its leadership, but to their weakness. As long as such a loyal and orthodox party existed in Poland, the Soviet leadership could at least retain the hope that developments could be arrested, the situation stabilized, and reforms and concessions brought to a standstill and, in the long run, at least partially reversed. Under such conditions, and knowing how high the costs of invasion would be, the Soviets could wait and hope for the best and rely on external intimidation. However, the disintegration of the Polish party and its selection of a self-reforming path have invalidated the logic of this position.

At present the Soviet Union is facing a no-win situation in

Poland. The costs of a decision not to intervene—and thus to let the Polish situation deteriorate further without realistic hopes of reversal—would be enormous. It would mean, first of all, that the political and military reliability of the crucial country in the Soviet empire, the main Soviet route to its forward position confronting NATO in East Germany, would be sacrificed. This is an unacceptable alternative for the Soviets. Secondly, while the precise conditions that led to the Polish upheaval do not presently exist in other East European countries, the example of a pluralistic communism in Poland may in the near future act as a contagion for the working classes and intelligentsia in other parts of the Soviet Union's East European empire. All of Eastern Europe will confront a harsh economic situation in the 1980s, a situation that, as history has demonstrated, can be easily translated into social and political unrest. Thirdly, the Polish example may even prove contagious to the Soviet Union. As we will discuss later, the Soviet Union itself in the 1980s will in all probability not be immune to social unrest, especially labor unrest. Thus, the specter of "Polonization" is probably never far away from the thoughts of the Soviet leaders.

If one weighs these costs of nonintervention in Poland against the costs of intervention, then one must conclude that this is the most difficult decision—particularly in its international ramifications—that has faced the Soviet leadership in the post-Stalin era. To date, the threshold of Soviet tolerance for developments in Poland has been so high because of the leadership's reluctance to bear the enormous costs incurred by an invasion. The five following consequences would be particularly dangerous:

1   In all probability an invasion of Poland would lead to a virtual state of war with the Polish workers and the Polish nation. While it is highly unlikely that the Polish armed forces would stand united against the invaders, it is very probable that individual major units would resist. All in all the exercise might become a very bloody and protracted affair. Such a military operation in the heart of a divided Europe could prove unpredictable and risky even in its military consequences. Even the behavior of the Warsaw Pact countries and armies could not be surely predicted.
2   After the inevitable subjugation of the Polish nation the Soviet Union would acquire a staggering burden. It would not only have to maintain its occupying army, but would also have to deliver extensive support to a nation of 35 million people. It would have to feed them, sustain their economy,

and service their $22-billion debt to the West. The Soviet economy, already beset with serious domestic difficulties, could ill afford the strain.
3 An invasion of Poland and the possibility of a massacre of Polish workers will almost certainly shatter the last ties between the Soviet Communist party and the leading Communist parties of Western Europe. In all probability the break between the Italian and Spanish parties and Moscow would become final, and the intensity of their conflict with Moscow would rival that between the Soviet Union and China.
4 An invasion of Poland would destroy one of the foundations, perhaps the cornerstone, of Soviet foreign policy since Afghanistan—the political, cultural and especially economic détente with Western Europe which survived the dissolution of détente with the United States. A bloody invasion would not only shock both the Left and the Right in Europe and unite them in condemning the Soviets, but it would also probably go far to heal the ailing Western alliance. The most serious repercussions of invasion for the Soviet Union would be military—particularly the question of Theater Nuclear Forces in Europe, which has been a principal source of disruption within the Western alliance. The Reagan administration regards the deployment of TNF in Europe as a first priority and a factor that will strengthen the Western bargaining position in negotiations with the Soviet Union. The West European position, which required progress in negotiations on arms control with the Soviet Union—specifically ratification of SALT II – as a precondition for the introduction of TNF into Europe, afforded some consolation to the Soviet Union when SALT II was not ratified. A Soviet invasion of Poland would most probably alter the West European governments' policy in favor of the American desire for the introduction of TNF without SALT II.
5 An invasion of Poland would doubtless create revulsion in the United States and intensify the anti-Soviet mood that helped Reagan into office. At a time when the Reagan administration is beginning to define its global policies, an invasion would ensure American policy choices most injurious to Soviet interests. It would spur the United States to stress military buildup over arms control—to intensify the deployment of TNF, to expand the capabilities of the Rapid Deployment Force, and to accelerate the search for U.S. bases in the Persian Gulf. It would also step up the

momentum toward closer U.S.-Chinese relations which began during the last year of the Carter administration.

6 Finally, an invasion of Poland would surely affect the scale and nature of the Soviet military threat to NATO. It is quite possible, for example, that close to one million Soviet troops might be used for the invasion, and that a large number of these—perhaps 300,000—would remain in Poland as an occupation force. In the short run this might mean some thinning of the twenty-two Soviet divisions in East Germany that now form the spearhead of the Soviet military force directed against NATO. But the overwhelming likelihood is that the Soviets would call up or retain reserves to make up the difference rapidly, and the very state of mind revealed in a decision to invade could hardly be reassuring to the members of NATO, who will certainly want to reaffirm and carry through NATO's present increased defense program, and possibly to increase the number and readiness of troops stationed in the Federal Republic of Germany.

Along with these international repercussions, the decision to intervene in Poland will, in all probability, have two major repercussions on the Soviet internal political scene, including the leadership and the forthcoming succession.

1 It is not far-fetched to assume that the Soviet leadership is divided about Poland. In all probability there is already acrimony from those in Soviet leadership circles who suggested an intervention long ago and can now rightly say that an early intervention would have been much less costly. The standing of various leaders within the Soviet leadership—along with their political prospects in the Brezhnev succession—has probably been influenced by their position on Poland.

2 More importantly, the decision to intervene in Poland and its repercussions would raise the most basic questions about the inclinations of those leaders now in office and those who will replace them in the near future. How would these two leadership groups react to the total disintegration of détente and international isolation that would follow an intervention in Poland? How would they react to the treatment of the Soviet Union as a pariah state? One likely response would be to consolidate its position, stand firm, and hope that after perhaps a year or two the damage done to détente can be partly repaired, at least in Europe. But there is also the

possibility of a belligerent attitude that would reassert the right of the Soviet Union as a truly global power to do what it wants without fear. This attitude of injured frustration would seek to establish a Soviet position of immunity to the censure of both its adversaries and the neutral community. I believe that the first response is more likely from the leadership now in office, but I am not at all sure that the new, incoming leadership will respond the same way.

A major Western assumption is that Soviet international behavior is determined by a low-risk foreign policy posture. According to this view, the Soviet Union is inclined to engage in external expansion only when the risks to its key security interests or the chances of costly defeat are very low. I would propose that Soviet behavior in the 1970s, a period of increasing Soviet expansion which included the use of military force, does not contradict this assumption or imply that the Soviet Union has redefined their concept of risk. Soviet expansionism in the 1970s, for the most part, simply reflected the growth of Soviet capacities and the range of opportunities as well as the apparently temporary retreat of American power.

A major dilemma will confront the Soviet Union in the 1980s: while engaging in expansionist activities they will have to face much higher risks of confrontation with the United States, much higher risks of retaliatory measures against Soviet security interests in other areas, much higher risks of costly failures, and much higher direct economic costs on the homefront. The Soviets have not yet faced up to this dilemma, nor can we know how they will respond. It is unclear whether the Soviet response will be to take higher risks, to redefine their concept of risk, or to conduct a more moderate policy. If I had to guess, I would not expect the present aged leaders to make a change in Soviet foreign policy that would involve a redefinition of risk, but I think all bets are off with regard to the new leadership that will eventually replace them.

The shape of Soviet politics and policies changes very slowly, and one must always allow for the built-in tendency of the current Soviet political system to retain the characteristics and directions typical of the 1970s. Yet, in the 1980s, the Soviet Union will be facing issues and events which may produce incremental—or even, conceivably, fundamental—changes in the nature of politics and the directions of policies.

We have discussed some of the foreign-policy issues that face the Soviet policy-makers in the 1980s. We will discuss now some of the key domestic issues. The most important stimulus for political change in the Soviet Union in the 1980s may not be the new policy issues, but the policy-making process itself. The impending turnover of the leaders and elites injects a pronounced element of unpredictability and uncertainty into the entire Soviet political process, with profound consequences for the political system. There is a greater probability of deep personal and policy conflicts among the top leaders—and of more extreme methods for resolving these conflicts.

Such a period offers opportunities for destroying the bureaucratic inertia of the departed leaders and for changing the inertial drift of their policies. It is a period with a high potential for ferment, for greater responsiveness to pressures—real and anticipated—for broadening political participation and for an opening of the political process. In sum, the succession, aside from its intrinsic importance, releases pressures which already exist within society, but which previously had limited opportunity for expression.

The 26th Party Congress was the first one in Soviet history at which no changes in the upper echelons of the leadership took place. This congress made abundantly clear that the destabilizing effects of the eventual succession may be even stronger than had been envisaged. By not preparing even in a rudimentary way for changes at the higher levels of the leadership, the aged Soviet oligarchs are delegitimizing their own rule and increasing the chances of a disorderly struggle for power and the emergence of alternative policies when they leave the scene.

The approaching succession is in many respects different from those in the past. It combines a number of characteristics which give it very important political implications for the 1980s. Most importantly, this succession almost inevitably will combine the replacement of the top leader with that of the core leadership group and a large part of the central elite, and with the beginning of a generational turnover among the Soviet elites. Moreover, because of the age-cohort characteristics of the Soviet leadership and elites, the massive replacement will be compressed into a relatively short time-span.

The importance of the passing of the top leader himself should not be minimized Leonid Brezhnev has led and dominated Soviet political life longer than all but one leader in Soviet history. If one can say that the period of his leadership has represented the maturation and the stabilization of the Soviet system, one can argue similarly that his departure could be handled at least as routinely as the post-Khrushchev succession. If it were only a matter of the replacement of the top leader, however, the potential for stress and change would be limited. Given the required combination of qualifications for the top leadership position and the extraordinary circumstances which at present severely restrict the field of available candidates, the man selected for the top post—if Western evaluations are correct—will certainly be an interim leader. The most important questions concern who will succeed Brezhnev's immediate successor. Thus, we will in all probability see two successions to the top leadership in the 1980s.

The coming succession will inevitably bring about a massive replacement of the top leadership stratum and will compress the turnover into a relatively short time-span. It will especially affect the inner core of leaders who have worked together for such a long period of time. This massive replacement will occur quickly because of the remarkably advanced age of this group as a whole; it is older than any inner core of leaders in Soviet history and older, incidentally, than the leadership of any industrial society. There is also no precedent in Soviet history for the clustering of such a high proportion of the members of the leadership group in the very highest age-bracket. What is even more important from the point of view of our inquiry is the lack of a precedent for the described type of age configuration on the eve of the succession.

The age structure of the central elite closely resembles that of the top leadership, both in the advanced age of the group as a whole and the clustering of so many of its members in the highest age bracket. Its massive replacement in the 1980s is also unavoidable.

Massive replacements at the levels of the top leadership and central elite, which will certainly accompany the second if not the first stage of the upcoming succession, will most probably produce political conflicts over policies and procedures, regardless of who the new leaders will be. Such a prospect is especially likely because the succession will follow a period of extraordinary and long-lasting stability, during which policy differences were submerged in the name of unity and compromise, and bold initiatives—especially on the domestic scene—were lacking. Furthermore, the succession will come at a time when the Soviet Union will begin to face difficult economic choices, and it will be harder to accommodate diverse interests and pressures through compromise solutions than it has been in the Brezhnev period.

Finally, the succession and the subsequent replacement of large segments of the elite will coincide with the emergence of distinct differences between the incoming group and the outgoing group, irrespective of the diverse personalities within each group. In addition to the imminent replacement of the top leader and a large part of the highest leadership, a generational change within the Soviet elite will also occur; a large proportion of the new elite will have entered politics after Stalin's death. The approaching succession, whatever the form and results of its initial stage, will eventually involve a replacement of the top leadership and the central establishment on a scale much greater than the last two successions and will be combined with an increased generational turnover of the Soviet political elite. This conjunction of successions in both the broad and the narrow sense has no precedent in Soviet history. It will be a political development of long duration and significance.

What will be some of the characteristics of the new generation of leaders who will make their mark on the Soviet political scene during the 1980s? Given the fragmentary evidence at our disposal, we must at the outset underscore the tentativeness of this profile of the post-Stalin generation. Because this generation entered Soviet politics immediately after Stalin's death, it did not experience the paralyzing and destructive terror which continued to corrode and influence the behavior of the earlier generations (despite the renunciation of mass terror as an instrument of rule). Consequently, the post-Stalin generation cannot directly—out of its own hide, so to speak—appreciate the enormous price paid for the Soviet achievement. Perhaps the most crucial formative political experience for this generation took place during the protracted ferment and shock of Khrushchev's anti-Stalin campaign, a campaign that admitted the monstrosities no one hitherto had dared to name and that stimulated critical thought by questioning authority and established truths. The post-Stalin generation's entrance into Soviet politics also coincided with an open recognition of the gross inadequacies of Soviet development and the backwardness of Soviet technology and, at the same time, with extravagant predictions of matching Western achievements in the foreseeable future, predictions whose collapse caused considerable embarrassment.

The new generation is clearly a Soviet generation in its typical and persistent adherence to the cult of the state. One cannot doubt the sincerity of its members' commitment to the basic forms of Soviet political organization, or their belief that the system is right and proper for the Soviet Union. At the same time, they do not seem to believe that this system is suitable or desirable for developed Western societies. Although they share with their predecessors a devoted patriotism, they exhibit little of their predecessors' xenophobia. Rather, they display a curiosity that surely reflects intense concern about the patent inadequacies in the workings of the Soviet system.

Some traits of the new generation may appear contradictory. On the one hand, one detects a sense of security and self-confidence that contrasts with the old generation's sense of insecurity or even inferiority. At the same time, however, their attitude toward the Soviet system is defensive. They are more conscious than their predecessors of the failures, shortcomings, and backwardness of the Soviet society and polity and less willing to overlook them. Unlike their predecessors, many of them are ready to engage outsiders in frank and serious exchanges of opinion.

The post-Stalin generation perceives not only the backwardness of Soviet society, but also the inability of the Brezhnev administration in recent years to lay out a direction for Soviet development and to rectify the functional deficiencies of the system. At the same time it is probably confident in its own ability to make necessary changes. This generation is less likely to accept actual or potential international achievements as substitutes for internal development, and may be willing to tolerate a certain degree of political and social change if persuaded that such change would assure substantial improvement in the growth and efficiency of the productive and distributive processes.

Even if our portrait of the new generation of Soviet officials were less provisional and patchy, we would still be presumptuous and unwise to use it as a basis for specific predictions about their future behavior. The formative political experiences and the predilections which we have tried to identify suggest only that these officials might be different as a group from their predecessors in the older generation.

The pressures created by the forthcoming succession, in combination with the political issues which will become a part of the political agenda, will probably lead to the destabilization of the central policy-making system. In a highly centralized polity such as the Soviet Union, these developments may have very important consequences. The destabilization will involve a breakdown of the consensus among the leadership and the elites, the intensification of factional struggles at the top and middle levels of the bureaucracy, possible realignments of existing alliances, the exploitation of policy issues for the accumulation of power by individual leaders and groups, and sharp twists and turns in central policies.

In the 1980s, the impact of economic problems on the political system and its relations with the society will be extremely significant, probably more so than it was in the 1970s. What are the major economic problems which the Soviet Union is facing?

1   In the 1980s the Soviet Union will face a secular decline in the growth rates of its economy, involving almost all sectors. Extensive development has reached such limits that retention of the high growth rates of the past is no longer possible. Even without the intervention of other negative factors, and assuming no decline in the quality of the traditional Soviet leadership of the economy, the growth of the Soviet GNP in the 1980s will only be approximately 2.5 percent per year.
2   The Soviet political-economic system of management, pricing, and incentives is ill prepared to maximize the possibilities for intensive growth. The fundamental changes which are needed in the political-economic system are unlikely to be accomplished in the foreseeable future. None of the steps already undertaken by the Soviet government to counteract declining economic growth rates will have any major impact on the Soviet economy.
3   The Soviet Union in the 1980s is also facing unfavorable demographic trends. There will be a rapid decline in the growth of new labor resources, and the new labor force that does emerge will be overwhelmingly non-Russian.
4   The Soviet Union will face an energy balance unfavorable to its economic growth, particularly in the production of oil. How much this production will decline is a matter of major contention among economists, but there is a growing consensus that a decrease will take place. Even if one rejects the worst-case scenarios, which predict oil production levels of 8 million barrels a day, the decline will probably be sufficient not only to impose major constraints on economic growth, but also to limit the Soviets' ability to utilize fully their existing economic capacities.
5   The enormous agricultural investments of the Brezhnev era have produced limited and—at best—uncertain results. Soviet agriculture in the 1980s will remain a highly volatile sector of the Soviet economy. Moreover, because of the

decline in secular growth in other sectors, the unavoidable agricultural fluctuations will have an increasing influence on the size of the Soviet GNP.

Just how difficult the Soviet economic situation will be in the 1980s is a matter of conjecture. According to the worst-case scenarios, it will be a period of low growth intermingled with economic stagnation. But even according to the more optimistic scenarios, the Soviet Union will face an economic crunch far more severe than anything it encountered in the 1960s and 1970s.

I must reiterate that the differences between the optimistic and pessimistic scenarios are a matter of great importance; they signify the difference between a difficult situation and a deep crisis. Moreover, the choice of the most likely scenario from among the various scenarios is not the result of a belief in more or less precise and complex computations (or, for a political scientist, the result of his faith in the skills of one or another group of economic forecasters), but a result which should include unpredictable elements, such as vagaries of nature and, as importantly, the seriousness and the effectiveness of corrective economic policies adopted by the Soviet leadership. Even assuming that the more optimistic scenario better reflects the reality of the 1980s, what will be the effects of the growing economic difficulties on the Soviet political scene? The two most important consequences will be sharply increased competition for scarce resources, among sectors as well as among regions.

During its history, the Soviet political system, at both its micro- and macro-economic decision-making levels, has become accustomed to scarcities, shortages, and stringencies, and dealing with those problems has been its normal *modus operandi*. Yet it must be remembered that these conditions have gone hand in hand with a process of highly uneven development, concomitant with rapid overall economic growth. Moreover, during times of extreme stringencies and particularly one-sided development, the system was guarded by a mass terror apparatus introduced by Stalin and dismantled by his successors. In the post-Stalin period, the relatively high ratios of growth, while still accompanied by uneven development, assured the flow of new resources to all sectors of the economy, including those totally neglected during the Stalin era. Though accustomed to shortages, the Soviet political system is not accustomed to dealing with prolonged periods of low overall economic growth.

The Soviet system is ill prepared to deal with the problems of how to stimulate higher growth rates and how to overcome critical bottlenecks for exactly the same reason that growth has declined: the decrease in effectiveness or exhaustion of the extensive factors of growth. Its past responses to economic difficulties were based on a mass mobilization of capital and labor—a policy not of the scalpel but of the hammer.

On the distributive side of the equation, the Soviet political system will have difficulty in dealing with prolonged low overall rates of growth for three reasons: (1) the absence of a paralyzing mass terror apparatus which would make all sacrifices and demands palatable; (2) the existence of powerful organizational groups and issue-alliances in the decision-making apparatus which inhibit the implementation of cutbacks and restraints; and (3) the emergence of new social constraints to such cutbacks.

The sharply increased sectoral competition for resources and the dilemmas which it will create are not difficult to envisage. The policy of guns, butter and growth—the political cornerstone of the Brezhnev program—is no longer possible. To keep the rate of growth in *military spending* at the level of the last decade will necessitate a redirection of resources from other sectors. Yet for a number of reasons—past Soviet behavior, growing Soviet insecurity about what they consider the formation of an alliance among the United States and NATO and China, the growing determination of the United States to change the existing balance of military power, the breakdown of SALT talks—it is highly unlikely that any configuration of Soviet leaders will decide to slow down the growth in military expenditures, let alone cut actual arms spending, without a major breakthrough, or without a major disavowal of their global ambitions. If arms spending continues at the same pace as in the past decade, the burden of keeping the Soviet military juggernaut in shape will be felt more acutely than at any time in the Brezhnev era and will constitute one of the key contentious issues of Soviet internal politics.

Another even more divisive issue concerns the rate of growth and direction of Soviet nonmilitary investment resources. Throughout their history, the Soviets have persistently kept their share of investment in their national economy and the levels of investment growth very high. Recently, however, they have been unable to maintain such high rates of investment. But if there ever was a period when the Soviet Union needed a very large investment in their national economy, it is now. It is difficult to envisage how the Soviet leadership can compensate for the limitations of the existing pattern of extensive growth without keeping the percentage of investment in the economy —and even the growth rate of investments—at high levels.

Intensive growth, given Soviet conditions, requires a thorough modernization of the industrial plant and major investments in new technology. Without a large-scale, persistent and creditable effort in this direction, there is little chance that any increased productivity of Soviet labor will overcome the downward pull of the exhaustion of the extensive factors of growth.

The energy problem facing the Soviets in the 1980s will demand mammoth and prolonged investments, which have already begun. The development of the Siberian oil and gas reserves will constitute a major and increasing burden on Soviet investment resources, but it is a burden that the Soviets can neglect only at their own peril.

The achievements of Soviet agriculture under Brezhnev—the growth in grain production, but especially the stress on meat production—have required extraordinarily large expenditures of capital. Yet even with those expenditures, Soviet agricultural productivity remains uneven from year to year, and the agricultural sector continues to be highly volatile. The Soviets have not yet devised a way to assure even the present inadequate levels of agricultural production without massive infusions of capital. In the coming decade, when the Soviet economy slows down, the divisive pull of conflicting claims on investment resources will increase to a level unknown during the Brezhnev era.

One of the most significant accomplishments of the Brezhnev era was the prolonged and substantial growth of Soviet *mass consumption*. The last fifteen years saw a growth in the standard of living of the Soviet people that was rapid by any—but especially by Soviet—standards, particularly in the area of durable consumer goods. This gain is especially notable because it was achieved simultaneously with the rapid growth of Soviet military power. In other words, Brezhnev successfully pursued a guns-and-butter policy. The stability of the Brezhnev period in the absence of terror can be explained to a large degree by the leadership's basic ability to satisfy more fully the demands of the Soviet consumer. The Soviet citizen—worker, peasant, and professional—has become accustomed to an uninterrupted upward trend in his standard of living and has come to expect more goods and services from the government. In view of the major demands placed by other sectors on Soviet resources in a period of decreasing growth rates, it will be extremely difficult for the Soviet leadership to continue its policy of consumption growth even at the lower rates of the last five-year plan.

It is probable that even without major agricultural disasters or a particularly severe energy crisis, Soviet consumption will stagnate in the 1980s, with undeniably negative results. First of all, it is difficult to see how the crucial goal of increasing Soviet productivity can be attained without an increase in remunerative incentives for the labor force. Secondly, the stagnation of the standard of living will be experienced by the working population at a time when the other basic avenue of betterment—upward mobility—is also being blocked off. Thirdly, and most importantly, neither we nor the Soviet leaders know how the Soviet industrial working class will react to such changing circumstances. The post-Stalin society without terror has never been at the same time a society with a stagnant standard of living.

As far as we know, the desire of the Soviet population for a better life has never become unmanageable or assumed the form of a revolution, or of a vicious spiral of rising expectations. The key to the stability of the Soviet system has been the leadership's successful management of the expectations of the population. Yet one should not forget that it was a management of expectations which went hand in hand with a steadily (sometimes rapidly) growing rate of consumption, which may have been a substitute for and a damper on growing political expectations. Whether the existing police controls and the management of mass expectations can keep the Soviet working class docile in the absence of increases in their living standards is an open question. One has the impression that the specter of "Polonization" of the Soviet working class is never far from the minds of the Soviet leadership and the elites.

Of course, not only the intersectoral competition for resources, but also the intrasectoral competition for specific priorities will be much sharper. Specific elite constituencies represent each of these priorities in the national leadership. In addition, these types of competition for resources will be intertwined with and complicated by a stronger, more tenacious competition for resources among the various regions of the Soviet Union. Such a competition was a normal facet of Soviet politics in the 1970s. The regional budgetary conflicts—such as those between the Ukraine and Siberia—over economic development plans have been well documented. They are certain to increase in the 1980s.

The difficult political decisions of how to distribute the available resources are complicated by the underlying economic dilemma: the European part of the Soviet Union has a well-developed infrastructure, and investments here would be relatively cheap and would provide a higher return. But at the same time, the European part of the Soviet Union is on the verge of exhausting new labor resources and it is poor in natural resources. Central Asia has a limited infrastructure, especially in the technological sector. In addition, the political claims of Central Asian elites in seeking new resources would probably be fiercely debated by the dominant Slavic elites. The regions in the Russian Republic where the natural resources are located are extremely poor in labor resources and lack any infrastructure; investments will be extremely expensive and difficult to manage.

The regional struggle for resources will be conducted during a period of leadership succession. During such periods, the political clout of the provincial and the republican elites traditionally increases. For example, the regional leaders became real king-makers during Khrushchev's rise to power. The temptation to sacrifice sound economic policy in the upcoming political bargaining will be strong.

The first and foremost response of the Soviet authorities to their economic and political difficulties will be to strengthen the authoritarian character of the Soviet party-state. The emphasis on law and order, social discipline, unswerving loyalty, nationalism, and punitive and restrictive measures taken against anti-social behavior may become more pronounced than in the 1970s. We can also expect the role of the secret and not-so-secret police to increase. Whenever the situation becomes difficult, whenever no prospects for rapid improvements are in sight, and whenever a tightening of the belt is in order, the natural response of any Soviet leadership—old or new—is to tighten the screws of political and social control. The capacity, the potential and the instruments for such policies already exist.

It is an open question whether such policies will be sufficient to maintain order under the conditions of new and prolonged economic stringencies. After the Soviet population realizes that it will experience a prolonged decline in the growth of its living standard, the basic stability of the Brezhnev period and the compact between the elites and the workers may be weakened, and the industrial labor force may grow restless. An increase in labor unrest, work stoppages, industrial demonstrations, and communal dissatisfaction is a clear possibility. Such developments will have an effect upon the allocation policies adopted by the government.

In the new situation, the nationality problem may also become aggravated no matter what policy the leadership adopts vis-à-vis the non-Russian regions. The Soviet leadership managed to contain the nationality problem in the 1970s partly because the nationality areas enjoyed a quicker growth than the rest of the country, especially in the standard of living and the conditions of the rural sector. If the party, under more stringent economic conditions, decides to slow the growth of those regions, the relative peace in existing relations among the nationalities will be strained.

The leadership's response to the new demographic trend in the growth of Soviet labor resources will be the most important issue in Soviet policy toward the nationalities in the 1980s. The need to exploit the growing non-Slavic—particularly Central Asian—labor resources presents two options for the Soviet policy makers: migration of the non-Slavic labor force to the industrial areas, or a dramatic increase in the industrial development of Central Asia. Both options could seriously destabilize nationality relations in the USSR. In my opinion, the second option is more likely to be adopted. This course of action would produce, in some Central Asian regions, the type of major social displacement associated with rapid industrialization. It will also involve a rapid and massive influx of Russian bureaucrats into those regions, creating dissatisfactions and tensions between the local, native elite and the newcomers. The non-Russian republics, including those of Central Asia, have only recently developed native administrative and technical cadres capable of administering their own affairs without Russian help. Under these conditions, local elites are developing more of a sense of their own identity, a trend which may provide difficulties for the central authorities.

The economic realities of the 1980s will sharply strengthen the tendency toward a markedly less benign political climate than that of the 1970s, and will contribute immensely to a political environment of sharp competition, confrontation, and discord. Without a doubt, these difficult economic issues will play a crucial role in the disputes, conflicts and realignments which will accompany the Soviet succession.

The scenario for a two-stage succession presented above is the most probable one, but one cannot exclude the possibility of another scenario in which no interim leader emerges and the replacement of the old generation is much more massive from the outset. This second scenario is unlikely because no leadership is ever ready to liquidate itself, especially in a country like the Soviet Union, where retirement is tantamount to political death. However, one can underestimate the degree of frustration in the Central Committee of the CPSU over the old generation's handling of the affairs of state. If a revolt is brewing among the younger members of the Central Committeee and if they succeed in arranging a one-stage succession, then there will be a much stronger push towards changes in the Soviet domestic scene, particularly towards economic reforms.

I should like to make one thing clear. The new generation of Soviet officials believes in reform within the Soviet framework, but we cannot expect them to exhibit reformist tendencies similar to those of the Dubcek regime in Czechoslovakia. Nor do I expect them to be favorably disposed to the highly ideological, frantic, and campaign-like reforms associated with Khrushchev. I also doubt that they will be easier to deal with in the international arena. They may be less cautious and more prone to take risks than the present leadership, precisely because they have no firsthand experience of the costs of building Soviet might and may take the Soviet Union's great power status for granted. I am in no way making a judgment here on whether the new generation of Soviet officials is better or worse from the standpoint of our value system and interests. I only suggest that the new generation seems to be different from the old.

The Soviet leaders of the 1980s will have limited knowledge of international relations and will have to learn on the job. Their presence in the top Soviet leadership, along with the confrontational internal politics of the succession process and the difficult Soviet economic situation, will add an element of volatility and uncertainty to Soviet relations with the West.

The new generation of leaders certainly will make a major effort to reform the antiquated Soviet economic system. I doubt, however, that even these leaders will succeed in a wholesale revamping of their economic system. The obstacles to restructuring the Soviet system of management and planning are simply too formidable. First of all, the vested political and economic interests opposing such reform are very powerful, and will remain so in spite of the high turnover in the elites and the growing pressure to get the country moving again. Secondly, the initiative for such reform in the face of widespread opposition must come not only from below but also, to be even moderately successful, from above—especially from a strong general secretary. On its own, an oligarchic leadership, which by its very nature has to rely on bargaining, trade-offs, and compromises is ill suited for initiating and executing major structural, procedural, or even policy reforms. For this reason the future of such reforms depends largely on the initiative and persistence of the top leader. Certainly, one cannot expect this kind of initiative from Brezhnev during his last days in power. But can a more innovative leader emerge during the coming succession? Even assuming that the new leader becomes convinced of the necessity for such far-reaching reforms—and this is a very big assumption—it will be a long time before he is strong enough to make serious progress in this direction.

Furthermore, the professional groups, especially the economists, usually provide the greatest support for radical reforms. In order to take advantage of their significant advisory capacity, these groups must agree on what proreform advice they provide to the leadership. (This unity, incidentally, was an important factor in the implementation of Hungary's radical reforms.) In the Soviet Union, however, these groups are divided about what kinds of reforms are needed. Moreover, they are easily manipulated by the various factions in the leadership and the elites. If they cannot resolve their differences, they will neutralize their potential for bringing about reform. Both the proponents and opponents of reform in the leadership will be able to find or to mobilize the support of experts for their positions.

One should also not minimize the purely economic and technical difficulty of large-scale reform in the Soviet Union. Such reform would most certainly involve a temporary decline in production and in productivity, would significantly increase the need for real incentives, and would entail the enormous task of reeducating the labor force and the management. The difficult transitional period from the old to the new system would require very large reserves of capital and consumer goods. During the 1980s, however, the Soviet economy will be stretched to its limits, and planning will be especially difficult, with reserves dwindling. Radical reform will be extremely difficult in such conditions.

Eastern Europe very often is regarded as the funnel through which Western influence and reformist tendencies are channeled to the Soviet Union. There is undoubtedly truth in this assertion, but Eastern Europe is more often a thoroughly conservative influence on the *domestic* Soviet scene. The very fact of the Soviets' total commitment to the existence of Eastern Europe as their imperial sphere of influence, along with the potential instability of the East European domestic and international situation, exerts a powerful pull on Soviet domestic policy: the more restless Eastern Europe becomes, the more conservative this influence becomes. When attempting to implement a reform in the Soviet Union, any configuration of Soviet leaders must anticipate its potential impact upon Eastern Europe, where it would only encourage liberal forces whose growth can only endanger Soviet rule. Under these circumstances, only an enormously confident—or desperate—Soviet leadership would initiate internal policies which could undermine its external holdings, especially holdings which will be facing severe economic, social, and political strains in the 1980s.

The multinational and nominally federal nature of the Soviet system also exerts a conservative influence on reformist tendencies among the Russian leadership and elites. A thorough liberalizing reform would undoubtedly diffuse economic authority within the Soviet Union. If the pay-offs are sufficiently high, the leadership might tolerate such a delegation of authority to the Russian elites and subelites, but not to the non-Russians. To institute a thorough liberalizing economic reform in the Soviet Union could and probably would, upset the existing balance. In the minds of the Russian leadership, it may be tantamount to accepting the restructuring of the relationship between the nationalities in the Soviet Union, a risk which I highly doubt they are willing to take.

A thorough overhaul of the economic system would require a basic change in the working style of the leadership, elites, and subelites. One does not embark on such an extremely serious undertaking without being convinced that the old system is really exhausted and absolutely needs to be abandoned. This is not the case with the old leadership, and there is also no compelling evidence that the emerging leadership and elites are ready to make such a commitment. As a result, it will be extremely difficult to place the question of the basic viability of the system on the Soviet political agenda. But without such discussion, a thorough overhaul of the system is highly unlikely. The Soviet leaders' perceptions of their economy's long-range prospects will help them decide whether to undertake major reforms. If they see the difficulties of the 1980s—particularly the energy problem—as temporary aberrations which can be corrected in the 1990s, they will have another reason not to revamp the system.

Finally, a key obstacle to successful liberal reform is the reform mechanism itself, that is, the usual process by which reforms have been adopted and implemented under the conditions of post-Stalin Soviet politics. To be effective, far-reaching reforms must be carried out across the board without hesitation, and not in piecemeal fashion. As we know from past experience, however, the Soviets tend to adopt the self-defeating approach of waiting for proof of a program's effectiveness before agreeing to pursue it with determination. From the various possibilities for reform, the leadership selects a compromise solution which will cause the least disturbance and requires the least cost and effort. Instead of introducing an across-the-board reform with determination, they try it on an experimental basis and on a limited scale. Consequently, the results of the reform are inconclusive and even disappointing, an outcome that, in turn, fuels the argument of opponents who prevent its further implementation. The leadership reverts to the traditional way of doing business and continues to tinker half-heartedly with the system. Instead of transforming the traditional economic system, the well-intentioned, piecemeal reforms are absorbed and neutralized by the system. This political mechanism explains the inherent stability of the traditional economic system and the inherent instability of reform efforts in the Soviet Union.

To sum up, I am arguing that despite the unprecedented pressures brought about by the difficult economic situation and the very rare opportunities offered by the coming succession, the odds are against a successful, far-reaching reform which would move in the direction of market socialism. I am not arguing that reforms in this direction will not be attempted. Rather, such reforms will be hesitant, limited in scope, and ultimately absorbed by the system that they are meant to change.

Each period of Soviet history, each decade of Soviet development, has posed new dilemmas for the leadership. The dilemmas of the 1980s are more difficult than any the Soviet leadership has had to face since Stalin's death. The Soviet Union is clearly at a crossroads socially, politically, economically, and with regard to its military and foreign policy—a crossroads which is no less important than those which it faced at the end of NEP (the New Economic Policy of the 1920s) and after Stalin's death. So far, the Soviet Union is still designing its policy according to the guidelines of the 1970s. We may, however, expect that in the 1980s this inertia will be broken and a new outline of Soviet policies will emerge.

2

Changes in Soviet Elite Composition

Jerry F. Hough

In substantial part, the Soviet Union has achieved the basic goals established by Stalin in 1928-9—the building of an industrial base and the attainment of military equality with the West. Precisely for this reason, it now faces a series of decisions and policy dilemmas as difficult as those which existed sixty years ago. Yet a strong majority on the Politburo—including the inner core of five leaders—are part of a historic generation created by Stalin to administer the industrialization drive, and these men seem quite incapable of facing up to the need for new priorities and planning mechanisms. Any significant change in policy will almost surely depend on a significant change in personnel, and for that reason alone the character of Soviet elite composition is a question of intense interest.

In practice, the personnel developments associated with the 26th Party Congress show a continuation of the basic trends of the last decade. Enormous stability in personnel is found in the leading party bodies, while normal turnover is present at middle levels. The very large "postwar generation" of officials who were born in the second half of the 1920s and who were too young to have their college education destroyed by World War II—and who are now in their early fifties—has been penetrating the higher elite in increasing numbers.[1] Excluding the new military members,[2] over 80 percent of the officials who were elected full or candidate members of the Central Committee for the first time at the 26th Party Congress were 55 years of age or younger at the beginning of the year. Over 20 percent of them were under 50. For the first time, a member of this new postwar generation has been elected a full member of the Politburo, and three others have become deputy chairmen of the Council of Ministers.

This article is based on work done for the Brookings Institution.

40 *Jerry Hough*

The Politburo

At the 26th Party Congress itself no change was made either among the full or the candidate members of the Politburo—the first time that this had happened since the 15th Congress in 1927. The basic structure of the group of full or voting Politburo members remains essentially what it has been since the early 1970s: an inner core of five who are the crucial decision-makers (now Brezhnev, Chernenko, Kirilenko, Suslov, and Tikhonov), the three top governmental officials handling foreign policy (Gromyko, Ustinov, and Andropov), the Central Committee secretary for agriculture (now Gorbachev, who is actually directing the new agro-industrial complex that is now being formed),[3] four regional leaders (Grishin, Kunaev, Romanov, and Shcherbitsky), and an old Bolshevik who was a deputy to the Petrograd Soviet in 1917 (Pel'she) (see Table 2.1).

As before, the candidate members of the Politburo include the minister of culture and the head of the International Department of the Central Committee, but five of the other six candidate members are representatives of the country's largest republics. In general, the degree of the representation of the republic reflects its relative population. The giant Russian Republic (RSFSR) has two men among the voting members of the Politburo, and the second most populous republic (the Ukraine) and the long-time third (Kazakhstan) have one each. The first secretaries of the fourth through seventh most populous republics (Uzbekistan, Belorussia, Azerbaidzhan, and Georgia), as well as the chairman of the Council of Ministers of the RSFSR, serve as candidate members. (Uzbekistan has moved into the third spot in population—although not in the size of its party organization—and it would not be surprising if this were reflected in one way or another in the end of the present status difference between it and Kazakhstan in the future.)[4]

If, however, we focus our analysis not on the 26th Party Congress but on the period between the 25th and 26th congresses, the Politburo membership looks far less stable. Of the sixteen voting members elected to the Politburo in 1976, five were no longer on it in 1981: three (Andrei Grechko, Aleksei Kosygin, and Fedor Kulakov) because of death, and two (Kirill Mazurov and Nikolai Podgorny) because of retirement. Only one of the six candidate members was not reelected (Petr Masherov died), but the expansion of the number of candidates to seven permitted the election of two new candidates (Kiselev and Shevarnadze).

Table 2.1 Politburo Members, 1981

Member	Year of Birth	Position
		FULL MEMBERS
Brezhnev, L. I.	1906	General secretary
Andropov, Iu. V.	1914	Chairman, KGB
Gorbachev, M. S.	1931	Secretary, Central Committee
Grishin, V. V.	1914	First secretary, Moscow City Party Committee
Gromyko, A. A.	1909	Minister of foreign affairs
Kirilenko, A. P.	1906	Secretary, Central Committee
Kunaev, D. A.	1912	First secretary, Kazakhstan Party Central Committee
Pel'she, A. Ia.	1899	Chairman, Party Control Committee
Romanov, G. V.	1923	First secretary, Leningrad Regional Party Committee
Suslov, M. A.	1902	Secretary, Central Committee
Tikhonov, N. A.	1905	Chairman, USSR Council of Ministers
Ustinov, D. F.	1908	Minister of defense
Chernenko, K. U.	1911	Secretary, Central Committee
Shcherbitsky, V. V.	1918	First secretary, Ukrainian Party Central Committee
		CANDIDATE MEMBERS
Aliev, G. A.	1923	First secretary, Azerbaidzhan Party Central Committee
Demichev, P. N.	1918	Minister of culture
Kiselev, T. Ia.	1917	First secretary, Belorussian Party Central Committee
Kuznetsov, V. V.	1901	Deputy chairman, Presidium of the Supreme Soviet
Ponomarev, B. N.	1905	Secretary, Central Committee
Rashidov, Sh. R.	1917	First secretary, Uzbekistan Party Central Committee
Solomentsev, M. S.	1913	Chairman, RSFSR Council of Ministers
Shevardnadze, E. A.	1928	First secretary, Georgian Party Central Committee

Yet, except for one case—the replacement of Kulakov (born in 1918) as Central Committee secretary for agriculture by Gorbachev (born in 1931)—the Politburo changes brought little rejuvenation with them. The two departing members of the inner core, Podgorny and Kosygin, were born in 1903 and 1904, their successors (Tikhonov and Chernenko) in 1905 and 1911. The inner core averaged 71 years of age in 1976 and 74 in 1981. Two of the departing full members were not even replaced by new members. Grechko (born in 1903) was replaced by a man already on the Politburo (Ustinov), while Mazurov (born in 1914) was replaced as the number two man in the Council of

Ministers by Ivan Arkhipov (born in 1907). Surprisingly, Arkhipov was not even elected a candidate member of the Politburo, although that status is almost always conferred on the first deputy chairman of the Council of Ministers. Yet even this did not prevent a rise in the average age of the Politburo voting member from 65 to 69 between the two congresses.

Whatever the relative age of the officials, a Politburo change of the scale that occurred between 1976 and 1981 obviously has major political significance. Most clearly, it indicates that Brezhnev retained enormous political strength in the intercongress period. Of the men promoted during this period, Brezhnev had known Tikhonov and Arkhipov from his days in Dnepropetrovsk in the late 1930s, and as Moldavian first secretary in the early 1950s he had known Chernenko. Indeed, Chernenko had essentially worked as Brezhnev's personal secretary since 1960. Ustinov, as the country's top defense industry administrator from 1957 to 1963, had been Brezhnev's close associate in the late 1960s when the future general secretary had served as the Central Committee secretary for heavy industry, the defense industry, and the space program.[5] Ustinov was one of the two Politburo members to whom Brezhnev spoke in public in the familiar form of "you"—*ty*—when Brezhnev awarded him an order on his 70th birthday in 1978. (The other was Kirilenko in 1976.) The appointment of so many old cronies must be weakening Brezhnev's legitimacy and even power over time—and, in fact, also that of the system as a whole—but his ability to make these appointments demonstrates the extent of his power in the short run.

The appointment of the 75-year-old Tikhonov as chairman of the Council of Ministers and the election of the 49-year-old Gorbachev as a full Politburo member only three months before the congress also surely has important implications for the coming succession. If only we knew what they are!

One probable significance of Tikhonov's appointment is a further weakening of Kirilenko's hopes to succeed Brezhnev. Reasonably knowledgeable Soviet intellectuals with policy interests have always scoffed at the notion of Kirilenko as a general secretary, and his position has been undercut in recent years by the removal of his protégé, Iakov Riabov, from the Central Committee Secretariat, by the apparent assumption of some of his responsibilities for supervision of the lower party apparatus by Chernenko, and by the simple passage of time.[6] Even if we leave these factors aside, however, it boggles the mind to think of the party going to the people in a time of crisis with a team of Kirilenko and Tikhonov, both in their mid-seventies, both without significant foreign policy experience, and both promoted out of the same province (Dnepropetrovsk) because of personal connections with the old leader.

Gorbachev, by contrast, has all the appearance of an eventual general secretary. The only man in the leadership to graduate from prestigious Moscow University (and, in fact, one of the few under 70 years of age with a full-time college degree, although he later added a second degree from the extension division of an agricultural college), he is carrying out a wide range of responsibilities. He not only is the Central Committee secretary for agriculture, but also supervises the Light Industry and Food Industry Department of the Central Committee as well. These may only be temporary assignments until the Central Committee departments are restructured to deal with the agro-industrial complex, but for the moment at least he is the major Politburo member with specific responsibility for consumer goods.

As a graduate of the law faculty of Moscow University, Gorbachev was named chairman of the Legislative Proposals Committee of one of the houses of the Supreme Soviet—the committee that participates in the drafting of all Supreme Soviet legislation and also has special responsibility for law-and-order questions. Finally, he has frequently been appearing at airports in connection with foreign visits. At first, one suspected that he was the only Politburo member stationed in Moscow who was young enough to be exposed to the Moscow winters at the airport, but then in the warmer month of April he was the only Politburo member at the airport to see Suslov off when he made his famous trip to Poland and to greet Suslov when he returned.[7] It appears more and more that a deliberate effort is being made to increase Gorbachev's experience and public status.

Gorbachev would almost surely be a reform leader. He is associated with the one apparent major reform in recent months—the expansion of the private sector in agriculture, which one middle-level Soviet official, rightly or wrongly, calls the beginning of a partial reintroduction of NEP (the New Economic Policy of the 1920s) in agriculture. He also must have close ties with the interesting editor of *Kommunist*, Richard I. Kosolapov, who, like Gorbachev was in Komsomol work in Moscow University's graduating class of 1955 and was also promoted to full membership in the Central Committee this year.[8] Perhaps most importantly, Gorbachev's age gives him every incentive to retire those in their sixties and seventies in the central state apparatus and to replace them with his own men (presumably, in order to gain their support in the Central Committee, many of them regional party secretaries), and talk of reform would at a minimum provide an excuse for personnel change.

Gorbachev's age and his likely desire to make personnel changes are, of course, certain to raise as many suspicions among those to be replaced as hopes among those young enough to be promoted. Nevertheless, he does have extraordinarily good political connections. He was Komsomol secretary at Moscow University when Ivan Kapitonov, the Central Committee secretary for personnel selection, was first secretary of the Moscow Provincial Party Committee and Grishin was second secretary.[9] Gorbachev then spent twenty years in Suslov's old province of Stavropol and was the direct protégé of Kulakov, his predecessor as first secretary of Stavropol. Kulakov also had worked closely with Chernenko in the Penza region (*oblast*) in the mid-1940s, and conceivably this tie extends to Kulakov's protégé Gorbachev. For whatever reason, Vedernikov, the head of the Organizational-Party-Work Department and then the organizational secretary of the Stavropol Territorial Party Committee (*kraikom*) under Gorbachev, now serves as head of the Organizational-Party-Work Department of the National Central Committee in charge of Moldavia and the Ukraine (or at least the Western Ukraine) and presumably has some power over personnel selection there.[10]

Thus, Gorbachev clearly has the type of quality education and the set of experiences and connections that mark him as a potential leader, but if the succession occurs in the near future, his youth and his relative inexperience with the non-Russian nationalities and with foreign policy will count against him. The choice is likely to go to a transitional figure, and in the transition others of his generation will arise as competitors. For example, the man in the postwar generation with the best combination of industrial and foreign-policy experience, Konstantin Katushev, remains a deputy chairman of the Council of Ministers, but he was shifted in late 1980 from work in Comecon and given overall coordinating responsibility for transportation, one of the most critical sectors. He and Gorbachev would complement each other nicely—or make natural competitors.

Assuming that the leadership does not want to court the enormous dangers to regime support that would be produced by another general secretary from the Brezhnev generation and with the Brezhnev priorities, the obvious candidates to serve as transitional leader are Andropov, Chernenko, Grishin, and Shcherbitsky. The selection of the poorly educated Chernenko, who has been a Brezhnev personal assistant for so long (reminiscent of Stalin's personal assistant Poskrebyshev) and who himself will be 70 this year, seems improbable, and Shcherbitsky, the Ukrainian first secretary, surely cannot be named the top choice, so long as another Ukrainian—Tikhonov—is chairman of the Council of Ministers.

Of Grishin and Andropov, the former is clearly the cautious choice—the man who is not terribly bright, who does not have a college education, and who instinctively seems to seek the compromise solution. As long-time chairman of the trade union, he is likely to distrust greater wage differentiation, greater incentives, and other economic reforms that could generate unemployment, higher prices for meat and other basic items, and other disturbing social consequences. If he is allied with Kapitonov, with whom he worked in the early 1950s, and if Kapitonov has had the key role in the selection of regional party officials,[11] he may start with a significant political machine, and he seems the natural choice if the leadership is looking for Brezhnevism without Brezhnev.

Andropov, by contrast, is a far more natural choice for a time of crisis and choice. First and foremost, he is a man with an immense amount of foreign-policy experience (really the only candidate with it) at a time when this issue should be critical. His secret police background would likely reassure the conservatives, while he has the knowledge of East Europe that a reform leader needs, and he has good connections with some leading liberal intellectuals. He was essentially a protégé of the reformer, Otto Kuusinen,[12] and a number of important progressive intellectuals worked with him when he was in the Central Committee handling relations with socialist countries from 1957 to 1967. The fact that he has a history of heart trouble may also be reassuring to those who want the next leader to be transitional, but who fear that some "transitional" leader will turn out to have the physical constitution of a Tito.

The signs about the relative strength of the two major contenders that emerged at the 26th Party Congress were rather meager, but they tended to point to Andropov. Three deputy chairmen of the KGB were promoted to full membership in the Central Committee, and some of the other foreign-policy specialists named to that body may also reflect Andropov's influence. By contrast, the number of secretaries of Grishin's Moscow City Party Committee elected to the Central Commit-

46 Jerry Hough

tee fell from four to two. The significance of these indicators is difficult to judge—and, indeed, it is hard to say whether any status which may be conferred by Brezhnev provides any clue about the power situation after he is gone—but recent events also demonstrate the party's great need for a leader with foreign-policy expertise, familiarity with East European reforms, and some propensity to think more decisively than the present general secretary. The crucial question about the Soviet political system is whether the structure of power within the party will permit the decisions that are needed or whether the system as a whole is as petrified as the Brezhnev administration seems to be.

The Central Committee

Any change in the Soviet leadership must be made or at least ratified by the Central Committee, and the Central Committee elected at the 26th Party Congress gives the impression of even more continuity than the Politburo. If the worker and peasant members are excluded, 89 percent of the living full members of

Table 2.2 *Types of Employment of Central Committee Members, 1976 and 1981*

Type of Employment	Full Members		Candidate Members	
	1976	1981	1976	1981
National party apparatus	17	29	13	14
Provincial party apparatus	103	106	35	37
National government*	70	78	26	26
Provincial government	24	20	20	19
Military*	20	22	10	13
Lower foreign affairs officials	17	16	4	8
Police	2	5	4	1
Media or cultural figure	5	6	9	10
Scientist or designer	9	11	5	4
Trade unions	3	5	2	3
Workers	8	15	7	8
Peasants†	0	0	0	4
Farm management†	2	1	1	3
Miscellaneous	7	5	3	1
Total	287	319	139	151

* The minister of defense was included in the military category in 1976 when he was a professional military man, but in the national government category in 1981 when he was a life-long civilian.
† Farm brigadiers are included in farm management. In practice, there is one in each of the full "farm management" figures.

the Central Committee were reelected at the 25th Party Congress in 1976, and this year at the 26th Congress in 1981 the percentage was identical. Of the thirty living officials not reelected to the Central Committee, twenty-three were over 65 years of age. Were it not for the removal of several younger men of political importance (notably Dmitrii Poliansky, former Politburo member, and Vasilii Tolstikov, former first secretary of Leningrad), one could say that Central Committee membership in the Brezhnev era almost became a near-life peerage —something that one normally retained until one died or was forced to retire for reasons of health.

If looked at in terms of new membership, however, the picture is not quite so stable. Once again the Central Committee was expanded—this time from 287 voting members in 1976 to 319 in 1981 (see Table 2.2). (Of course, the real size of the Central Committee fluctuates, and the death of the minister of the gas industry, S. A. Orudzhev, in April 1981 reduced the size of the Central Committee to 318.) The expansion of the Central Committee, together with twenty-four deaths of Central Committee members and thirty-three removals (thirty officials and three nonofficials), meant that eighty-nine new members were elected—28 percent of the total.[13] The turnover is even larger if looked at in longer-term perspective. Only twenty-seven of the present voting members had that status in 1970.

The new voting members continue to come mainly from two traditional sources. First, the Central Committee has come to be composed largely of occupants of high-status posts rather than of politically important men and women who are moved around the administrative chessboard. When a post held by a Central Committee member is vacated, his or her successor is usually elected to the Central Committee at the next party congress. This occurred in 78 percent of the cases in 1971, 77 percent of the cases in 1976, and 82 percent in 1981. Secondly, a number of candidate members of the Central Committee are normally promoted to full membership at the next congress, sometimes because they are moved to a more important post, but more usually because the Central Committee has been expanded and the candidate members are in posts whose status is just below that of the full members. In 1971, 49 percent of the new full members had been elected a candidate at the previous congress, and this figure stood at 48 percent in 1976 and 45 percent in 1981. (This time, eight of the candidate members were actually promoted between the congresses.)

With 28 percent of the voting members newly elected in 1981,

Table 2.3 Occupations of Members of Republican Party Bureaus, 1976 and 1981

Occupation	1976 Full Members	1976 Cand. Members	1981 Full Members	1981 Cand. Members
Central Committee secretary	70	2	75	2
Chairman, Council of Ministers	14	0	14	0
Chairman, Presidium of Supreme Soviet	14	0	14	0
First secretary, capital city or region	14	2	11	5
First deputy chairman, Council of Ministers	13	3	13	1
Chairman, People's Control Committee	8	3	c 7	3
Military officer	7	1	8	0
Chairman, Trade Union Council	5	8	6	7
Chairman, KGB	5	7	7	7
First secretary, outlying city or region	3	5	3	11
Head, Organizational-Party-Work Dept., Cent. Comm.	2	9	3	6
Deputy chairman, Council of Ministers	1	3	1	3
Worker	0	0	4	1
Miscellaneous	0	6	1	2
Total	156	49	167	48

two obvious questions arise. First, are there changes in the personal characteristics of the new members that may have significance for the future? Secondly, does the pattern of posts represented on the Central Committee suggest anything about changes that may have occurred in institutional status and, perhaps, influence? We will leave the first question to the next section, and, in dealing with the second, we will supplement the data from the national Central Committee with data from the party elections in the republics just before the congress.[14]

One change in institutional representation in the leading party organs involved regional party officials, but the results were somewhat paradoxical. On the one hand, a conscious policy seems to have been followed in recent years to increase the regional representation on the Politburo and the republican party bureaus, where meaningful discussions are actually held. Not only has the number of regional representatives among the Politburo full and candidate members now risen to nine (really ten, if Pel'she is considered a representative of the Baltic Republics), but between 1976 and 1981 the number of first secretaries of outlying cities and regions among the candidate members of the republican bureaus rose from five to eleven —the most dramatic change in bureau membership (see Table 2.3).

On the other hand, the composition of the voting membership of the broader Central Committee reaffirmed the existence of an old trend: a decline in the representation of provincial officials. Over the years, the proportion of provincial officials among the full members declined steadily from 56 percent in 1956 to 40 percent in 1971. In 1976 the figure rose to 44 percent, but this year it has reached a post-Stalin low of 39 percent. At the same time the basic trend towards representation of republics on the Central Committee in proportion to their percentage of party members has continued, especially if the largely Russian regions in Kazakhstan are really counted as part of the RSFSR[15] (see Table 2.4). With the regional officials so neatly balanced, it is difficult not to see the decline in their percentage representation as a reflection of a growth in the importance of leading personnel

Table 2.4 *Party Members and Central Committee Representation of Union Republics, 1956-1981*

Republic	Percentage of Party Members		Percentage of Provincial Officials on Central Committee					
	1956	1980	1956	1961	1966	1971	1976	1981
Armenia	1.0	.9	1.4	1.2	1.0	1.0	.8	.8
Azerbaidzhan	1.6	1.9	2.7	1.2	1.0	1.0	.8	.8
Belorussia	2.2	3.4	4.1	4.8	6.9	5.2	4.0	4.0
Estonia	.3	.5	1.4	1.2	1.0	2.1	1.6	1.6
Georgia	2.7	2.0	2.7	2.4	2.3	2.1	.8	1.6
Kazakhstan	3.6	4.2	2.7	4.8	6.9	8.3	7.9	8.7
Kirgizia	.7	.7	1.4	1.2	1.0	1.0	.8	.8
Latvia	.8	.9	1.4	2.4	1.0	1.0	.8	.8
Lithuania	.6	1.0	1.4	1.2	1.0	1.0	.8	.8
Moldavia	.6	.9	1.4	1.2	1.0	1.0	.8	.8
RSFSR	68.5	62.1	64.4	51.2	52.9	53.1	60.3	58.7
Tadzhikistan	.5	.6	1.4	1.2	1.0	1.0	.8	.8
Turkmenia	.5	.5	1.4	1.2	1.0	2.1	.8	.8
Ukraine	13.8	16.9	9.6	20.0	16.1	15.6	15.1	15.1
Uzbekistan	2.1	3.2	2.7	4.8	5.2	4.1	4.0	4.0
Total (Absolute Numbers)			73	84	87	96	126	125

Table 2.5 Types of Employment of Full Members of Republican Central Committees, 1976 and 1981

Type of Employment	Armenia 1976	Armenia 1981	Azerbaidzhan 1976	Azerbaidzhan 1981	Belorussia 1976	Belorussia 1981	Estonia 1976	Estonia 1981	Georgia 1976	Georgia 1981	Kazakhstan 1976	Kazakhstan 1981
Central Committee apparatus	13	18	13	15	16	21	14	17	19	20	16	19
Lower party organs	23	21	21	25	33	34	25	26	32	38	41	39
Republican government	34	34	28	27	33	39	36	36	29	37	34	37
Lower governmental organs	1	1	3	3	7	8	7	7	4	4	20	19
"Intelligentsia"*	12	10	10	11	14	14	12	11	13	13	10	9
Military†	2	1	4	2	8	8	3	5	4	3	5	5
Industrial-Construction manager	2	3	2	3	4	4	1	3	4	1	10	12
Farm management‡	4	2	10	10	4	6	8	7	6	5	7	6
Peasant‡	3	5	5	5	3	1	1	2	6	6	9	6
Worker	7	9	20	24	8	11	11	10	13	13	14	9
Miscellaneous	4	3	4	3	2	2	2	5	2	3	3	2
Unknown	16	14	5	3	7	9	5	2	5	4	12	21
Total	121	121	125	131	139	157	125	131	137	147	181	184

Table 2.5—Continued

	Kirgizia 1976	Kirgizia 1981	Latvia 1976	Latvia 1981	Lithuania 1976	Lithuania 1981	Moldavia 1976	Moldavia 1981	Tadzhikistan 1976	Tadzhikistan 1981	Turkmenia 1976	Turkmenia 1981	Ukraine 1976	Ukraine 1981	Uzbekistan 1976	Uzbekistan 1981
CCa	15	15	15	18	13	15	19	20	16	16	14	18	19	21	18	16
Lpo	29	32	32	31	32	35	29	30	26	28	30	33	54	56	45	48
Rg	31	32	37	40	36	38	43	47	38	38	34	35	34	38	42	50
Lgo	5	4	2	1	2	2	2	3	4	5	7	6	12	11	15	14
Int	7	9	9	9	17	17	7	7	11	6	5	7	16	17	10	10
Mil	2	4	6	7	8	7	1	1	3	3	4	4	6	6	2	1
Ind	3	5	3	4	3	3	1	1	4	7	3	3	9	7	8	8
Farm	8	7	7	5	7	6	2	3	15	13	13	11	13	12	7	7
Peas	7	11	5	5	2	2	1	1	2	2	2	4	1	3	2	3
Work	9	10	10	10	14	14	6	6	8	6	15	9	18	14	7	8
Misc	3	3	8	8	4	3	2	3	4	4	3	2	3	4	3	4
Unk	6	5	5	3	7	7	4	3	5	11	10	23	7	6	8	7
Total	125	137	139	141	145	149	117	125	137	139	140	155	191	195	167	177

* Includes cultural figures, newspaper and magazine editors, scientists, and designers
† Includes border guards (KGB) and draft board chairmen (*voenkomy*)
‡ Brigadiers are included among management, link leaders among peasants

in other institutions. (In the republican central committees, although this is not reflected in Table 2.5, there has also been a gradual decline in the proportion of the rural district first secretaries among the full members, probably for similar reasons.)[16]

A second change in the institutional representation on the Central Committee is the obverse of the decline in provincial representation. As Table 2.2 shows, the number of national governmental officials on the Central Committee grew approximately at the same rate as the Central Committee itself, but the representation of the central party apparatus increased from seventeen to twenty-nine. In some part, this increase resulted from the transfer of men who were already Central Committee members to work in the Central Committee apparatus,[17] but the more basic reason was clearly a conscious decision to promote the leading assistant of each of the Central Committee secretaries (and of the chairman of the Party Control Committee) to full membership in the Central Committee. If the Central Committee secretary also serves as department head, then the first deputy head was normally elected to full membership in the Central Committee. Conceivably, the purpose of this maneuver was to free all the secretaries from the duties of department head by promoting the relevant first deputies to those posts, but this did not occur immediately after the Congress.[18] If the secretary did not serve as department head, then the head of the leading department he supervised received this honor (see Table 2.6). As Table 2.5 indicates, a similar expansion occurred in the number of republican central committee officials on the republican central committees.

A third change in institutional representation on the Central Committee in 1981 was an expansion in the number of men from the foreign-policy establishment. This development is not fully visible in Table 2.2, for the seventeen full members of the Central Committee in the category "lower foreign affairs officials" in 1976 were primarily former party officials serving as ambassadors to Communist countries. If we define the foreign-policy establishment more broadly, then we find twenty-four representatives in 1976 instead of seventeen, but only four were long-time foreign-policy professionals. In 1981 the number of representatives had risen to twenty-seven, but the number of professionals had increased from four to eleven.

In the republics too, the number of heads of foreign-ties departments of republican central committees who were elected full members of the national Central Committee rose from two

Table 2.6 Central Committee Secretaries and Their Direct Subordinates on the Central Committee

Secretary*	Subordinates Who Are Full Members of the Central Committee
L. I. Brezhnev	A. M. Aleksandrov-Agentov, personal assistant
	G. E. Tsukanov, personal assistant
M. A. Suslov	Presumably the secretaries, Ponomarev and Zimianin
A. P. Kirilenko	B. I. Gostev, head, Planning and Financial Organs Dept.
M. S. Gorbachev	V. A. Karlov, head, Agriculture Department
	N. E. Kruchina, first deputy head, Agriculture Dept.
K. U. Chernenko	K. M. Bogoliubov, first deputy head, General Department
	N. I. Savinkin, head, Administrative Organs Dept. (probably)
B. N. Ponomarev	V. V. Zagladin, first deputy head, International Dept.
I. V. Kapitonov	N. A. Petrovichev, first deputy head, Organizational-Party-Work Department
V. I. Dolgikh	I. I. Sakhniuk, head, Agricultural Machinery Dept.
M. V. Zimianin	E. M. Tiazhel'nikov, head, Propaganda Dept.
	S. P. Trapeznikov, head, Science-Education Dept.
K. V. Rusakov	O. B. Rakhmanin, first deputy head, Socialist Countries Dept.

Note: The first deputy (I. S. Gustov) of the chairman of the Party Control Committee (A. Ia. Pel'she) was also promoted to full membership in the Central Committee this year. The bosses of the head (N. M. Pegov) and first deputy head (V. N. Bazovsky) of the Personnel Abroad Department, of the head of the Foreign Information Department (L. M. Zamiatin), and of the head of the business office (G. S. Pavlov) are not known for certain, but at least some of these men are probably direct subordinates of Brezhnev.

* The rank-order for Secretaries is that given in the Soviet press. After Brezhnev, it corresponds to tenure in office, first, of the Politburo members, then candidates, and then the non-Politburo members.

to five. One should also mention the new candidate member of the Politburo, Vladimir Kuznetsov, who had been first deputy minister of foreign affairs for over twenty years when he was named first deputy chairman of the Presidium of the Supreme Soviet—a post whose responsibilities include receiving new Western ambassadors.

The increase in foreign-policy specialists on the national Central Committee cut across many categories. The number of officials of the Central Committee apparatus in the foreign-relations realm (excluding the highest leaders such as Brezhnev and Suslov) rose from four to eight. Two directors of foreign-policy institutes (the Institute of the World Economy and International Relations and the Institute of the USA and Canada) were promoted from candidate membership to full membership. Even outside the twenty-seven full members in the foreign-policy establishment proper, the two new military posts represented on the Central Committee were primarily oriented to foreign relations (the chief of staff of the Warsaw Pact and the deputy minister of defense for weapons development). Although the deputy chairman of the KGB who is probably directly in charge of foreign espionage (V. A. Kriuchkov) was not named to the Central Committee,[19] at least one of the three KGB deputy chairmen promoted to full membership in the Central Committee—almost surely the first deputy chairman at a minimum—should have some foreign representatives to go with his domestic ones.

The fourth institutional change is more problematical. The Western press reported an increase in the representation of the security apparatus—the KGB and the military—on the Central Committee, but this is only partially accurate. The military showed no significant increase in membership. The military officers among the full members increased roughly in proportion to the increase in the size of the Central Committee, and the percentage of the line officers among the candidate members actually declined, since the number of political officers increased from two to four. The change in the republican bureaus—shown in Table 2.3—from seven full members and one candidate in 1976 to eight full members was hardly significant, especially if it is noted that the commander of the Kiev military district was elected a candidate member of the Ukrainian bureau several months after the 1976 congress and should be added to the 1976 figures. Table 2.5 suggests a slight percentage decrease in the military representation on the republican central committees, and even if full identification of all members would change this conclusion, clearly there was no significant increase.

The increase in the status of the KGB was more real. The total number of KGB officials among the full and candidate members of the Central Committee remained steady at four, but only one of the four was a full member in 1976 while all were in 1981. Since the three deputy chairmen who were raised in status all came from the old Brezhnev strongholds of Dnepropetrovsk or Moldavia, it is possible that institutional status was less a factor than cronyism in their promotion, but KGB representation also increased marginally in the provinces. In 1976 the chairman of the KGB was a full member of all republican central committees, and his first deputy was usually a candidate member, and, except in the Ukraine, this situation did not change in 1981. However, the number of KGB chairmen on the party bureaus both of the

Table 2.7 *Representation of KGB Chairmen on the Bureaus of the RSFSR Obkomy and on Republican Central Committees of the Union Republics*

Year	Full Member	Cand. Member	Not a Member
Republican Central Committees			
1966	2	2	10
1971	3	3	8
1976	5	7	2
1981	7	7	0
Obkomy, RSFSR*			
1966	31	15	8
1971	32	17	5
1974	35	17	2
1976	34	18	2
1979	38	16	0

* *Obkomy, RSFSR* includes the territorial party committees (*kraikomy*), but excludes the Moscow region (*oblast*) (where the relationship with the city is a complicating factor), the autonomous regions within the territory (*krais*) and the autonomous republics.

republican central committees and the regional committees (*obkomy*) of the RSFSR continued to increase gradually (see Table 2.7).

Finally, changes in representation were observed in several key social groups. Peasant representation remained surprisingly low both in the central and provincial party bodies, but the number of workers among the full members of the national Central Committee rose from eight to fifteen between 1976 and 1981 (see Table 2.2). The substantial number of workers among the unidentified members of the republican central committees makes generalization about the trend at this level more dangerous, but there was probably a very slight rise in worker representation here as well.

It was at the all-important bureau level that workers made an important breakthrough. In the cities and regions, more workers had been getting elected members of the party bureaus, but between 1976 and the party elections of 1979 the proportion of regional committee bureaus in the RSFSR with a worker among their full members rose from over 40 percent to over 75 percent. In 1981, for the first time, workers were elected as full members of the bureaus of the republican party central committees of Armenia, Azerbaidzhan, Georgia, and Latvia; in addition, a worker was elected a candidate member in Lithuania (see Table 2.3).

The representation of women was a very different situation.

The number of women among the full members of the Central Committee remained the same (which meant a decrease in representation from 2.8 percent to 2.5 percent), and at the republican level a substantial decline took place. In 1976, republican bureaus elected four women full members and four women candidates. In 1981 these figures were one and five respectively, an overall decline which is explained by a decrease in the number of women secretaries of the republican central committees from four to one. The picture among middle-level female republican officials is more mixed (the proportion of women on the republican councils of ministers—essentially the top fifty governmental officials in each republic—rose from 4.4 percent to 5.0 percent, but that among the heads of the departments of the republican central committees fell from 6.2 percent to 4.5 percent), but the result is still paradoxical in the face of the unprecedented increase in the number of women admitted to the party that has occurred during the Brezhnev years.

For the first twenty years after the war, the proportion of women in the party remained steady at roughly 20 percent. Then the proportion of women among those admitted to candidate membership rose to 25.7 percent in the 1966–70 period, 30.8 percent in 1976, and 33.5 percent in 1980. Women now comprise 26.5 percent of the total membership compared with 22.2 percent in 1971.[20] Eventually this development almost surely will be reflected in some increase in the number of women among high officials, but the age groups that provide most party members are very different from those from which high officials are drawn. The proportion of women among high officials is influenced by developments that shaped men and women now in their fifties—and by the prejudices of men now in their seventies.

The Rise of the Postwar Generation

The changes in institutional and group status both in the center and in the republics are more the result of past trends and current pressures than reliable indicators of future ones. At the national level in particular, the changes are made or at least confirmed at the Politburo level, and a man as careful in guarding his power position as Brezhnev would not permit what he considers dangerous changes in the Central Committee, which has the power to remove him. Any important changes in the 1980s will almost surely be made by men who come after Brezhnev—if they have the will and the ability.

The Politburo, of course, continues to be dominated by the Brezhnev generation. Only three of the fourteen Politburo voting members were born in 1918 or later (that is, are 63 years of age or younger in 1981), and only five in 1914 or later. If the future trends were to be determined by the Politburo alone, little would be likely to change. In reality, however, the key decisions are the ultimate responsibility of the Central Committee. They will be influenced by social forces outside the Politburo which are reflected mainly in the middle levels of the various bureaucracies which employ nearly everyone in the country.

This is not the place for a comprehensive examination of the generational changes taking place within the various Soviet hierarchies, all the more so since two recent books are devoted to the subject. It should be noted, however, that the rates of turnover among officials, especially in the provinces, continue to be quite substantial (see Tables 2.8, 2.9 and 2.10). Some of the turnover simply consists of normal promotion from one category on the table to another or even lateral movement within a single category, but the figures on the turnover among voting members of the republican and regional committee bureaus and repub-

Table 2.8 *Turnover among Top Officials, 1971–81 (in Percent)*

	1971–76		1976–81		1971–81	
	1971 Officials Not in Office in 1976	1976 Officials Not in Office in 1971	1976 Officials Not in Office in 1981	1981 Officials Not in Office in 1976	1971 Officials Not in Office in 1981	1981 Officials Not in Office in 1971
Officials						
Deputy chairmen, USSR Council of Ministers	18	10	45	57	64	71
Other members of USSR Council of Ministers	23	26	30	32	50	55
Central Committee secretaries	10	18	27	20	40	40
Head of Central Committee depts.*	26	26	11	27	42	48
Republican party first secretaries	29	29	21	21	50	50
Obkom party first secretaries	36	39	41	41	68	69

* When a Central Committee secretary headed a Central Committee department, the first deputy head is counted as department head for purposes of this calculation.

lican central committees show movement in and out of the leadership pool of an area. Except in isolated cases (for example, the republic of Georgia in the early 1970s), the Soviet Union has not witnessed the kind of sweeping changes in the middle bureaucracies that have been seen in Poland recently, but over a ten-year period, the gradual replacement of personnel now taking place can have a major cumulative impact.

Table 2.9 *Turnover among Republican Officials, 1971–81 (in Percent)*

Officials	1971–76		1976–81		1971–81	
	1971 Officials Not in Office in 1976	1976 Officials Not in Office in 1971	1976 Officials Not in Office in 1981	1981 Officials Not in Office in 1976	1971 Officials Not in Office in 1981	1981 Officials Not in Office in 1971
Republican party first secretaries	29	29	21	21	50	50
Other republican party secretaries	55	55	59	62	88	89
Dept. heads, repub. central committee	57	59	64	67	86	88
Chairmen, republican Council of Ministers	36	36	50	50	71	71
Members, republican Council of Ministers	45	46	47	50	74	76
Raikom first secretaries (10 republics)	66	68	63	64	88	89
Full members, repub. party bureaus	39	45	38	43	67	72
Full members, repub. central committees	47	54	41	43	66	70
High officials among full members, repub. central committees*	38	43	31	36	59	65

NOTE: The figures are based on all the republics except the Russian Republic. In the first six categories, a movement from one post to another, even within the same category, is counted as turnover. In the last three categories, a change of job is not counted as turnover, only departure from or election to the bureau or Central Committee. The right-hand column of the three pairs usually shows greater turnover, for an expansion in the number of officials (which often occurred) meant that there were more new officials in the last year than old officials who departed.

* Includes officials of the republican central committees, members of the republican council of ministers, a few other republican officials (for example, trade union officials), regional (*oblast*) level officials, district (*raion*) officials in republics other than Belorussia, Kazakhstan, the Ukraine, and Uzbekistan, and newspaper editors. Military officers, almost all of whom left the republic between congresses, are excluded.

Table 2.10 Turnover among RSFSR Regional Officials, 1971–80 (in Percent)

Officials	1971–75	1975–80	1971–80
First secretary, regional party committees	24	24	47
Chairman, executive committee of regional soviets	40	47	73
Other secretaries, regional party committees	41	40	63
Deputy chairmen, executive committee, regional soviets	43	43	72
Heads of administrations, regional soviets*	37	38	65
First secretaries, capital city party committees	50	62	79
Voting members of bureau, regional party committees†	—	—	56

NOTE: Data on first secretaries of regional committees, chairmen of executive committees of regional soviets, and bureau members reflects all 55 regions. In the other four categories of this table, the data reflects only 34 regions.

* This is based on 13 administrations (*upravleniia*) and departments (*otdely*): agriculture, communal economy, consumers' services, culture, education, finance, food industry, health, internal affairs, local industry, planning, road construction, and trade.
† Bureaus were not elected in 1975, and it would have taken more time than was available to determine the bureau membership at that time. In this one case, the final date for the turnover calculation was 1979—the year of bureau elections. This is the one category in the table in which expansion has occurred from 1971 to 1979. In 1979, 60 percent of the voting members had not held their seats on the bureau in 1971.

Turnover does not, of course, necessarily mean rejuvenation. The replacement of the 76-year-old Kosygin as chairman of the Council of Ministers by the 75-year-old Tikhonov may have brought to power a man younger in heart (certainly one sounder in heart), but it does not lead one to think of generational change. In the provinces, however, turnover has brought much younger men to the fore. The 1975 data of Table 2.11 is the most recent available in comprehensive form on the non-Russian republics, for the republican newspapers did not publish the year of birth of the 1980 deputies and the republican biographical directories for that year are not yet available. Nevertheless, scattered information suggests that younger officials are continuing to be appointed and that the 1980 pattern found in the Russian Republic (see Table 2.12) is also present in the other republics.[21]

The characteristics of the new officials are difficult to summarize, for they differ from specialized hierarchy to hierarchy. Moreover, the first members of any age group to reach a certain administrative level have been on an especially fast track, and it is easy to jump to the erroneous conclusion that their characteristics will be found in other members of the age-group who are promoted at more normal speeds.[22]

Table 2.11 *Average Age and Representation of the Post-Stalin Generation among Republican Elites (7 non-Slav Republics) 1975–6*

Position	No.	Average Age	Representation of Post-Stalin Generation (%)
Republican secretaries	37	55.3	27.0
Presidium of Council of Ministers	42	55.7	33.3
Department heads, Central Committee	89	51.1	46.1
Council of Ministers	210	54.2	35.2
First secretaries, district and city party committees	267	47.8	66.6
Chairmen, executive committees of city and district soviets	71	47.2	73.2

SOURCE: Seweryn Bialer, *Stalin's Successors: Leadership, Stability, and Change in the Soviet Union* (Cambridge: Cambridge University Press, 1980), p. 111.

The most noticeable general feature of the new officials populating the middle levels of the bureaucracy is that they come from a new generation who were educated in the postwar period and have had almost all of their work career in the post-Stalin period. Especially because of the emphasis placed on engineering and agricultural education for important political and administrative work in the Soviet Union, World War II had a devastating impact on the generation who should have been in college during those years (essentially those born between 1919 and 1926). By the time that the war was over, they had forgotten much of their mathematics but many of them had gained administrative and political experience, and a disproportionate number moved into the type of second-level political work which

Table 2.12 *Age Distribution of RSFSR Regional Officials, 1980*

Age and Period of Birth	Regional Party First Secretaries	Other Regional Party Secretaries	Chairmen Regional Soviets	Dept. Heads Soviets
Under 40 (post-1939)	0%	2%	0%	4%
40–44 (1935–39)	0%	18%	8%	12%
45–49 (1930–34)	20%	24%	27%	19%
50–54 (1925–29)	25%	34%	41%	36%
55–59 (1920–24)	16%	13%	14%	21%
60–64 (1915–19)	25%	8%	8%	7%
65 and over (pre-1915)	13%	1%	2%	1%
AVERAGE AGE	57	50	52	51

SOURCE: Jerry F. Hough, *Soviet Leadership in Transition* (Washington, D.C.: Brookings Institution, 1981), p. 74

was not thought to require technical education. (Women of this age group did especially well because they gained early political experience at home while the men were at the front.)

Those who were too young to fight in World War II or who fought in it only briefly had a much different set of experiences. They spent the war in secondary school, and they entered college at a time when those of lower class origins were not given any preference in admission. Only the best students passed the highly selective entrance exams (and naturally they tended to come from white-collar homes which emphasized education and transmitted cultural values), and they passed through college during the rigorous period which became famous in the West at the time of the first Sputnik. The officials in this age-group, a group much larger than its predecessor because it had been spared the battlefield, began reaching their fifties during the late 1970s and have come to dominate the provincial administration.

Members of this postwar generation have begun moving into the higher positions, often "jumping" the preceding wartime generation in the process. Although the slow rate of turnover among Central Committee members has retarded the rise of younger officials, the election of eighty-nine new voting members in 1981 created the opportunity for considerable promotion, and Table 2.13 dramatically shows the jumping of the generations. The officials among the voting members of the 1976 Central Committee who were not on it in 1981 were born in 1912 on the average. Even though a half-dozen of the new voting members were 70 years old, the average year of birth of the officials named voting members for the first time was still 1924. As a result, the average age of the voting members of the Central Committee fell from 63 on the eve of the Congress to 61 or perhaps even 60.

Table 2.13 *Age Distribution of Obkom First Secretaries and Central Governmental Officials Elected to the Central Committee, 1981*

Years of Birth	Obkom First Secretaries	Central Govt. Officials*
Pre-1910	2	16
1910–14	7	25
1915–19	21	19
1920–24	17	7
1925–29	30	17
Post-1929	22	3

NOTE: Table includes both full and candidate members.
* Includes members of the Council of Ministers (excluding *ex post facto* republican members) and deputy chairmen of the USSR Gosplan.

The great uncertainty about the Soviet political system is the set of attitudes within the Central Committee. Members of the Central Committee under Brezhnev must have enjoyed a likely prospect of life tenure, and they must recall that both Stalin and Khrushchev used their power to follow a very different personnel policy toward earlier Central Committee members. Although officials of the postwar generation surely have more "modern" attitudes on the average than officials of the Brezhnev generation,[23] those on the Central Committee might well allow any general views to be overridden by their interest in personal political survival and might, therefore, support a leadership candidate who promises not to change the status quo.

If the Central Committee does choose such a course, the dependence of the leader on a body composed largely of administrative officials who in turn owe their jobs to him will be seen in retrospect to be the fatal flaw in the Soviet political system. It will have hindered the system's ability to adjust to changing conditions without the type of unrest that developed in Poland. The petrification that has marked the last years of the Brezhnev regime will have proven to be the first sign of the petrification of the system. And, in the Soviet Union, there is no outside army whose threatened intervention could inhibit the spread of revolution to the internal army.

The difficulties that have always attended the prediction of the Soviet future in the 1980s have been further deepened by the events in Poland. An article written at the time of the Extraordinary July Congress in Poland cannot be certain about the ultimate Soviet response to the Polish developments nor about the response of the Soviet leadership to what may be the general secretary's indecisiveness in the face of the crisis or of the possible spread of the unrest to the Baltic States. If the Polish crisis is resolved more or less to the satisfaction of the Soviet leadership, one would think that they would conclude that they should avoid the grandiose, reckless program launched by Gierek, but should gradually move to correct the type of economic imbalances that would require Draconian action in the event of a crisis. A Central Committee whose members are over a decade younger than the members of the inner core of the Politburo should find the threat to the system and the possibility of promotion of key regional officials to key central posts sufficient incentives to entrust the party to a mildly reformist leader,[24] but it is never guaranteed that political institutions *will* do what they *should* do.

Notes

1 For a discussion of this generation, see Jerry F. Hough, *Soviet Leadership in Transition* (Washington, D.C.: The Brookings Institution, 1980), pp. 57–60. My "postwar generation" is marginally different from Seweryn Bialer's "post-Stalin generation" (the latter includes, besides members of the "postwar generation," officials who were slightly older but whose wartime experience delayed their rise into responsible work until the post-Stalin period), but the two are basically the same. Bialer's definition has the consequence of increasing the number of high officials with a "new" set of attitudes, and in this respect it almost surely corresponds with reality. See Seweryn Bialer, *Stalin's Successors* (Cambridge, Eng.: Cambridge University Press, 1980), pp. 102–124.
2 New commanders of military districts were almost all born in the early 1920s and hence had low-level exposure to World War II.
3 *Pravda*, 6 March 1981, p. 2.
4 The importance of population in determining regional representation was neatly shown in the Georgian and Azerbaidzhani cases. During the Khrushchev years, Georgia ranked sixth in population, and its first secretary (Mzhavanadze) was a candidate member of the Politburo. By the time that he was retired, however, Azerbaidzhan had passed Georgia in population, and when Mzhavanadze was replaced on the Politburo, it was by the Azerbaidzhan first secretary rather than the Georgian. Then when the regional representation was expanded by one in 1979, it was the leader of Georgia—now next in line in population—who was named.
5 At the end of the war, special organs were created under the Council of People's Commissars to develop rockets and nuclear bombs. Ustinov headed the rocket program and V. L. Bannikov the atomic. See V. Tolubko, "Osnova boevogo mogushchestva," *Tekhnika i vooruzhenie*, no. 11, 1974, p. 3. From 1956 to 1960 "the office of the Central Committee secretary [Leonid Brezhnev] was a special kind of staff, where the most important questions of rocket construction were decided," and Ustinov, as deputy chairman of the Council of Ministers for the defense industry for most of this period was the chief governmental official involved. See V. Tolubko, *Nedelin: Pervyi glavkom strategicheskikh* (Moscow: Molodaia gvardiia, 1979), p. 183.
6 For recent indications of Kirilenko's decline, see Boris Meissner, "The 26th Party Congress and Soviet Domestic Politics," *Problems of Communism* XXX, no. 3 (May-June 1981), p. 5.
7 *Pravda*, 24 April 1981, p. 4, and 25 April 1981, p. 5.
8 Kosolapov's biography only states that he entered Komsomol work immediately after graduation in 1955, but that would not have occurred if he had not been active in it in the university.
9 At a time when the Moscow Regional Committee (*obkom*) supervised the city as well as the outlying region, Kapitonov was first secretary of the Moscow City Committee from 1952 to 1954, while Grishin was second secretary of the regional committee. (Khrushchev was then first secretary of the Regional Committee and supervised them both.) Then from 1954 Kapitonov became first secretary of the Regional Committee and Grishin remained his second secretary before becoming the national trade union chairman in 1956.
10 For Vedernikov's posts in Stavropol, see *Stavropol'skaia pravda*, 21 February 1971, p. 1, and 23 February 1974, p. 1.
11 From 1952 to 1956 Grishin was second secretary of the Moscow Regional Committee having worked the previous two years as head of that committee's Machinery Industry Department. Kapitonov was Grishin's predecessor as second secretary, and then from 1952 to 1954 served as first secretary of the Moscow City Committee (*gorkom*) and from 1954 to 1959 as the Moscow Regional Committee first secretary (and, therefore, as Grishin's direct boss from 1954 to 1956). N. A. Petrovichev, the first deputy head of the Organizational-Party-Work Department of the Central Committee since 1968, worked as head of the Propaganda-Agitation Department of the Moscow Regional Committee under Kapitonov in the late 1950s. See *Directory of Soviet Offtcals* (Washington, D.C.: Department of

State, August 1960), Vol. 1, p. 154. The only regional committee secretary in the RSFSR to be shifted from one region (*oblast*) to another in recent years, was head of one of the departments of the Moscow regional committee from 1951 to 1955 under Kapitonov and Grishin. (Of course, since he then became head of the Urals and Western Siberian section of the Central Committee's Party Organs Department—as the Organization-Party-Work Department was then called—he obviously also came to know Kirilenko very well in the latter's capacity as first secretary of the Sverdlovsk Regional Committee.) See *Kalininskaia pravda*, 10 February 1979, p. 1.

12 Andropov worked for eleven years in Komsomol and party work in the Karelo-Finnish Republic, where Kuusinen was chairman of the Presidium of the Supreme Soviet. As Kuusinen became more prominent in policy making towards foreign Communists after Stalin's death, Andropov was named ambassador to the extremely sensitive country of Hungary, and in May 1957—less than two months before Kuusinen was named a full member of the party Presidium, Andropov was appointed head of the newly created Socialist Countries Department of the Central Committee. For a description of Kuusinen in these years, see F. M. Burlatsky, "O. V. Kuusinen—marksistskoleninskii issledovatel' i teoretik," *Rabochii klass i sovremennyi mir*, no. 6, 1979, pp. 99–104.

13 Actually eight of the new full members had already been promoted to that status from candidate membership in the period between the 25th and 26th congresses.

14 The membership of the republican bureaus and central committees, along with the members' occupations, were printed in the respective republican newspapers at the conclusion of the republican congresses, which were held in late January and in early February.

15 In nearly half the regions the Kazakhs comprise less than one-quarter of the population.

16 The proportion of rural district first secretaries among the full members fell from 11 percent in 1976 to 10 percent in 1981.

17 For example, the Komsomol first secretary, Evgenii Tiazhel'nikov, became head of the Propaganda Department of the Central Committee, while Ivan Sakhniuk, the first secretary of the Kharkov Regional Committee became the head of the newly created Agricultural Machinery Department.

18 See *Pravda*, 29 May 1981, p. 4; 13 June 1981, p. 4; 2 August 1981, p. 4.

19 When a monument was dedicated in Baku to the famous spy of the prewar period, Richard Sorge, the head of military intelligence (Sorge's direct superior) and one deputy chairman of the KGB (Kriuchkov) attended. Almost certainly this was the deputy chairman with overseas intelligence responsibilities. See *Bakinskii rabochii*, May 8, 1981, p. 1.

20 *Ekonomicheskaia gazeta*, no. 10 (March) 1981, p. 15.

21 For example, when new ministers are appointed in the Ukraine, their biographies are now always published. The new ministers are almost invariably born in 1930 or later.

22 Thus, the men born in 1927 or later who were elected regional committee first secretary before being named to the Central Committee at the 25th Party Congress had attained this job at the average age of 41 and had had only nine years of work outside the party apparatus. Those born in 1927 or later who were elected first secretary between the 25th and 26th congresses and named to the Central Committee in 1981 for the first time became regional committee first secretary at the average age of 47 and had worked for twelve years outside the party apparatus.

23 This hypothesis is also presented in Bialer, 1980, pp. 102–107; and Hough, 1980, pp. 103–108, 127–30, 144–49.

24 By the time any succession occurs, other changes too may have occurred in the elite. Already in the months since the 26th Party Congress, one of the older regional committee secretaries on the Central Committee (the 69-year-old A. M. Borodin from the Kustanai region has retired). He was replaced by the 51-year-old V. P. Demidenko from the North Kazakh region (already a member of the Central Committee), but the latter was replaced by V. T. Stepanov, who was born in 1928 (*Kazakhstanskaia pravda*, 10 April 1981). For Stepanov's year of birth, see *Leninskoe znamia* (North Kazakhstan), 31 May 1977.

3
Reformism, Conservatism, and Leadership Authority at the 26th Party Congress

George W. Breslauer

The purpose of this chapter is to examine the speeches of Leonid Brezhnev and Nikolai Tikhonov at the 26th Party Congress, to determine their stated approaches to domestic policy and foreign economic ties, to place this analysis in the context of the history of reformist and conservative policies during the Brezhnev era, and to offer evidence bearing on the relationship among reformism, conservatism, and political authority in Soviet elite politics.

My argument, in brief, is that since 1973, Brezhnev has led a political coalition on behalf of conservative domestic policies and reformist foreign policies. He has avoided economic decentralization and slashes of the defense budget, but has sought to increase economic efficiency and consumer satisfaction by importing Western capital, technology, expertise, and consumer goods (including grain). At the same time he has sought to buttress the long-term viability of this program through the development of Siberia. Siberian development holds out the hope that, by the 1990s, the Soviets will possess an inexhaustible supply of mineral wealth to trade for Western consumer goods, and would therefore be able to maintain indefinitely a relatively conservative political, economic, and administrative regime.

Alexei Kosygin was not a vocal advocate of this approach. He was rather consistent in advocating greater experimentation with reformist approaches to domestic economic organization. And he engaged in polemical debate with Brezhnev on these matters at the 25th Party Congress in 1976. But by the time of the 26th Party Congress in 1981, Nikolai Tikhonov had taken

Kosygin's place, and was singing a very different tune. He sounded like a Brezhnev loyalist, neither advocating domestic policy reformism nor challenging the workability of Brezhnev's program. This change has important implications (explored below) for our interpretation of the link between Politburo members and various types of "constituency pressures" in the Soviet political establishment.

There are many definitions of reformism in the literature on Soviet politics. Minimalist definitions equate reformism with any policy change, of whatever magnitude, in a liberal or progressive direction.[1] Maximalist definitions of the term equate it with a commitment to market socialism and political democracy.[2] I use the term differently in this paper, for these definitions do not strike me as very useful. The minimalist definition trivializes the concept by applying it to both insignificant and significant changes. The maximalist definition demands so much change that it leaves us without a conceptual apparatus for understanding the "great issues" that have animated Politburo-level conflict throughout the Brezhnev era. That definition identifies a policy of change which would be more appropriately called radicalism than reformism.

As I use the term, reformist policies are those which challenge core traditional values that became ingrained during the Stalin era: priority status for military and heavy-industrial interests in the budgetary process; the sanctity of a planning and administrative structure that combines central ministerial dominance over local economic units with the interventionist prerogatives of central and local party organs; a pattern of political participation that protects official political authority against unregulated criticism or challenges "from below"; and a confrontational foreign policy that justifies economic self-sufficiency. Thus, reformism is not a one-dimensional term. Leaders may, for example, pursue political reformism without pursuing budgetary, administrative, or foreign-policy reformism. Other variants are possible, though interdependencies in the Soviet economic system probably ensure that only a few variants will work effectively—but that is another issue.

Conservative policies, then, are those which stay within the limits defined by the core traditional values just noted (but which do not entail a return to Stalinism, for that would be not a conservative but a reactionary course). Those policies may take many different forms. My use of these terms will perhaps be clarified by a glance at the evolution of reformist and conservative policies and programs in the Brezhnev era.[3]

Reformism and Conservatism Under Brezhnev and Kosygin: 1965-76

During the first year after Khrushchev's dismissal, a rather broad consensus formed in the Soviet Politburo on behalf of reversing Krushchev's populist political reformism, and on behalf of rejecting calls for evolution toward liberal-democratic constitutionalism. Within this politically conservative consensus, conflict centered on the preferred approach to administrative and budgetary policies. The Kosygin reforms were modest in scope, but that is no reason to label them conservative. For the premises that underlay them reflected a reformist inclination to experiment with movement in the direction of decentralized economic authority and formalized restraints on ministerial and party intervention in managerial policy decisions. Naturally, this inclination provoked opposition, in both the administrative structure and the Central Committee and Politburo, from those inclined toward conservative variants of economic administration—both the computerizers and the mobilizers.

On budgetary policy, the debate within the Politburo revolved around two alternative approaches: (1) a simultaneous massive infusion of funds into the agricultural and defense sectors, with much more modest (though increased) allocations to light industry and consumer services; and (2) a more substantial infusion of funds into light industry, a defense buildup, and substantial (but not massive) investments in agriculture, coupled with experimentation with forms of agricultural decentralization that might make the investment yield a higher return. Brezhnev leaned toward the first policy, while Kosygin leaned toward the second, more reformist policy. The forces led or encouraged by Brezhnev carried the day, both in administrative and budgetary policy.

During 1969-71, Brezhnev expanded both his policy-making authority and his power base in the leadership. Yet his behavior at the 24th Party Congress revealed that his conservatism of 1965-1968 was, at least in part, exaggerated for politically opportunistic reasons. In his accountability report, Brezhnev tempered his budgetary and administrative conservatism, moving in a moderately reformist direction. He announced that Group B industries would grow at a higher rate than Group A industries in the 9th Five-Year Plan, and he legitimized this with doctrinal innovations. He launched a campaign to pressure officials in heavy-industrial and defense industries to produce "industrial consumer goods" above plan, and buttressed this campaign with a series of doctrinal revisions that reduced the ideological status of traditional heavy-industrial priorities. He also coopted the production-association issue, and pointed out its reformist implications by warning the central ministries against obstructing the creation of associations that cut across ministerial jurisdictions, while similarly warning provincial party officials against obstructing creation of associations that cut across, and diluted, regional committee (*obkom*) jurisdictions. Finally, he publicly praised the Shchekino experiment for the first time in his administration.

Kosygin had been outflanked, both politically and programmatically. The issue of reformism had been coopted by Brezhnev and rechanneled in a more moderate direction. Kosygin accepted this redefinition—or was forced to accept it— as his speech to the 24th Party Congress shows. In that document, one finds an extraordinarily high level of agreement with Brezhnev's moderate budgetary and administrative reformism. The polarized polemics of 1967–68 are nowhere in evidence. A new consensus had been reached or imposed.

By 1976, the consensus had unraveled. Before that, Brezhnev's program had been frustrated by the harvest failure of 1972. During 1973, Brezhnev redefined the program, largely eliminating the reformist components and reverting to a conservative approach to problem solving. Brezhnev's speech to the 25th Party Congress (1976), which reflected that redefinition, offered a new program with the following components:

1   Massive investment in agriculture, and rejection of agricultural decentralization as an alternative (though agro-industrial complexes were the preferred form of deconcentration);
2   No mention of campaigns to pressure heavy-industry and defense officials to produce consumer goods above plan; an end to projections that Group B would exceed Group A in rates of growth; reassertion of the doctrinal priority of heavy-industrial growth rates;
3   No special lauding of production associations; no criticism of oppositions to their establishment as long as it was based on criteria of economic efficiency and not of political jurisdiction;
4   No mention of the Shchekino experiment:
5   Endorsement of huge projects and campaigns (development of the Non-Black-Earth Zone, Siberian development, the

Baikal-to-Amur Railroad that fit in with the conservative mobilizational tradition.

The one reformist feature of the program was in the foreign-policy realm. To buttress the credibility of the program (as well as its actual workability), Brezhnev linked his domestic policies explicitly to the expansion of foreign economic ties—something he had not done at the 24th Party Congress. Brezhnev's discussion of such ties, which had appeared in the international-relations section of his 1971 speech, now received twice as much space and a section of its own, located in the economic portion of the report. Finally, Brezhnev's statements explicitly conceded that expanded foreign economic ties would improve the chances of achieving domestic economic goals, including improved consumer satisfaction.

Thus, Brezhnev proposed to balance off his conservative policies at home with a reformist foreign policy that was collaborative and antiautarkic, in hopes of demonstrating that he too could do what Soviet party leaders had been trying to do since Stalin's death—provide the mixture of conservatism and reformism that would promote both national security and consumer satisfaction.

Doubts about the viability or desirability of Brezhnev's program, though, appear to have emerged sufficiently to be in evidence at the 25th Party Congress. The two indicators of this that I have studied are the language of insistence, urgency, and accusation in Brezhnev's speech, and the refusal of Kosygin to endorse Brezhnev's program this time around.

Brezhnev's language of insistence took several forms. In defense of his agricultural program, the general secretary proclaimed that it "has passed the test of time ... it is correct ... the Party will, in the future as well, follow this line." In apparent rebuttal of those who might favor a different approach to raising agricultural efficiency (such as decentralization *à la* link system?), Brezhnev argued, "This is a complex matter; there are no ready recipes." On light industry, Brezhnev laid responsibility for failure on the "central planning and economic organs," and on all those who "plan and direct this sector of the economy." With respect to public administration, Brezhnev covered his retreat on the production-association movement by dramatically embracing the cause of project planning and interbranch programs, calling structural changes toward these ends "an unpostponable matter" and insisting that the changes must "take effect in the immediate future." He told the delegates that they had "measured the cloth" enough and now had to act on the need for these changes. For the first time in the Brezhnev era, he return to these matters in his closing remarks to that congress, tempering their usual optimism with the warning that the delegates must "concentrate on the remaining shortcomings and unsolved problems." Finally, Brezhnev's language of accusation found expression in escalated threats against cadres who did not shape up. In 1971, his remarks on cadre policy had been balanced and conciliatory. In 1976, they were harsh indeed, threatening forced retirements.

I have assumed that Brezhnev's language of insistence was a response to growing skepticism in the political elite about the workability of his program, and reflected his effort to parry responsibility for failure, seize the initiative with new directions in policy, and basically insist that "there is no other way!" Kosygin's speech suggests that, if this interpretation is correct, Brezhnev faced skepticism (if not challenges to his policy effectiveness) from within the Politburo itself.[4] For a close analysis of Kosygin's speech indicates that the consensus of 1971 was dead, and that Kosygin now reembraced reformist causes in response to Brezhnev's conservatism, while simultaneously seeking to counter Brezhnev's efforts to parry responsibility for failure.

On agricultural matters, Kosygin failed to echo Brezhnev's assertion that agriculture constituted a "task of all the people," and he challenged Brezhnev by enumerating agricultural shortfalls at length and declaring that "everything cannot be attributed to the weather." Kosygin also failed to echo Brezhnev's definition of heavy industry as "the foundation of the economy" or his definition of the party's "main task" as priority development of that sector. On matters of light industry, the Kosygin "dissent" was elaborate:

1 He did not blame ministers and planners for shortfalls;
2 He blamed agricultural problems for many of the problems in the food and light industries;
3 He stressed that all sectors of the economy should contribute to consumer-goods production (whereas Brezhnev had pointed to "huge reserves" in Group B industries, and had demanded that all sectors contribute to agricultural development);
4 He did not endorse importation of consumer goods in his discussion of foreign economic ties (for, I assume, such importation would undercut the case for expanded investment in Group B industries);

5   He invoked the language of insistence on this issue, referring to the urban and rural masses' "urgent...persistent demands" for more and better consumer goods.

An analogous dissent by the Soviet prime minister was in evidence on matters of public administration. Whereas Brezhnev had retreated to a muted and conservative discussion of production associations, Kosygin now embraced them and insisted that movement be initiated once again in the direction of exploiting their *reformist* potential. Kosygin lauded production associations as a "qualitatively new phenomenon in the management of industrial production." He resurrected the language of the 1965 reforms, calling for "signed contracts," "direct, long-term ties," and "long-term credits" as the basis for new forms of horizontal ties among these production units. And in contrast to Brezhnev's emphasis on project and regional planning through programs conceived in Moscow, Kosygin demanded an "active role" for local soviets and Union-republic councils of ministers in such planning.

The breadth of this dissent was striking. What was its source? Was Kosygin speaking for himself or was he echoing the skepticism of a broader constituency within the Soviet political elite? If Kosygin was speaking for himself, it is not likely that he was challenging Brezhnev's power (the man was never that ambitious, and was in poor health). It is more likely that he was defending himself against efforts by Brezhnev to deflect responsibility for poor performance. For the 25th Congress was held in the shadow of the disastrous 1975 harvest, abrogation of the Soviet-American Trade Agreement, and the apparent decline of détente in light of Angola, Vietnam, and the exile of Solzhenitsyn. Brezhnev, by using the language of insistence in his speech, seemed to be responding to skeptics by going on the counteroffensive—a shrewd tactic in any political system. Kosygin was vulnerable to such an effort, and may have been trying to protect himself by taking to the counteroffensive as well.

But Kosygin may also have been echoing the sentiments and interests of a broader, more reformist constituency. There is no way to know for sure which was the case at the time, but we might gain some insight on the problem by examining the speeches of Brezhnev and Tikhonov at the 26th Party Congress in 1981, when Kosygin was dead and buried, replaced by a "Brezhnev man."

The 26th Party Congress (1981)

An examination of Brezhnev's speech to the 26th Party Congress (*Pravda*, 24 February 1981, pp. 2–9) reveals the expected: the general secretary has reshuffled his program somewhat, but the program remains largely a conservative one.

Agriculture remains a priority sector in Brezhnev's program. After the harvest failures of 1979 and 1980, the Soviet leader was candid about the difficulties, but reiterated that further elaboration of his approach to the problem—not an alternative approach—was required:

> Difficulties in supplying food to the population are still occurring.... In order to achieve a radical solution to the problem, it has been deemed necessary to work out a special food program.... The foundation of the food program is the further development of agriculture (p. 6, col. 1).

Later in the speech, when discussing the peasantry as a social class, he devoted most of his attention to the need for a comprehensive program to make rural areas economically attractive places to live. He declared such development to be a necessary condition for the success of the food program, and pointed out that it would require "much effort, time, and resources" (p. 6, col. 3). Still further, he addressed the Non-Black-Earth Zone development project, calling it "so complex and urgent [or unpostponable—*neotlozhnyi*] that it has to be tackled through the joint efforts of all republics and in as short a time as possible" (p. 7, col. 2).

The one new wrinkle—which would be counted as reformist by most definitions—was a big pitch for easing restraints on the private sector in Soviet agriculture as a contribution to improving the food supply problem. This approach had already taken on campaign proportions in the fall of 1976, well after the 25th Party Congress, where the private sector had received a much more modest endorsement in Brezhnev's speech. Now the program has escalated still further, gaining support not only from the general secretary (p. 6, col. 2) but also from a series of new legal enactments. Thus, Brezhnev's political support stands behind a highly costly agricultural program based on centralist principles, and supplemented by greater largesse for the private sector.

A major change in Brezhnev's program from that of February 1976—though one that still falls under the conservative rubric —was his advocacy of energy development.[5] This sector is to receive large new investments in the 11th Five-Year Plan, a priority that is reflected in Brezhnev's Party Congress address. Energy simply dominated the speech, to such an extent that I am tempted to propose that Brezhnev embraced it as the heroic campaign of the decade, by which he would retain the policy initiative and demonstrate his policy effectiveness. In his discussion of economic progress, territorial production complexes for oil, gas, and coal received first attention (p. 4, col. 4). When he discussed the importance of heavy-industrial growth, energy development provided the first examples (p. 5, col. 1). When outlining bottlenecks to be overcome, he cited the development of heavy industry, "especially, and in the first place, the fuel and energy branches" (p. 5, col. 2), as well as the need to increase expenditures for development of the East and North (p. 5, col. 1). In his section on the "more efficient use of production potential," much of the discussion dealt with the need to reduce wastage of energy resources, adding that "successes in the entire national economy will greatly depend on raising the efficiency of the extraction industry" (p. 5, col. 3). When he discussed concrete administrative changes in the national economy, his examples of models to be followed were the interbranch departments and commissions created to coordinate development of the West Siberian oil and gas complex (p. 6, col. 3). The central importance of energy development in Brezhnev's speech was summed up in the following quotation:

> I consider it necessary to single out the rapid increase in extraction of Siberian gas as a task of primary economic and political importance. The deposits of the West Siberian region are unique. The largest of them—Urengoi—has such a gigantic amount that it could, for many years, meet the internal needs of the country as well as export needs—including exports to capitalist countries.
> I would like only to emphasize that the task of improving the structure of the fuel and power balance is becoming more and more pressing.
> The extraction of gas and oil in West Siberia, and their transport to the European section of the country, will have to be considered the most important links in the energy program of both the 11th and even the 12th Five-Year Plans. Such is the aim of the Party's Central Committee, and, I hope, it will be supported by the Congress. (p. 5, col. 2)

On top of these commitments, Brezhnev reaffirmed the priority development of heavy industry as the main task of the 11th Five-Year Plan. Given the slowdown in the rate of increase in capital available for investment, and given that Brezhnev is not pushing behind the scenes for defense budget cuts, it would be a great surprise to find Brezhnev realistically advocating much expanded investment in light industry and consumer services. Yet the draft of the 11th Five-Year Plan apparently calls for expanded investment in consumer-goods production,[6] and Brezhnev's speech contained faint echoes of his 1971 speech. At the 26th Party Congress, Brezhnev announced that the rate of growth of Group B industries would exceed that of Group A. He called on heavy-industrial enterprises to produce more industrial consumer goods. And he urged the new Ministry of the Chemicals Industry to "make real strides in the production of synthetics" for use in consumer soft goods (p. 6, col. 2).

Despite all this, there is substantial reason to doubt Brezhnev's commitment to the cause of consumer goods; that is, he did not appear willing to incur much in the way of political or economic costs to advance progress in these sectors. Several indicators of this low priority were in evidence in his speech (p. 6, col. 2). First, his advocacy of "industrial consumer goods" production was low-key and brief. It had none of the campaign rhetoric he had invoked in 1971, nor was it coupled with doctrinal innovations to reduce the political status of traditional heavy-industrial tasks. Secondly—and again in contrast to 1971—the discussion of these matters was very short, and came at the very end of the section of the speech on matters of public welfare. Thirdly, while Brezhnev spoke of the need for new technologies and better supply for light-industrial enterprises, he reserved the language of insistence for aspects of the problem that do not require increased central funding: "It may be that in no other sphere of the national economy do local possibilities and local reserves play so great a role in satisfying everyday consumer demand, and in serving the population" (p. 6, col. 2). His subsequent invocation of the threatening mass mood for the purpose of warning the cadres against poor performance in this area comes across as a reaffirmation of the importance of mobilizing local resources, rather than an indication of Brezhnev's commitment to increased central funding (p. 6, col. 2). In sum, Brezhnev's stated budgetary priorities of 1981 more closely resembled those of 1976 than those of 1971. And when the inevitable investment crunch arrives, we are not likely to find him defending the cause of light industry and consumer services.

As for foreign economic ties, Brezhnev's current program has tentatively abandoned (or substantially toned down) the reformism of 1976. In the 1981 speech, he uncoupled key features of his domestic program from dependence on foreign imports. First, there was no longer a separate section on foreign economic ties. Secondly, discussion of the matter was moved back from the section on domestic policy to the section on foreign policy. Thirdly, that discussion was both brief and entirely open-ended; he no longer specified the actual or potential benefits of such ties for domestic economic progress (p. 2, col. 3). Fourthly, when discussing technological development, Brezhnev unexpectedly called on Soviet industry to concentrate more on producing its own advanced technology, and less on purchasing technology abroad (p. 5, col. 4).

On the other hand, Brezhnev appeared to be leaving his options open on the issue of foreign economic ties, a position that is consistent with his collaborative offerings in the foreign-policy section of his address (p. 3, cols. 3–4; p. 4, cols. 1–4). I detect four indicators that Brezhnev was leaving his options open. First, when specifying the causes of the breakdown of foreign economic ties, Brezhnev predictably blamed the West, and alluded to Western policies that Washington had touted, but did not mention the United States by name (p. 2, col. 3). Secondly, Brezhnev was optimistic and forthcoming about the possibility of further developing economic intercourse with West Germany and France (p. 4, col. 1), though his failure to include this subject in the discussion of foreign economic ties *per se* may imply that he considered U.S.-Soviet ties to be central. Thirdly, Brezhnev cited trade—twice in the course of eight column lines (p. 6, col. 1)—as a component of the program for alleviating the food problem (though he did not link such trade to détente *per se*). Fourthly, Brezhnev justified Siberian development (p. 5, col. 2) in part by noting that it would "for many years" provide natural gas for export to capitalist countries.

On matters of public administration, Brezhnev's speech reaffirmed the conservatism of 1976. He suggested a regrouping of scientific forces to enhance technological innovation in machine building (p. 5, col. 4). He acknowledged that variants on the structure of enterprises and associations are needed, but seemed to refer the whole issue back to committee: "Great and varied experience has been accumulated. And it is precisely this experience that tells us that the search must be continued [*poiski nado prodolzhat*]" (p. 6, col. 3). Brezhnev's continued preference was rather for structural alterations within central planning organs to improve interbranch project planning (p. 6, col. 3). As for the rest of the economy, Brezhnev defined the work of public administration primarily as a set of mobilizational tasks. Thus, he devoted an entire subsection to the need for thrift, which he called the "core" (*sterzhen'*) of the party's economic policy (p. 5, col. 4). In addition, he defined the main cause of shortcomings in public administration as subjective inertia (p. 5, col. 2). In like manner, he proclaimed increased "demandingness" to be the "only path" toward improved administrative efficiency (p. 5, col. 2). Finally, he presented "discipline" and "personal responsibility" as the primary current needs, and greatly downplayed the need for more balanced and realistic plans for greater managerial effort (p. 6, cols. 2–3).

In sum, Brezhnev's budgetary and administrative program of 1981 is roughly as conservative as his 1976 program, while his approach to foreign economic ties is substantially more conservative than in 1976. Moreover, there is a tentativeness about Brezhnev's program that was not in evidence in 1976. Having backed off from the earlier close association between foreign economic ties and domestic economic progress, Brezhnev nevertheless indicated a desire to salvage détente and keep open the possibility of using foreign trade to alleviate Soviet economic difficulties. And well he might, for such an association between foreign-policy reformism and domestic conservatism had been the foundation of his policy program for eight years. Viewed in this light, Brezhnev's new-found advocacy of a storming approach to energy development is subject to a variety of interpretations. It could be an effort to legitimize his leadership through the sudden forcing of huge mobilizational projects. Alternatively, it could have little to do with political authority, and represent instead an effort to commit the elite to a project that will *require* substantial Western investment, thereby firming up support for foreign policy reformism. In other words, this could be an effort to "rig" the policy agenda for years to come.

Support for the second interpretation can be found by marshaling evidence that undermines the first. In 1976, we found evidence of defensiveness on Brezhnev's part, of apparent skepticism about the workability of his program. We might therefore expect, at a minimum, a continuation of that skepticism and defensiveness this time around, for conditions today are, if anything, worse than they were in 1976 relative to promises and expectations.

But we don't find such defensiveness in Brezhnev's address to the 26th Party Congress. The language of insistence, urgency, and accusation was strikingly diminished. To be sure, that language was used at points to buttress the general secretary's demands for energy development, thrift, local party attentiveness to mass consumer and welfare demands, and a reduction of mass and official corruption.[7] But consider the other side of the ledger:

1 Agriculture was not referred to as an "all-people's task," and there was no language in the agricultural section comparable to his insistence in 1976 that his program "is correct ... the Party will, in the future as well, follow this line ... there are no ready recipes."
2 In the matter of light industry, Brezhnev did not lay blame for shortcomings—as he did in 1976—on those "who plan and direct this sector of the economy."
3 On administrative affairs, the language was equally timid: there was nothing about 'unpostponable' reform needs; no particular need was defined as the "foundation of foundations of the science of administration"; the language of urgency was gone; and Brezhnev's optimistic closing speech to the Congress (*Pravda*, 4 March 1981, pp. 1–2) did not echo the warning of 1976 to "concentrate on the remaining shortcomings, on unsolved problems."
4 On cadre policy, Brezhnev very much toned down threats against incompetent or dishonest officials (we are assuming that his great candor about corruption was not meant to be taken as such a threat). Since 1970, there had taken place a steady escalation of such threats in Brezhnev's speeches, with the notable exception of the address to the 24th Party Congress. In 1976, Brezhnev had threatened forced retirements. In 1981, Brezhnev *never even raised the issue* of the balance between "respect for cadres" and "exactingness" toward them, much less elaborate on the need for placing greater weight on "exactingness."

What accounts for this decline in the language of insistence and accusation? It would be difficult to argue that Brezhnev's conservative program is now more credible, for the harvest failures of 1979–80 and the demise of détente were greater shocks to the viability of that program than the events of 1975 had been. So if skepticism and defensiveness are the issue, we would expect these still to be in evidence.[8] But who are the skeptics now? A constituency within the Central Committee and the political establishment at large? Or skeptics with independent power bases and prestige in the Politburo? In 1976, we saw that Kosygin dissented from Brezhnev's program, proposing a reformist alternative and defending himself against Brezhnev's efforts to parry responsibility for failure. By 1981, Tikhonov had replaced Kosygin, and the defensiveness disappeared from Brezhnev's speech. What's more, the "Kosygin dissent" also disappeared from Tikhonov's speech, to which we now turn (*Pravda*, 28 February 1981, pp. 2–4).

On agricultural issues, Tikhonov's stated perspectives were almost identical to those of Brezhnev, and he made no effort to emphasize Brezhnev's personal responsibility for the situation (p. 3, col. 4–p. 4, col. 1). Kosygin's detailed enumeration of shortfalls and his insistence that "not everything can be attributed to the weather" found no counterpart in Tikhonov's speech.

On heavy-industrial priority, Tikhonov (p. 2, col. 3) echoed Brezhnev's definition of the main task of the new five-year plan (Kosygin had not), and endorsed Brezhnev's energy development priority: "The Eleventh Five-Year Plan period is the first stage of the implementation of the USSR's energy program, which is being worked out on the initiative of Leonid Ilyich Brezhnev" (p. 3, col. 3).

On matters of light industry, which had evoked Kosygin's most broad-based dissent, Tikhonov faithfully echoed Brezhnev (p. 3, col. 2). He praised the 11th Five-Year Plan for projecting higher rates of growth for Group B than Group A industries, but he, like Brezhnev, then went on to define the requisites of success largely in mobilizational terms. He said nothing about investments *per se*, demanded more "initiative and persistence" in using "all the existing possibilities and reserves," called for the fuller use of "local resources," and called expanded consumer-goods production "a matter of the honor and professional pride of all those who produce consumer goods." In contrast to Kosygin, he did not blame agricultural shortfalls for adversely affecting consumer-goods production.

On issues of public administration, Tikhonov's speech was also an echo of Brezhnev's conservatism. He cited subjective "forces of inertia and tradition" as "the main reason for the difficulties, shortcomings, and bottlenecks in the national economy" (p. 2, col. 2). He called for enlarging and improving the role of central planning organs in setting economic priorities and coordinating interdependencies (p. 4, col. 3). In sharp contrast to Kosygin, he did not use any of the decentralist terminology of the 1965 reforms (p. 4, cols. 3–4). He spoke of the transition to production associations (as had Brezhnev), but did not use the laudatory terms that Kosygin had chosen ("a qualitatively new stage ... "). He did make one statement with potentially reformist implications. After calling for a struggle to overcome bureaucratic obstacles to the proper functioning of production associations, Tikhonov raised the following question: "Are the rights and duties of associations and their constituent units distributed in a sufficiently well-founded way?" (p. 4, col. 3). If this was intended for reformist consumption, it was tepid fare indeed. Not buttressed by the terminology of 1965, nor by any mention of "enterprise rights," and stated as a question rather than an imperative, these words do not come across as any less conservative than Brezhnev's analogous statement about the need for further "searches." In short, Tikhonov's treatment of this subject does not indicate a will to incur the political costs of taking action.

On foreign economic ties, there was greater divergence between Brezhnev and Tikhonov than on other issues—though the difference may not be very significant. As we saw, Brezhnev vastly toned down his association with the issue, though he kept his options open. Tikhonov (in contrast to Kosygin as well as to Brezhnev) devoted a headlined section of his speech to the topic (p. 4, cols. 1–4). Like Brezhnev, however (but unlike Kosygin), he twice mentioned foreign economic ties as a source of consumer goods. Unlike Brezhnev, he called on planning organs to "constantly work on raising the efficiency of foreign economic ties in the interests of economizing on labor and material resources, accelerating technological progress, and gaining time" (p. 4, col. 4).

On issues of reformism and conservatism, then, the gap between the general secretary and the chairman of the Council of Ministers, in evidence in 1976, is absent in 1981. Moreover, on issues of political authority, the dissension of 1976, in which both men were trying to parry responsibility for failure, is also gone. This last point can be further substantiated by one final indicator—the terms in which Kosygin and Tikhonov paid homage to Brezhnev. In his opening remarks in 1976, Kosygin had praised Brezhnev, but emphasized the position Brezhnev occupied:

> The Central Committee and Politburo, headed by the distinguished political figure of our time, the General Secretary of the CC KPSS, Leonid Ilyich Brezhnev ...
> The progressive tendencies of world development, profoundly laid out by the General Secretary of the CC KPSS Leonid Ilyich

> Brezhnev in the Accountability report to the Congress...
> (*Pravda*, 2 March 1976, p. 2, col. 1)

In contrast, Tikhonov's opening remarks gave billing as well to Brezhnev the man, omitting his last name and his title:

> With particular profundity, Leonid Ilyich characterized the multifaceted activity of the Central Committee, the titanic work of the party and people ...
> In conceiving and realizing this course, the leading role belongs to Leonid Ilyich Brezhnev. The party and people see in Leonid Ilyich a wise and experienced leader. (p. 2, col. 1)

Whereas Kosygin had praised Brezhnev's 1976 report as a "distinguished contribution to the theory and practice of Communist construction," Tikhonov called Brezhnev's 1981 report a "distinguished creative contribution to the development and enrichment of Marxist–Leninist teaching."

Conclusion

This paper has focused on one type of evidence about Soviet elite politics—the speeches of top leaders at party congresses. I have traced a moderately reformist "consensus" in 1971, a conservative-versus-reformist "clash" in 1976, and a conservative "consensus" in 1981. How one interprets this pattern depends in large measure on whether one views Soviet politics primarily as *corporate* or *clientelistic*. These, it seems to me, have been the two most prevalent images of power and accountability relations within the Soviet establishment that have informed analyses of Soviet elite politics.

Clientelistic models emphasize an imbalance of power relations, both within the Politburo and between the Politburo and other institutions. They emphasize the power of the general secretary to pack the Central Committee and the Politburo with men beholden to him for their jobs and/or with men who share his past experiences and policy orientations. Clientelistic models do not entirely deny the flow of influence upward from the political establishment, nor do they deny that various members of the Politburo have power bases and prestige of their own. But they emphasize the relative concentration of political leverage vis-à-vis his Politburo associates in the hands of the general secretary, and the relative concentration of political leverage vis-à-vis the Central Committee (and institutions represented therein) in the Politburo.

Corporate approaches do not deny the fact of asymmetrical power relations within the Politburo and between the Politburo and other institutions. But the emphasis in corporate models is nonetheless on balance. Such an image posits the existence of political constituencies within the broader political establishment (the Central Committee and beyond) of which Politburo members act as representatives. Moreover, the corporate model downplays the asymmetry of power relations within the Politburo, positing a norm of broad representation of elite interests in that body, or a norm against excessive imbalance in the representation of given institutional interests.

I would argue that neither of these models, on its own, is adequate for understanding the dynamics of Soviet elite politics. But each of them captures a good measure of that process, so that together they explain a very great deal. The dynamics of power and accountability relationships in Soviet elite politics are a product of the tension and interplay between clientelistic and corporate tendencies. In the course of the Brezhnev era, the relative weights within this mix have shifted. In the early and middle years, it would appear, corporate norms were considerably stronger than they have been in the past five years. If we were to adhere to a corporate perspective on Soviet elite politics today, we would find it difficult to explain the turn of events at the most recent party congress. We would have expected Tikhonov to articulate the interests and beliefs of reformist constituencies that are skeptical of, or threatened by, Brezhnev's conservative program. Tikhonov's broad endorsement of Brezhnev's conservatism probably reflects both the death of Kosygin (who had a different career background, different policy orientations, and independent personal stature and prestige within the political elite) and the strengthening of clientelistic ties and norms in Soviet elite politics in the late Brezhnev era—especially since 1976. Tikhonov is clearly a "Brezhnev man" by patronage, by past associations, and by apparent past policy orientations. His assumption of Kosygin's position apparently did not lead him to assume Kosygin's policy preferences, political commitments or ostensible role obligations—at least as far as the reformism-versus-conservatism issue is concerned, and in as much as political conflict over that set of issues is aired in speeches at party congresses. A more powerful test of the strength of clientelistic ties would have been possible had Tikhonov been a reformist by inclination, but a client of

Brezhnev's by political obligation. A conservative speech under those circumstances would have been still more compelling evidence of the strength of clientelism. But since Tikhonov's policy orientations and political obligations are mutually reinforcing, we do not enjoy the luxury of such a test. Nonetheless, the strength of corporate explanations would not be enhanced in either case. They cannot explain recent events.

Several hypotheses could still be advanced in hopes of salvaging a corporate explanation, but I do not find any of them convincing. One hypothesis would be that Tikhonov only very recently succeeded Kosygin, and that it will take time for reformist constituency pressures to impinge on his behavior. But Tikhonov had been Kosygin's deputy for several years, during which time he would already have been exposed to, and influenced by, alleged constituency pressures. A second hypothesis would be that, since the writing of party congress speeches is a collective endeavor, and since Kosygin resigned while the process was well under way, Kosygin would have given much the same speech—perhaps because sentiments and power relations within the establishment had shifted since 1976. But there is no evidence to suggest that underlying reform sentiments and pressures have slackened in recent years. Moreover, while the process of speech writing is based on rather broad input, the final speech does not necessarily reflect a tolerant compromise among conflicting viewpoints, especially over basic issues of reformism and conservatism. Then too, the final character of the report is likely to be decisively shaped late in the speech-writing process by the immediate staff of the chairman of the Council of Ministers, or by personal decisions of the chairman himself.

Still another hypothesis would be that the international situation at the time of the 26th Party Congress, when a siege mentality was taking hold in Moscow after the failure of détente, led the leadership to submerge differences and present a united front to the outside world. But in 1961 and 1966, the international environment of the party congresses was also hostile, yet elite differences on fundamental issues were in evidence.

The power of the corporate perspective to explain many features of contemporary Soviet elite politics lies in its emphasis on three factors: (1) the collective interest of most Politburo members in preventing an excessive concentration of power in the hands of the general secretary: (2) the collective interest of Politburo members in developing norms of compromise, and a division of labor, to regulate the bargaining process; and (3) the existence of political bases in bureaucracies outside the party apparatus, which serve as nominal constituencies that Politburo members feel inclinations or pressures to represent.

Since I have dealt in this paper with the "grand" issues of reformism versus conservatism, the clientelistic perspective on contemporary events appears to have been bolstered. But it is important not to overstate the case. For on issues of less systemic moment—for example, debate over variants on a conservative program—the corporate perspective gains greater credibility. Thus, Tikhonov has worked for several years with all-union planners and ministerial officials whose perspectives on concrete issues of economic policy, administrative change, and bureaucratic interest might be expected to differ from those of officials in Central Committee departments. We might further expect that Tikhonov would have absorbed certain of those planners' perspectives and/or found it politically necessary to articulate their interests in Politburo discussions. A closer, line-by-line comparison of Brezhnev's and Tikhonov's reports to the 26th Party Congress—which I have not undertaken—might yield interesting differences that reflect variants on a conservative program.

Let me cite a few examples of such divergencies that struck me in reading the speeches. In Brezhnev's remarks on planning, the concepts of "balance" (*sbalansirovannost'*) and realism in planning received short shrift; they were mentioned only in dependent clauses and in caveats in a hard-hitting critique of officials who seek lower plans (p. 6, cols. 2–3). By contrast, Tikhonov devoted several paragraphs to the importance of balance in planning, introducing the discussion by saying, "I would like to speak in particular about improving balance" (p. 4, col. 3).

Analogous differences may be in evidence on the issue of energy policy. Brezhnev invoked the language of insistence in support of his program for forced extraction of West Siberian natural gas, using terminology suggesting that the issue is controversial (see above, p. 73). Tikhonov's remarks on energy development (p. 2, col. 1; p. 3, col. 1; p. 3, col. 3), while endorsing Brezhnev's programs, appeared to give greater weight to atomic energy and electric energy, and did not make the energy issue the centerpiece of his speech, as Brezhnev's did. Then too, it *may* be significant that Tikhonov sandwiched his main remarks on energy (p. 3, col. 3) with introductory and concluding statements that emphasized *balanced* energy development: "Our duty, however large our supply of natural resources might be, is to search constantly for the most rational means of extracting them and the most economical means of using them.... We must work more actively to find new and more efficient sources of energy and to use them more rationally" (contrast the spirit of these remarks with the first lines of the Brezhnev quote on p. 73). Finally, as Robert Campbell has argued, there may be a note of subtle dissent on Tikhonov's part in his attribution to Brezhnev of credit (and responsibility?) for the unbalanced energy program the general secretary is pushing:

> Great national economic significance will attach to the timely and all-round solution ... of all questions connected with the task put forth by Leonid Ilyich Brezhnev of organizing the production of liquid fuel from Kansk-Achinsk coals. (p. 3, col. 3)

Further tentative support for Campbell's interpretation that remarks like this one were an effort to register Tikhonov's and Gosplan's skepticism of Brezhnev's energy program can be found in the following two bits of evidence: (1) Tikhonov here used Brezhnev's full name, in contrast, for example, to his use of only the given name and patronymic in his citation of Brezhnev's support of "intensification of the economy" (p. 3, col. 1); (2) In his discussion of "foreign economic ties," Tikhonov made no mention of Brezhnev's claim that the export of Siberian gas to capitalist countries was a component of regime plans or expectations.

Thus, it should be possible to pick up on valid indicators of political conflict over "within-system" issues, and to interpret this conflict, not as a mighty clash of intransigent and opposing forces, but as the usual fare of bureaucratic politics in the USSR. Moreover, we can feel confident that such bureaucratic politics may transcend patron-client obligations.

At this point, a word of caution is in order. The documentation of this kind of conflict solely on the basis of party congress speeches can be a hazardous exercise. For another insight from the corporate perspective is that Politburo members also share common interests simply as members of that body. These shared interests might lead Politburo members to coordinate their congress speeches to reflect agreements to mollify under-rewarded constituencies, norms against the display of certain types of differences, or simply a division of labor in the leadership. On the grand issues of reformism and conservatism, such a common interest or division of labor is not likely to invalidate the methodology used in this paper, both because of the intensity of conflict such issues provoke, and because a division-of-labor theory cannot explain the remarkable changes over time in these leaders' speeches. The less politicized and systemic the issues, however, the more likely that such coordination will occur. To take an example discussed in this chapter, such coordination may explain why Tikhonov's speech gave greater billing to the subject of foreign economic ties than Brezhnev's speech, for it would serve to keep the issue on the political agenda and mollify offended bureaucratic constituencies, without committing the general secretary's program or authority too closely to the issue. Of course, such coordination would not be inconsistent with a clientelistic perspective, for, in this particular case, the coordination would have taken place between a patron and a client. We may never know whether similar coordination would have taken place between Brezhnev and Kosygin.

Notes

1. See, for example, Donald R. Kelley, "The Communist Party," in Donald R. Kelley, ed. *Soviet Politics in the Brezhnev Era* (New York: Praeger Publishers, 1980), especially pp. 28–30.
2. See, for example, George R. Feiwel, "Economic Performance and Reforms in the Soviet Union," In *Ibid*., especially pp. 80, 101. For a wide-ranging discussion of these concepts, see Stephen F. Cohen, "The Friends and Foes of Change: Reformism and Conservatism in the Soviet Union," *Slavic Review* (June 1979), pp. 187–202; and comments by T. H. Rigby, S. Frederick Starr, Frederick Barghoorn, and George Breslauer, in *Ibid*., pp. 203–19.
3. I have not provided citations for assertions about the years preceding the 26th Party Congress. Full exposure of my evidence will appear in my book, *Patterns of Leadership in the Soviet Union Since Stalin*. Meanwhile, some of the evidence has already been displayed in George Breslauer, "The Twenty-fifth Party Congress: Domestic Issues," in Alexander Dallin, ed. *The Twenty-fifth Congress of the CPSU* (Stanford: Hoover Institution Press, 1977).
4. Thus, "authority" must be distinguished from "power." A leader can continue to consolidate his grip on power (that is, office) while suffering challenges to, or skepticism about, the desirability or workability of his proposed policies.
5. Actually, Brezhnev launched a campaign for energy development in December 1977. At that time, the preference was for forced oil extraction; now it is for forced extraction of natural gas, and the investments are much larger (see chapter by Thane Gustafson, in this volume).
6. Allan Kroncher, "Prospects for the Eleventh Five-Year Plan," Radio Liberty Research, RL 46/81, 26 January 1981.
7. Then too, Brezhnev called for publication of a revised edition of the 1961 Party Programme (p. 9, cols. 2–3), which could be interpreted as an "insistent" effort to ensure the continuation of his distinctive program into the future.
8. In fairness, we should note that the language of insistence and accusation has not been reduced in Brezhnev's other speeches. If anything, Brezhnev's speeches at end-of-year Central Committee plenary sessions since November 1978 have been more candid about shortcomings, and more accusatory, than those which preceded them. Indeed, one Soviet observer has referred to Brezhnev's November 1978 plenum address as a "bombshell" (noted in Jerry F. Hough, *Soviet Leadership in*

Transition [Washington, D.C.: The Brookings Institution, 1980], pp. 11–12). My impression, however, is that plenary session speeches perform somewhat different functions from party congress speeches. Plenary session speeches reflect efforts by the general secretary to seize the initiative on pressing issues, to preempt and redefine those issues in order to "disarm" *potential* anatagonists, and to use the campaignist atmosphere thereby created to justify increased control over the central ministries by organs of the Central Committee apparatus. Indeed, closer inspection of these speeches reveals that Brezhnev did not concede the systemic character of the problems, for he laid heavy blame on personnel—ministers in particular. Moreover, in contrast to his 26th Party Congress speech, Brezhnev delivered these attacks at a time when Kosygin, or his immediate clients, were still in positions of leadership in the Council of Ministers. All of this suggests a power play, rather than an effort to mobilize support for systemic reforms.

4
The 11th Five-Year Plan, 1981–85

Daniel L. Bond
and
Herbert S. Levine

Introduction

The aim of this chapter is to describe and analyze the Soviet 11th Five-Year Plan (1981–85) in broad and brief terms. We will begin with a short review of recent Soviet economic performance, which will serve as a background for the discussion of the new Soviet plan that will follow. The final section of the paper will present the results of some calculations, made with the use of the Wharton Econometric Model of the Soviet Union (SOV-MOD IV), which represent, roughly, our baseline projection for the plan period, and several alternative projections involving assumptions of low productivity growth, and high and low growth of defense expenditures.

Background: The 1970s

In his speech on the 11th Five-Year Plan at the 26th Party Congress, the new (75-year-old) Soviet premier, Nikolai Tikhonov, criticized Western observers for speaking of a "crisis" in the Soviet economy. He was probably right, for it still may be a little premature to use that term. But clearly the Soviet economy is in trouble. Soviet rates of growth have been declining since the 1950s, partly for reasons associated with the maturing of the economy, such as diminishing returns on capital investment, the aging of the capital stock, and the exhaustion of easily accessible sources of raw materials. But some of the downward trend is attributable to particular policies of Soviet leaders and aspects of the Soviet economic system, such as the policy followed until recently of relying heavily on the rapid expansion of the stock of fixed capital, and the systemic barriers in the centralized, bureaucratized Soviet economy to the introduction and diffusion of new technology (the crucial source of growth in mature economies).

It is not so much this downward trend, however, that has led serious students of the Soviet economy to begin to speak of a crisis, as the sharp drop in growth that has taken place in the last five years, particularly in the past two years. Soviet GNP, which grew at an average annual rate of slightly over 5 percent in the 1960s, fell to a growth rate of 3.8 percent in the first half of the 1970s, 2.8 percent in the second half of the '70s, and in the last two years an average rate of 1.2 percent.[1] Some of this is a reflection of agricultural failures caused by bad weather in the years 1977, 1979, and 1980. Agricultural output grew at an annual rate barely above 1 percent during the past five-year period, but in each of the last two years it fell, by an officially reported 4 percent in 1979 and 3 percent in 1980. The grain harvests of the last two years were considerably below plan and below the average level of the previous three years. Through heavy imports of grain in 1979, the Soviets were able to achieve a slight increase in both the production of meat and the size of livestock herds. In 1980, however, the U.S. grain embargo appears to have had some impact. Estimates indicate that while the Soviets were able to make up much of their desired grain imports, ending up with a total of about 31 million metric tons in calendar 1980, they probably would have imported close to 38 m.m.t.—the limit of their import-handling capacity—if it had not been for the embargo. According to official data, Soviet meat production in 1980 fell by 2.6 percent, and though cattle herds remained constant, other livestock herds decreased.

But bad weather and agricultural failures were not the only causes of Soviet economic troubles in the second half of the 1970s. Industrial growth also has slowed down, from about 6.5 percent per year in the 1960s, to 5.8 percent in the first half of the 1970s, 3.4 percent in the second half, and about 3.0 percent in each of the last two years. In 1979, for the first time in Soviet peacetime history, steel output fell, and then in 1980 it fell again, so that steel output last year—148 m.m.t.—was 3.5 million tons below the level of 1978. Coal output also fell.

Accompanying these sharp decreases in economic growth during the past five years has been a dramatic worsening of the growth of factor productivity. Overall labor productivity in the economy, which grew at a rate of about 3.5 percent per year in the 1960s, fell to a rate of 2.1 percent in the period 1970–75, and 1.4 percent in 1975–80; in the past two years it has not grown at all. Labor productivity growth in industry dropped sharply in the last half of the '70s. From a rate of 3.5 percent per year in the 1960s, it rose to a rate of 4.3 percent per year in the first half of the 1970s, and then plummeted to a rate of 1.9 percent per year in the second half of the '70s and 1.4 percent per year in the last two years. The picture is even more trenchant when we consider labor and capital productivity together: in regard to overall GNP, total factor productivity grew at a rate of 1.5 percent per year in the 1960s, fell to 0.1 percent per year in the first half of the 1970s and then *decreased* at an average rate of 0.4 percent per year in the second half of the 1970s.[2] Furthermore, in 1979 and 1980, the growth of total factor productivity was strongly negative, at a rate of about −2 percent per year. Again poor agricultural performance is part of the story, but only part, for a similar picture is painted by the data for industry. While total factor productivity in industry grew at the low rate of 0.2 percent per year in the 1960s, it rose to 1 percent per year in the period 1970–75, but then fell to −0.7 percent in the period 1975–80 and −1 percent per year in 1979 and 1980.

It is against this background that the new Soviet five-year plan was constructed and against which it must be analyzed. The erosion of output and productivity growth is the dominant theme. In many ways the Soviet economy has been performing at historic lows over the past five years, and in the view of a growing number of foreign observers it is approaching crisis levels.

Clearly the next five years will be very difficult ones. Labor and capital growth will both be severely limited. The growth of the labor force will be constrained by demographic factors which have been much discussed in both the Western and Soviet literature.[3] The projected precipitous drop in the growth of the working-age population (in part, the second echo of the heavy Soviet population losses in World War II) will be felt in full force during the next five years. The working-age population, which grew at a rate of 1.9 percent per year in the period 1970–75 and 1.5 percent per year in 1975–80, will slow down to a growth rate of 0.3 percent per year in 1980–85. Furthermore, what little growth is projected will be accounted for primarily by the Muslims of the Central Asian republics. The absolute size of the working age population in the Russian Republic, where a large part of the industrial capacity is located, will actually be slightly lower at the end of the five-year-plan period than at the beginning. These demographic developments, it is expected, will lead to a slowing down in the growth of the labor force, which will contribute to reducing output growth; and this, in turn, makes it even more important to reverse the productivity-growth slump, if output growth is to be increased or even maintained. In the past, the Soviets have often resorted to above-plan labor-force growth to compensate for below-plan productivity growth. In the 11th Five-Year Plan period, the possibility of this type of trade-off will be severely limited, although it is interesting to note that in 1980, while the working-age population grew only 1 percent, Soviet authorities were able to get a labor force growth of 1.7 percent (presumably, primarily through increased employment of pensioners).

The growth of the capital stock over the next five years will also be limited. It is clear that Soviet authorities have decided to reduce their growth of investment, for a number of reasons. First, the aim is to focus investment activity on completing the large number of unfinished projects rather than undertaking many new ones. The hope, it can be surmised, is that with less of an increase in investment, it will be more feasible than before to control the runaway growth of new projects. If this reduction in investment does lead to a concentration of investment funds on the completion and commissioning of projects begun in earlier periods, it will not immediately reduce the growth of capital stock very much.[4]

A second, related benefit of limiting investment will be a new emphasis on equipment instead of construction. The strategy is to add to and modernize the stock of machinery in existing structures rather than to continue expanding the structures as in the past. The crucially important goal of this strategy is to increase capital productivity, a need which is particularly acute at this period of time because of the aging and obsolescence of the capital stock in so many Soviet industries. In the ferrous metals and coal industries, for example, the difficulties and delays of the ongoing programs of replacing old capital with new, technologically more advanced capital may be a factor in the recent poor production levels. The need to replace existing capital is also called for by the tight energy situation and the reduced growth and expected leveling off of oil production. It would be well to replace old, energy-inefficient machinery with more modern, energy-efficient machinery rather than repair and retain the old equipment and just add new equipment to the capital stock.[5] Such a policy would have positive effects on productivity, but only after a period of time. In the short run

—that is, during the period of the 11th Plan—it will probably lead more to a reduction in the growth of capital than to an increase in capital productivity.

Finally, the reduced growth in capital stock will be intensified for many sectors of the economy by the needs of the energy and transportation sectors. During the next five years, the energy sectors will require substantial additions to their capital stock if they are to meet the demands placed upon them. The transportation sector also requires a significant increase in capital because it has proved to be a bottleneck in recent years, and, because it will be called on to transport fuel and energy over greater distances in the forthcoming years. These high-priority capital requirements during the period of the 11th Five-Year Plan will restrict the flow of capital to the other sectors of the economy and branches of industry, including the important machinery branch.

The 11th Five-Year Plan

A *General Characteristics*

Before going into the main indicators of the plan, we must say a few words about the plan documents themselves. The CPSU Central Committee's Draft Basic Guidelines on the 11th Five-Year Plan appeared in the Soviet press on 2 December 1980. This inaugurated a public discussion of the plan that culminated in the speeches and discussions of the 26th Party Congress, 23 February–3 March 1981, and in a ratified version of the Basic Guidelines, published in the press on 5 March 1981. A quick comparison of the Draft Basic Guidelines and the version ratified by the Congress indicates that there were very few changes made, particularly in the quantitative indicators. For example, there were slight changes in the growth figures for fiberboard panels, cardboard, and wood pulp, and the planned production in 1985 of beans and peas (pulses) was reduced from 14–15 million metric tons to 12–13 m.m.t. Also a minimum wage of eighty rubles per month was established for 1985, whereas in the draft no specific figure had been given, only the open-ended statement, "gradual increase in the minimum wage."

One new feature of the 11th Five-Year Plan (FYP) was embodied in the official title of the plan document (and of the draft): "Basic Guidelines for the Economic and Social Development of the USSR in 1981–1985 and in the Period to

1990." The extension to 1990 reflects the joint resolution of the Central Committee and the Council of Ministers in July 1979 on improving the mechanisms of planning and economic management.[6] This resolution called for the strengthening of the role of the five-year plan in the system of planning and for the working out of balances for a ten-year period—all this to begin with the 11th Five-Year Plan. While there is not a single figure in the Draft Guidelines on the period to 1990, the ratified Guidelines state that national income in 1990 will be at least 40 percent higher than in 1985.[7] This, however, should not be viewed as a major breakthrough in long-term, ten-year planning, since the 40 percent figure works out to a simple extrapolation of the bottom of the 18–20 percent range for national income in the period of the 11th FYP.

When the plan document is compared with the two previous five-year plans in the Brezhnev era, several things stand out. One is the rather significant decrease in actual data in the plan—about 40 percent less than in the 10th FYP. Interestingly, there is no 1985 output target for crude steel. While this decrease in hard data in the plan is consistent with the general decrease in the publication of economic data in recent years, it might also betray a lack of agreement among Soviet officials on what the 11th Plan targets should be.

The 11th FYP also differs from the previous plan in the topics covered. Like the 9th FYP (1971–75) but unlike the 10th FYP, the new plan includes a section on the improvement of planning and management procedures. Presumably, Soviet leaders wish to revive the spirit of reform of the 9th FYP, hoping perhaps that this will help revive the dynamics of the economy. The 11th FYP also includes, for the first time, a section on protection of the environment.

B *Main Indicators of the Plan*

An analysis of the Basic Guidelines for the new five-year plan indicates that the Soviet authorities acknowledge almost all the problems mentioned in our discussion of the background of the current economic situation. Overall, planned growth rates are very low. Some are at historic lows, and even these low rates can only be fulfilled by relying primarily on quite high targets for productivity, particularly labor productivity.

Table 4.1 contains data on the main indicators of the 11th FYP. In the section on total national income and product, a growth of 18–20 percent over the five-year period is planned for national income (net material product) utilized, implying an average annual growth of about 3.5 percent for this Soviet measure. This translates into a rate of 4.0 percent per year for GNP produced (Western concept), which is somewhat higher than that achieved in the past five years (although the two bad agricultural years in 1979 and 1980 should be taken into account in such a comparison).[8] Almost all of this growth is to be accounted for by a growth in labor productivity of 17–20 percent over the 10th FYP period, or slightly less than 3.5 percent per year. This is substantially higher than the 1.4 percent-per-year growth in labor productivity achieved in the period 1975–80, and it is also higher than the 2.1 percent-per-year rate in 1970–75. The indicated rates of growth of output and labor productivity in the new plan imply a very low planned rate of growth of the total labor force engaged in material-product sectors—about 0.5 percent per year. This is in line with the drastic fall in able-bodied population growth projected by Western specialists for the 1980s.

The planned growth of industrial output of 4.9 percent per year (mid-point of range) is the lowest that has appeared in any Soviet five-year plan. It is roughly what was achieved on the average during the 1970s, although quite a bit above the growth rate of Soviet industry in the past five years (using the Western

Table 4.1 Five-Year Plan Targets and Performance (Average Annual Rates of Growth, in Percent)

	9th FYP (1971–75)		10th FYP (1976–80)		11th FYP (1981–85)
	Plan	Actual	Plan	Actual	Plan
National product:					
Soviet measure					
(Net Material Product)	6.7	5.7	4.4–5.1	4.4	3.4–3.7
Western measure					
(Gross National Product)	5.8	3.7	5.0	2.8	4.0
Industrial output:					
Soviet measure	8.0	7.4	6.2–6.8	4.5	4.7–5.1
Western measure	8.0	5.8	6.3	3.4	4.7–5.1
Agricultural output:					
Official (5-year average)	4.0	2.5	2.7–3.2	1.7	2.3–2.7
Western recalculation	3.5	−0.5	5.5	1.1	5.0
Investment (new fixed)	6.7	6.4	3.5	3.6	2.3–2.8
Consumption	5.0	3.5	4.0	2.8	3.6

SOURCES: 1. Soviet FYPs and Statistical Handbooks
2. OER data handout (as revised), Kennan Center, 6 Feb. 1981
* Average annual rates of growth linking output in last year of period to output in year before period (from source 2, above)

measure). Heavy reliance is again placed on growth in labor productivity, which is set at slightly below 4.5 percent per year—more than double the rate of productivity growth in the preceding five years, but almost equal to that of the first half of the 1970s.

As Table 4.2 shows, the much discussed problems of Soviet oil production are reflected in the almost ironic fact that the oil output target set for the year 1985 (620–45 million metric tons) is identical to that set in the 10th FYP for the year 1980 (620–40 m.m.t.). It is also interesting to note that the 1985 targets for coal and cement in the 11th FYP are a bit below the 1980 targets set for these products in the 10th FYP. This may indicate an increasing reluctance on the part of Soviet planners to continue basing plans on unrealistic expectations, when (as the Soviet expression has it) "life itself refutes" such expectations. Finally, as we have already noted, the 11th FYP omits a crude steel target for 1985, perhaps because of the difficulties that the Soviet steel industry has been having in recent years. There is, however, a 1985 target for rolled steel of 117–20 m.m.t., which implies a rate of growth of 2.8 percent per year in the 11th FYP period.[9]

Agriculture, as stated above, fared poorly during the 10th FYP period, largely due to very bad weather. In the Guidelines for the 11th FYP, agricultural output is planned on the average to be 12–14 percent higher than in the 10th FYP. As Table 4.1 shows, this means a growth of roughly 5 percent per year

Table 4.2 *Five-Year Plan Individual Product Targets and Performances (End-Period Output; Physical Units as Indicated)*

	9th FYP (1971–75)		10th FYP (1976–80)		11th FYP (1981–85)
	Plan	Actual	Plan	Actual	Plan
Electric power (billion kwh)	1,065	1,039	1,340–80	1,295	1,550–1,600
Oil (million metric tons)	496	491	620–40	603	620–45
Natural gas (billion cubic meters)	320	289	400–435	435	600–640
Coal (m.m.t.)	695	701	790–810	716	770–800
Steel, crude (m.m.t.)	146	141	160–72	148	NA
Cement (m.m.t.)	125	122	143–46	125	140–42
Grain (5-year average, m.m.t.)	195	182	215–20	205	238–43
Meat (5-year average, m.m.t.)	14.3	14.0	15–15.6	14.9	17–17.5

SOURCE: Soviet FYPs and Statistical Handbooks

(comparing output in 1985 with that in 1980), which is considerably larger than the growth achieved in the 1970s. Grain and meat targets also appear high. The planned growth is based on expectations of better weather, high productivity growth, continued high investment in agriculture, a substantial increase in fertilizer production, and on some changes in management methods. These would involve the expansion of agro-industrial complexes, and perhaps some moves in the direction of decentralization and increasing the number of private plots for collective farmers.

We turn now to the plan's implications for allocation. With a decreasing growth of national product, the growth of end uses—consumption, investment, defense, other government expenditures, exports and imports—must also decrease. The issue is which ones and in what balance.

Consumer welfare has been a strong political theme in the Soviet Union over the past decade, and it is one of the important elements of the plan. Inadequate growth in consumption, some Western observers argue, could contribute to political difficulties for the regime like the Polish troubles, though not as intense. Moreover, if the leaders' hopes for the growth of labor productivity in the 11th FYP are to have any chance of fulfillment, worker incentives and morale must improve, which in turn requires the growth of consumption. The Guidelines call for a consumption growth rate of 3.6 percent per year, about equal to that of the growth of the NMP (Soviet measure) and somewhat less than the planned growth of GNP. The growth in consumption is backed up in the Plan by a slightly higher planned rate of growth within industry for consumer goods (5.1 percent per year) than for producer goods (4.9 percent).

Perhaps the biggest surprise in the Basic Guidelines is the continued decline in the rate of growth investment to the range of 2.3–2.8 percent per year, a postwar low. This trend is not new: starting with the 10th FYP, the Soviets radically altered their investment policy. They cut investment growth drastically, from a former level of about 7–9 percent per year to less than 4 percent in the 10th FYP and now to 2.6 percent in the 11th FYP. As stated above, the Soviets in their recent investment policy have concentrated on new equipment to modernize existing factories rather than on continued construction of new factories, with the intention of introducing new technology to reverse the decline in productivity growth.

What about defense? Soviet plans—and indeed Soviet statistics—do not provide more than the sketchiest data on Soviet defense expenditures. The estimates made by CIA, which encompass the research-development-procurement cycle for Soviet weapon systems, indicate a continuation of the growth of defense expenditures through the next five years at the rate that has been maintained since the mid-1960s—4.5 percent per year. In view of the reduced growth of national product planned for the next five years, there may be pressure to reduce this rate, although it is probably fair to say that most Western analysts feel it will be maintained (see below). Also, a comparison of the past relationships among planned growth of machine-building output, investment, and defense procurement with those in the 11th FYP, indicates a general consistency that would support an assumed Soviet growth plan of 4–5 percent in defense expenditures.

The Guidelines to the 11th FYP do not discuss foreign trade very extensively. During the past decade, the Soviets have made a major effort to import advanced Western technology, as an important part of their strategy for increasing productivity growth. It is still not clear what effect Afghanistan, the post-Afghanistan sanctions, and the change of administration in the United States will have on this policy. The section on economic relations with the developed West in the Guidelines is significantly less enthusiastic than the one in the 10th FYP. It does, however, call for the maintenance of stable, mutually beneficial economic relations with those developed capitalist countries "which show interest in cooperation with the Soviet Union." Although this phrase clearly appears to be directed at the United States, the chairman of Gosplan, at the October 1980 meeting of the Supreme Soviet, went further in explicitly separating the United States from other developed capitalist countries. It should be noted that not only are technology imports at stake, but also the grain imports needed to maintain the growth of livestock herds and the production of meat, an item very dear to the hearts of Soviet consumers. In this regard, Tikhonov's speech at the 26th Party Congress is informative. After repeating the theme of the Guidelines, he went on to say that it was not the Soviet Union's fault that trade with the United States had decreased, but the fault of the United States for using trade for improper political purposes.[10] He concluded, however, that "as far as the Soviet Union is concerned, we are ready to develop economic relations also with the United States, on an equitable and mutually advantageous basis"[11]— thus opening the door for the Reagan administration, if it wishes to enter.

Some Key Issues

One key issue in the Guidelines is the leaders' recognition that serious problems will complicate economic performance in the '80s. Brezhnev, in his Report, lists them as follows: limitations on the growth of the labor force, the need to develop resources in the remote and difficult territory of the East and North, the increasing number of old factories which will need remodeling and modernization, and the inadequacy of the Soviet transportation system, roads and communication. With these he also includes the "inevitable growth in expenditure on environmental protection."[12]

Secondly, the crucial role of productivity growth is stressed again and, although in many places this is stated in the familiar form of intensive growth replacing extensive growth, Tikhonov goes so far as to say: "As regards its historic scale, importance and consequences, the present transfer of our national economy onto the path of intensive development can justly be put side by side with such a profound transformation as the socialist industrialization which radically altered the image of the country."[13]

Thirdly, in several places a reduction in the material intensity of output—especially the metal-intensity—is mentioned as a way to increase productivity. Brezhnev complains that the Soviet Union spends more than the other leading economies on raw materials and energy per unit of national income. The Basic Guidelines, in the section on the machine-building industry, devotes a rather long paragraph to a detailed, technical listing of many ways that metal can be saved in the production of machinery; and Brezhnev in discussing the ferrous metals industry, states that while of course steel production capacity will be expanded in the 11th FYP period, reductions in the utilization of metals and the development of metal substitutes are much more important than the "endless expansion of metal production."[14]

Fourthly, throughout the discussions of the 11th Plan at the Congress and in the Guidelines, there are frequent references to the paramount importance of developing a workable food program, based not only on increased production of food, but also on its effective distribution, storage, and supply. The theme is that improving the supply of food is the most important element in improving the standard of living of the Soviet citizen. In this regard, it is worth noting the creation, last December, of a new USSR Fruit and Vegetable Ministry. The new ministry will not only have control over specialized fruit and vegetable farms, but will also have responsibility for the procuring, transporting, processing, and marketing of fruits and vegetables.

The fifth and last issue is the broad area of planning and management reform. Since this is the subject of Nancy Nimitz's contribution to this volume, we shall confine ourselves to a few brief comments on the subject.

One intriguing thread in the discussions in this area is the repeated criticism of downward revisions of plans and the loss of plan discipline that this entails. Brezhnev's Report (this and his speech at the October 1980 plenum of the Central Committee are by far the most interesting contributions to the discussions of economic reform) stresses the importance of regarding the plan as law because, he argues, only its strict observance can ensure the smooth operation of the economy. And his call for strengthening the plan and making it more compulsory sounds like an appeal for centralization.

Another theme in the discussion is the emphasis on creating interdepartmental administrative units. The main element here is the campaign to develop the planning and institution of specific-purpose programs which will cut across ministerial lines. This is obviously a hot issue for the Soviet bureaucracy and requires much more study than we have given it. However, it would appear that Brezhnev's support of this potentially revolutionary/disruptive approach was more spirited at the October plenum than at the 26th Party Congress. In October, Brezhnev called for a detailed organization of the management of specific-purpose programs "that establishes precise personal responsibility for every sector of work and gives individuals the necessary authority. Without all this, a program is not really a program but only a summation of good wishes."[15]

A third part of the discussion of new management approaches concerns the perennial problem of the need to stimulate the introduction of new technology. In his Report to the Congress, Brezhnev called upon Soviet scientists to play an active entrepreneurial role in "disturbing the peace" to foster the innovation process. Both in his Report and in his address to the October plenum, he suggested the possibility of using scientists from the defense industries to work on the development of new technology in the civilian sectors, especially those concerned with consumer goods.

The Soviet Union sorely needs some new approaches to its planning and management processes. And while Brezhnev's October and February speeches have the virtue of calling for such approaches and attacking the power of inertia and tradition, they lack detail and specificity and do not offer a reform program. Furthermore, more than words one requires the energy to battle the bureaucracy and move it. The Soviet Union will have to wait for younger, more energetic leaders to take over the reins of government and test the Soviet economic system's true capacity for reform. The longer it has to wait, the closer the Soviet economy will come to what must be called a state of crisis.

Alternative Projections

In this section, we present some alternative projections for the 11th FYP period and the five-year period following it. These are derived from the twenty-year projections which we developed in our Airlie House Conference paper, as revised (see note 2). They have been calculated through the use of SOVMOD IV, the Wharton Econometric Model of the Soviet Union.[16] The alternative projections are the following:

‡ Baseline projection, with factor-productivity growth based on data from the period 1968–78.
‡ Low-productivity-growth projection.
‡ Baseline projection, with high and low growth of defense expenditures.
‡ Low-productivity projection, with high and low growth of defense expenditures.

Summary data from these projections are presented in Table 4.3.

Baseline Projections

The assumptions underlying the baseline projection include the calculation of factor productivity, outside the agricultural and energy sectors, from data for the period 1968–78. (Our assumptions are spelled out in greater detail in our Airlie House paper, as described in note 2). Agricultural output is modeled in a two-stage manner: first, as a function of labor, capital, land and material inputs; and secondly, as a function of weather (deviations from normal). Therefore, productivity in agriculture, as projected in our study, reflects variations in weather, which we capture by imposing the historical weather pattern of the period

Table 4.3 *Alternative Projections, 1980–85 and 1985–90 (Average Annual Rates of Growth, in Percent)*

	Baseline (1968–78 Productivity Growth) (1)	Low Productivity Growth (2)	Baseline Productivity Growth		Low Productivity Growth	
			High Defense (3)	Low Defense (4)	High Defense (5)	Low Defense (6)
GNP						
1980–85	3.71	2.73	3.70	3.72	2.73	2.74
1985–90	3.00	2.16	2.97	3.04	2.13	2.20
Industry						
1980–85	4.11	2.87	4.11	4.12	2.86	2.88
1985–90	3.48	2.51	3.45	3.52	2.47	2.54
Agriculture						
1980–85	4.53	4.60	4.53	4.53	4.60	4.61
1985–90	2.46	2.53	2.45	2.47	2.52	2.54
Investment						
1980–85	3.60	2.67	3.40	3.80	2.47	2.87
1985–90	2.48	1.66	2.07	2.84	1.20	2.05
Consumption						
1980–85	2.89	1.80	2.19	3.26	1.08	2.18
1985–90	2.16	0.91	1.18	2.53	−0.22	1.34
Consumption per capita						
1980–85	1.95	0.87	1.25	2.31	0.15	1.24
1985–90	1.38	0.14	0.41	1.76	−0.98	0.57
Defense						
1980–85	4.50	4.50	7.50	2.50	7.50	2.50
1985–90	4.50	4.50	7.50	2.50	7.50	2.50
Total Factor Productivity GNP						
1980–85	1.35	0.47	1.36	1.35	0.47	0.46
1985–90	0.97	0.31	0.98	0.95	0.32	0.29
Non-Agriculture						
1980–85	0.81	−0.26	0.80	0.80	−0.25	−0.26
1985–90	0.85	−0.09	0.73	0.72	−0.08	−0.10

1958–78 on the original twenty-year projection period 1980–2000, with each fifth year set at normal weather. Thus for the projection period 1981–85 the historical weather pattern of 1959–62 was imposed on the years 1981–84, and 1985 was set at normal weather; and similarly, for 1986–90, the weather pattern of 1964–67 was imposed on the years 1986–89, with 1990 being set at normal levels.

In the baseline projection, we make the following assumptions for fuel production. Oil output, which was 603 million metric tons in 1980, drops to 600 m.m.t. in 1981, remains at that level through 1985, and then drops to 550 m.m.t. by 1990. Gas output grows steadily from 435 billion cubic meters in 1980 to 600 b.c.m. in 1985 and 700 b.c.m. in 1990. Coal output grows from 716 m.m.t. in 1980 to 770 m.m.t. in 1985 and in 1990.

Following the CIA projections, we assume that defense expenditures will grow at a rate of 4.5 percent per year.

The summary data presented in column 1 of Table 4.3 generally depict the Soviet economy growing, in the period 1980–85, at somewhat lower rates than those set out in the 11th FYP, but not strongly inconsistent with those rates. In addition, the data indicate that in the succeeding years, 1985–90, the Soviet economy will be exhibiting slower rates of growth than in the first half of the decade (more on this below). For the 11th FYP period, the baseline projects the growth of GNP and of consumption to be below the rates in the 11th Plan, and the growth of investment to be above the rate of the Plan (see Table 4.1).

The agricultural growth rate in the baseline looks high, but it is the result of the assumption of a return to better weather conditions and the calculation of an average annual rate of growth relating output in 1985 to the very low output in 1980. If five-year averages were used, then the annual growth of agriculture in the baseline, for the period 1981–85 compared to the period 1976–80, would be 2.4 percent per year. Also the total factor productivity related to overall GNP of 1.35 percent per year is rather high, but it too reflects the calculated high growth of agriculture. The total factor-productivity growth in the nonagricultural sectors, 0.81 percent, is more in line with the record of the 1968–78 period. A comparison of individual industrial branch growth rates in the baseline projection with those in the 11th FYP also reveals a broad consistency between the two, with the baseline growth rates generally below those in the 11th FYP (see Table 4.4). In particular, the baseline growth rates for the two consumer-goods industries—light industries and food—are below those in the Plan, a finding which supports the inference that the Soviets will find it difficult to fulfill their goals for the growth of consumption.

One conclusion to be drawn from this general correspondence between the Plan data and the SOVMOD baseline is that the 11th FYP, in relation to the weather and productivity assumptions upon which it is based and with the exception of its consumer goods branches, exhibits a fair amount of internal consistency.

In regard to foreign trade, the assumptions made in the

Table 4.4 Industrial Branch Growth Rates, 1980–85
(Average Annual Rates of Growth, in Percent)

	11th FYP	SOVMOD Baseline Projections
Industry, total	4.90	4.11
Electric Power	4.06	6.19
Oil	0.96	−0.10
Gas	7.34	6.63
Coal	1.83	1.49
Chemicals	5.63	5.73
Machine Building and Metal Working	6.96	5.67
Construction materials	3.37	2.15
Forest product	} 3.37	0.87
Paper and pulp		2.49
Light industries	3.54	2.35
Food industry	4.48	2.26

baseline projection about the output of fuels, coupled with a moderately low rate of growth of GNP, allow the Soviets to maintain high total fuel exports to the West in the period of the 11th FYP, which would continue to account for about 70 percent of Soviet hard currency earnings. With oil output set at 600 million metric tons and domestic consumption calculated in the model to be 460 m.m.t., an exportable surplus of 140 m.m.t. of oil is projected for 1985. Allowing for oil exports to Eastern Europe of 80 m.m.t. (their 1980 level)[17], Soviet oil exports to the West are estimated at 60 m.m.t. in 1985, which is about 20 m.m.t. below the 1980 level. In the baseline projection, Soviet exports of gas to the West make up for this decrease.

On the whole then, the implications of the baseline projection are that with some luck in the weather, and a return to the average productivity growth of the 1968–78 period, the Soviets, while not fulfilling the 11th FYP, could come reasonably close to it.

Low-Productivity Projections

But it is not at all clear that the Soviet economy will be able to reattain the productivity-growth levels of the 1968–78 period during the next five years. With all the problems that the Soviets face, and with a growing perception among Western observers of serious erosion of morale among Soviet workers and managers,[18] lower productivity-growth rates might well be expected. Therefore, an alternative projection was run in which productivity growth was severely constrained. One percentage point was deducted from the combined factor productivity of the nonagricultural sector and the nonenergy branches of industry.

The results are shown in column 2 of Table 4.3. Overall total factor-productivity growth is reduced to 0.47 percent per year and nonagricultural productivity growth to −0.26 percent per year. This leads to a drop in GNP growth of one percentage point to 2.73 percent per year, and similarly substantial decreases in the growth of industry and investment. Of particular importance is the drop in the growth of consumption per capita below 1 percent per year. This low level may have dangerous political repercussions for Soviet authorities.[19]

With the drop in output growth, the domestic energy requirements are reduced, and thus the Soviet Union would have more surplus oil and gas. In fact, oil available for export in 1985 is estimated to be equal to that in 1980 (while the amount of gas available for export would increase substantially).

To estimate the impact of a drop in oil production (as opposed to the unchanged production levels we assumed in our other projection), we ran a projection with the same low rates of productivity growth but with oil output falling from 603 million metric tons in 1980 to 500 m.m.t. in 1985. In this projection, rates of growth (except for that of agriculture) slip somewhat, but oil production at that level does not appear to be a significant constraint on the economy. There is, however, a further erosion in the growth of consumption per capita, down to 0.69 percent per year, which could represent a very serious problem. In regard to oil exports, they are estimated to fall to 67 m.m.t. in 1985, which would most likely mean no hard currency oil exports and a reduction of Soviet oil exports to Eastern Europe—also a very serious problem.

Alternative Defense-Growth Projections

To throw some light on the oft discussed issue of Soviet defense expenditures in an era of constrained economic growth, we ran two variations of both our baseline and low-productivity projections with rates of growth of defense expenditures different from the assumed rate of 4.5 percent per year: one with a high rate of growth of defense expenditures of 7.5 percent per year, and the other with a low rate of growth in defense expenditures of 2.5 percent per year.

The summary results are shown in columns 3–6 of Table 4.3.

They indicate that changes in the growth of defense expenditures have very little impact on the growth of output—GNP, industry, and agriculture—over the period of the next five years, and just barely more impact on output growth in the second half of the 1980s, even though in both periods the impact on the growth of investment is not insignificant. This results mostly from the fact that the change in the absolute amount of annual investment that is caused by a change in defense expenditures (primarily procurement) is small relative to the size of the capital stock in the economy. It thus has a limited effect on the growth of the capital stock. In the four alternative defense projections over the decade of the 1980s, the range of capital stock growth is from a little above 6 percent per year to a little below 5 percent per year, while the range of investment growth is from 3.8 percent per year to 1.2 percent per year. This is then compounded by the rather low output elasticity of capital in the production functions of our Soviet model.

In contrast to the insignificant effect of variations in defense expenditures on the output of national product, there is more effect in our projections on the uses of national product. We have already commented about the effect on investment growth. The effect on consumption growth is of much greater significance. In the baseline productivity projections in Table 4.3, high 7.5 percent-per-year growth of defense expenditures reduces the rate of growth of consumption per capita, in the 1980–85 period, to 1.25 percent per year compared to the baseline rate of 1.95 percent to be found in column 1. On the other hand, a reduction in defense expenditure growth to 2.5 percent per year raises the growth of per-capita consumption to 2.31 percent per year, which is pretty close to the 11th FYP target. In the succeeding five-year period, if high 7.5 percent growth of defense expenditures were to be maintained, per-capita consumption would grow at a very low 0.41 percent per year compared to a baseline rate of 1.38 percent in column 1. Certainly, Soviet policy-makers would try to avoid a level of per-capita consumption growth so far below the 1 percent threshold.

The low-productivity-growth projections confront Soviet leaders with great difficulties in regard to consumption-growth standards. A continuation of the past 4.5 percent-per-year growth of defense expenditures in combination with low productivity growth, would lead to a 0.87 percent-per-year growth of per-capita consumption in the first half of the 1980s and an extremely low 0.14 percent per year in the second half of the 1980s. In such an environment, an increase in the growth of defense expenditures would be a difficult policy to pursue. Conversely, a policy of reducing the growth of defense expenditures from 4.5 percent to 2.5 percent per year would have the effect of raising per-capita consumption growth from 0.87 percent to 1.24 percent per year in the period of the 11th FYP. But in the period of the succeeding 12th FYP, the maintenance of this low defense growth would still leave per-capita consumption growing at a very low 0.57 percent per year. These projections illustrate how important it is to the Soviets to increase their factor-productivity growth over the levels observed in the last half of the 1970s.

To Soviet policy-makers, the impact of variations in the growth of defense expenditures may actually be much more significant than that indicated by the summary data just presented. This is so because policy-makers are more concerned with the allocation of the increments to output among competing claimants than with the distribution of the total flows of output, the past levels of which tend to be difficult to change and reallocate. The shares of incremental output going to defense, shown in Table 4.5, may thus provide a better illustration of what the burden of defense will be in the eyes of Soviet policy-makers.

The data in Table 4.5 show that the incremental effects of defense expenditures are greater than the average effects. In the baseline, with defense expenditures growing at 4.5 percent per year, the share of defense in GNP ("average burden of defense") increases from a level of 13 percent in 1980 to 15 percent in 1990. But the share of the increment to defense expenditures in the increment to GNP rises from 16 percent in 1980–85 to 21 percent in 1985–90. And most importantly for the issue of the impact of the growth in defense expenditures on Soviet policy-makers, the increment in the procurement of defense equipment grows from a share of 35 percent of the increment in machine-building and metal-working output, in the period 1980–85 (which is about the same as its incremental share in the 1970s) to a share of 54 percent in 1985–90. That is, in the period of the 12th FYP, the increase in defense procurement will be taking more than half of the increment in machine-building and metal-working output. This represents a serious problem for Soviet decision-makers, who will have a constrained residual with which to augment the flows of investment equipment which the heads of the economic ministries will be clamoring for. It indicates the likelihood, even in our baseline projection, of pressure at the top Soviet policy-making levels to reduce the rate of growth of defense below the 4.5 percent annual rate. The data in the high-defense-expenditure variant of the baseline case imply that the bureaucratic pressure from competing claimants for investment equipment would make it unlikely that a 7.5 percent rate of growth of defense expenditures could be maintained for very long, except in extreme circumstances.

The problems for defense expenditures produced by low productivity growth are clearly portrayed by the "incremental burden of defense" figures in column 3 of Table 4.5. In a low-productivity-growth environment, the baseline level of defense growth has the same impact as the high defense growth with baseline productivity growth; and low productivity growth combined with low defense growth have the same impact as the baseline defense and productivity growth. It is hard to see how, in such an environment, a decision to raise the rate of growth of defense expenditures could be arrived at by Soviet policy-makers (again outside of the direst of circumstances).[20] Indeed, it is hard to avoid the conclusion that, in the face of low productivity growth, Soviet policy-makers would not maintain their 4.5 percent rate of growth of defense expenditures for very long, most likely not past the mid-1980s.

Table 4.5 *Average Incremental Burden of Defense (in Percent)*

	Share of Defense in GNP (end of period) (1)	Share of Defense Increment in GNP Increment (2)	Share of Defense Procurement Increment in MBMW Increment* (3)
Baseline			
1980–85	14	16	35
1985–90	15	21	54
Baseline: high defense			
1980–85	16	29	45
1985–90	20	44	78
Baseline: low defense			
1980–85	13	9	26
1985–90	12	10	34
Low productivity			
1980–85	14	23	47
1985–90	16	32	82
Low productivity: High Defense			
1980–85	17	40	60
1985–90	22	65	117
Low productivity: low defense			
1980–85	13	12	34
1985–90	13	15	51

* The MBMW increment is the increment to that part of machine-building and metal-working output going to final demand.

Notes

1. Unless otherwise indicated, data are from the SOVMOD Databank. This draws on many sources including the reconstructions of Soviet data produced by the Office of Economic Research, CIA.
2. The data on total factor productivity for the periods 1960–70 and 1979–75 are from Abram Bergson, "Soviet Technological Progress: Trends and Prospects," prepared for the conference on "The Soviet Economy Toward the Year 2000" Airlie House, October 1980, Revised January 15, 1980, Table 1.
3. See the recent articles of Murray Feshbach, including his paper "Population and Labor Force" at the Airlie House Conference (Footnote 2).
4. Furthermore, abstracting from the issue of completed and uncompleted capital, it should be kept in mind that net investment is the annual addition to the capital stock. Therefore, even if net investment does not grow at all from year to year, as long as it is positive it will contribute an annual increment to the capital stock. Thus, net investment growing at a zero rate will still lead to capital stock growing at a positive (though declining) rate.
5. See Stanley Cohn, "Soviet Replacement Investment: A Rising Policy Imperative," in JEC, *Soviet Economy in a Time of Change*, GPO, Washington, D.C., 1979, Vol. 1, pp. 230–45.
6. For a summary statement of this resolution, see *Pravda*, 29 July 1979, and the *Current Digest of the Soviet Press*, XXXI:30 (22 August 1979).
7. In his report to the Congress, Brezhnev also stated that investment would grow at approximately the same rate as national income until 1990.
8. There are thus two differences involved: one, national income utilized and produced; and two, the Soviet concept—net material product, and the Western concept—gross national product. On the former, see the recent interesting article: Vladimir G. Treml, "Losses in Soviet National Income and Agriculture: A Puzzle," *The ACES Bulletin*, XXIII, 1, Spring, 1981, pp. 103–109.
9. If the growth of crude steel had been planned at the same rate, it would have a 1985 target of 170 m.m.t., which would be within the 10th FYP range for 1980.
10. Recent Soviet data show that in 1980, the United States dropped from second to seventh place among the Soviet Union's Western trading partners.
11. The Tikhonov speech was carried in the Soviet press on 27 February 1981. See also FBIS, "Proceedings of the 26th CPSU Congress," Volume V, 2 March 81, p. 26.
12. FBIS, *op. cit.*, Vol. I, p. 25.
13. FBIS, *op. cit.*, Vol. V, p. 23.
14. FBIS, *op. cit.*, Vol. I, p. 26 and Vol. X, pp. 12, 17.
15. *CDSP*, XXXII:42 (Nov. 19, 1980), p. 14. Brezhnev's address to the plenum was carried in the Soviet press on 22 October 1980.
16. For a detailed description of SOVMOD IV and its use, see D. L. Bond and H. S. Levine, "The Soviet Economy to the Year 2000: An Overview," (Revised May 1981), Airlie House Conference, *op. cit.*
17. In the absence of compensating policies, this will not be sufficient to meet East European energy needs. A full discussion of this issue is beyond the scope of the present paper.
18. It is argued that this erosion of morale is reflected in increasing alcoholism in the Soviet Union and such demographic developments as rising death rates among working-age males and rising infant mortality.
19. See the papers by Gertrude Schroeder and Seweryn Bialer at the Airlie House Conference, *op. cit.* Given the inefficiencies and the inequalities of the Soviet distribution system, an overall 1 percent per-capita consumption growth might well mean no growth or even negative growth for substantial segments of the Soviet population. To some extent, however, this could be ameliorated by increased consumer-goods production in the second economy.
20. In Table 4.5, column 3, a number greater than 100 indicates that in that period the flow of investment equipment to the sectors of the economy would be less than it was in the previous period.

5

Soviet Agricultural Plans for 1981–85

Douglas B. Diamond

Background

As the USSR enters the 1980s it is confronted with a marked slowdown in the secular growth of agricultural production at a time of steadily rising demand for farm products—a demand occasioned by population growth, increasing purchasing power, and rising expectations of improved diet. Annual farm output in 1976–80 averaged only 6 percent above the level posted in 1971–75, roughly the same growth as the increase in population. Nearly all of the 5 percent boost in per-capita availability of farm products in 1976–80 was attributable to a tripling of net imports of food and natural fiber. But even with record high levels of imports of farm products, the forward momentum achieved earlier in improving the quality of the Soviet diet has not been maintained.[1]

The near stagnation in agricultural production in the last half of the 1970s appears to be related to (*a*) less favorable growing conditions, (*b*) a decline in the rate of increase in resources committed to the farm sector, and (*c*) a failure to raise farm productivity through more efficient use of resources.

A review of climate trends since 1960 suggests that a major impetus to growth in farm output between the early 1960s and the mid-1970s was the result of unusually favorable weather.[2] By longer-run historical standards, the weather experienced in the 1976–80 period may have signaled a return to more "normal" conditions.[3] During the 10th Five-Year Plan (1976–1980), even by the standards of the previous decade, there were two years of very favorable growing conditions (1976 and 1978) and two years of exceptionally poor weather (1979 and 1980). Weather for

Table 5.1 USSR Indicators of Output Performance in Agriculture, 1976–80. Plan vs. Actual

	Average Annual Production			Change from 1971–75 to 1976–80		Actual Increase in 1976–80 as a Share of Plan Increase (Percent)
	1971–75 Actual (1)	1976–80 Plan (2)	1976–80 Actual (3)	Plan (4)	Actual (5)	(6) (Col. 5 ÷ Col. 4) ×100
Net farm output (billion 1970 rubles)	84.5	96.1	90.7	11.6	6.2	53
Selected commodities (million tons)						
Grain	181.6	217.5*	205.0	36.0	23.4	65
Cotton	7.7	8.5	8.9	0.8	1.2	150
Potatoes	89.8	102.0	82.5	12.2	−7.3	Absolute Decline
Sugar beets	75.9	96.5*	88.4	20.6	12.5	61
Meat (carcass weight)	14.0	15.3*	14.9	1.3	0.9	69
Milk	87.4	95.0*	92.7	7.6	5.3	70
Eggs (billion units)	51.4	59.5*	63.0	8.1	11.6	143

* Midpoint of ranges given in plan documents.

1977 was slightly unfavorable. However, growing conditions for 1977, 1979, and 1980 were strongly subnormal only by comparison to the average (favorable) conditions prevailing in the 1963–74 period.

In addition to less favorable growing conditions in 1976–80, there was a slowdown in the growth of agriculture's resource base. Total inputs for 1971–75 were about 10 percent above those in 1966–70. During the 1976–80 plan period inputs were only 5 percent above 1971–75 and considerably below the original targets.[4] Deliveries of industrially produced inputs, especially fertilizer and machinery, fell well short of plans. More importantly, the decline in the rate of increase in the resources committed to the farm sector in 1976–80 was not offset by an acceleration of growth in efficiency gains (output per unit of combined inputs). Since farm output averaged 6 percent above that in 1971–75, increases in production not explained by additional resource use were only 1 percent higher than during the previous period.

Some of the principal measures underlying these aggregate indicators of planned and actual performance for 1976–80 for output and inputs are presented in Tables 5.1 and 5.2.

Goals of the 11th Five-Year Plan

The regime's 1981–85 goals for agriculture, as contained in the new Directives, are essentially the same as those released in July 1978 at a Party plenum. The Directives call for a 10.5 percent increase in farm output in 1981–85 over that of 1976–80. Although specific targets for several inputs have not been announced, the implied plan for additions to the resource base in 1981–85 is only 3.5 percent above the average for each year in 1976–80, somewhat less than the increase registered in the last half of the 1970s. Since farm output is scheduled to be 10.5 percent above the annual average for the last half of the 1970s, a surge in increased productivity in the use of resources is required if the new five-year plan goals are to be attained. The ratio of additional output per unit of additional input is targeted at 7 percent in 1981–85, compared with 1 percent achieved in 1976–80.

Resource Plans

With respect to resource commitments, the highlights of the plan are:

Table 5.2 USSR: Selected Inputs in Agriculture, 1976–80. Plan vs. Actual

	1971–75 Actual (1)	Average Annual Inputs 1976–80		Change from 1971–75 to 1976–80		Actual Increase in 1976–80 as a Share of Plan Increase (Percent) (6) (Col. 5 ÷ Col. 4) ×100
		Plan (2)	Actual (3)	Plan (4)	Actual (5)	
Deliveries of:						
Tractors (thousand units)	334	380	360	47	27	57
Trucks (thousand units)	220	270	269	50	49	98
Agricultural machinery* (billions of rubles)	3.1	4.6	4.3	1.5	1.2	80
Mineral fertilizers† (million metric tons)	61	93	81	32	19	59
Gross additions of irrigated and drained land (thousand hectares)	1,784	1,920	1,598	136	−286	Absolute Decline

* Production of agricultural machinery; assumed equal to deliveries.
† Includes feed phosphates.

1 Total direct investments in agriculture in 1981–85, excluding rural housing and services, are scheduled to be 148 billion rubles. Meeting this goal will require agricultural investment to grow at an average of 3.3 percent a year, compared with a 2.5 percent average rate of increase in 1976–80.
2 Flows of other types of industrial goods are to expand at the relatively slow pace of 3 percent per year, somewhat below the rate in 1976–80.
3 Deliveries to farms of the most important of these industrial goods—mineral fertilizer—are slated to reach 115 million tons by 1985, the same amount planned for 1980 in the original 1976–80 Plan.
4 Completed reclamation projects are to include 3.5 million hectares of irrigated and 3.8 million hectares of drained land.

Other measures related to resource flows to farms in 1981–85 are shown in Table 5.3.

All of the increase in grain output is slated to come from higher yields; no further expansion in acreage is expected. (The output targets for principal commodities are reported in Table 5.4). The single most important factor in raising yields of grain and other crops will be the availability of fertilizer. Of the 115 million tons of fertilizer scheduled for delivery to farms in 1985, about 60 million tons are to be applied to grain crops. The total quantity of fertilizer used on grain will double, and the share of fertilizer allocated to grain crops will increase from 38 percent in 1980 to 52 percent in 1985. To the extent that further increases in fertilizer applications to nongrain feed crops will be suppressed because of the priority given to grains, additional dependence will be placed on grains as a source of livestock feed.

As Table 5.2 shows, a large shortfall in the delivery of fertilizer to farms occurred during the 1976–80 plan period. The USSR will have to overcome its current problems in operating Western-equipped fertilizer plants and boost output of requisite raw materials sharply if the gap between targeted output for mineral fertilizers and actual performance is to be substantially closed in 1981–85.

During 1981–85, 7.3 million additional hectares are scheduled to be irrigated and drained, compared with gross additions of 8.9 million hectares during 1976–80. Thus, despite huge expenditures on land reclamation projects over the ten-year period 1976–85 (roughly one-fourth of total agricultural investment outlays), the gross increase in irrigated and drained land in

Table 5.3 USSR: Selected Inputs in Agriculture, 1981–85. Plan

| | | Annual Average Amounts | | |
| | | | Change From: | Plan Change in 1981–85 as a Share of 1976–80 Actual Change (Percent) |
	1981–85 Plan (1)	1971–75 Actual to 1976–80 Actual (2)	1976–80 Actual to 1981–85 Plan (3)	(4) (Col. 3 ÷ Col. 2) × 100
Annual investment* (billions of rubles)	29.5	5.9	3.6	61
Deliveries of:				
Tractors (thousand units)	374†	27	14	52
Trucks (thousand units)	290†	49	30	61
Mineral fertilizer (million metric tons)	105‡	19	25	132
Gross additions of irrigated and drained land (thousand hectares)	1,460†	−286	−38	Further Decline

* Includes outlays for productive purposes, i.e., construction, electrification, acquisition of equipment. Data are in prices of 1 January 1969.
† Midpoint of ranges given in plan documents.
‡ Derived by interpolating between 1980 actual deliveries and 1985 planned deliveries. Totals include feed phosphates.

1981–85 will be nearly 20 percent below that attained in 1971–75. Even if the 1981–85 plan for reclaiming land is realized, the original goals for 1985 first promulgated in 1970 will be underfulfilled by more than 20 percent.

Meanwhile, the expected increases in state purchase prices for many farm products (to cover rising farm costs), will add a further burden to the state budget. Even at the present level of state procurements of livestock products, the higher prices would result in a marked increase in subsidies, if, as the government promises, retail prices remain unchanged. Between 1974–75 and 1978–79, the cost of producing a ton of animal liveweight on collective and state farms increased 19.5 percent for hogs and 23 percent for cattle.[5] State retail prices remained at fixed levels as they have for the past two decades. As a result of these divergent trends, the average retail price for all types of red meat is currently roughly one-half of the average cost in the meat industry. Subsidies to cover the difference between prices paid to farms and those charged to consumers during 1976–79 averaged more than 20 billion rubles annually. This is roughly the equivalent of two-thirds of agricultural investment in 1979 and 30 percent of agriculture's contribution to gross national product. Unless recent trends in costs are arrested or—equally unlikely—retail price policies are changed, subsidies will continue to mount.

Productivity Plans

Although the new program for agriculture in 1981–85 calls for a slower rate of growth of inputs than in the previous five-year plan, it is very costly and will require a steady effort. In addition, there will have to be a marked acceleration in productivity growth if the output goals are to be attained.

The two major points of attack on the problem of efficiency in 1981–85 are (a) better organization and management of agriculture and the supporting industries, and (b) relaxation of restrictions on private agricultural activity.

Organization and Management. Ever since the mid-1950s, Soviet leaders from time to time have enjoined the party and government to "stop exercising petty tutelage and usurping the functions of the leaders and experts" on the farms. While Soviet leaders—including Khrushchev, Brezhnev, and Kosygin —have in the past advocated a sharp increase in the power of individual farms to decide what crops to grow and to choose how

Table 5.4 USSR: Indicators of Output Performance in Agriculture, 1981–85. Plan

	Annual Average Amounts	Change From:		Plan Change in 1981–85 as Share of Actual Change in 1976–80 (Percent)
	1981–85 Plan (1)	1971–75 Actual to 1976–80 Actual (2)	1976–80 Actual to 1981–85 Plan (3)	(4) (Col. 3 ÷ Col. 2) ×100
Net farm output (billion 1970 rubles)	100.0	6.2	9.3	150
Selected commodities (million tons)				
Grain	240.5*	23.4	35.5	152
Cotton	9.3*	1.2	0.4	33
Potatoes	100.0†	−7.3	17.5	—
Sugar beets	101.5*	12.5	13.1	105
Meat (carcass weight)	17.3*	0.9	2.3	256
Milk	98.0*	5.3	5.3	100
Eggs (billion units)	72.0	11.6	9.0	78

* Midpoint of ranges given in plan documents.
† Based on plan data for major producing republics.

to distribute resources between crops and livestock, in the end the several regimes always undermined the promised autonomy for the farms.[6]

A decree published in December 1980 once again announces changes aimed at "correctly combining centralized leadership of agriculture with further development of the managerial independence of enterprises." Although the decree sharply reduces the number of plan indicators for farms, the state procurement plan for each farm will still be handed down from the center. The retention of a system of procurements dependent upon a rather arbitrary and detailed procedure for allocating quotas to farms weakens any set of proposals for decentralizing farm planning and decision making. In the past, when the center seemingly granted more room for initiative on the part of farm leaders, the highly developed system of bureaucratic control reemerged quickly when local managers took initiatives that the center perceived as threatening to the procurement plan. In addition, the recent emphasis on "interfarm associations," "agro-industrial complexes," and farm specialization runs counter to any notion of decentralization of decision making.[7]

In line with Moscow's desire to have a fully "integrated" food program, Brezhnev announced in October 1980 the creation of an agro-industrial food complex that would strengthen the ties between agriculture and the procurement, storage and processing of farm products. Soviet institutions have demonstrated a sometimes remarkable inability to receive, process, and market raw foodstuffs efficiently. As a result, prodigious quantities of perishable foodstuffs—20–25 percent of output according to official statements—have been left to deteriorate on the farms, have been fed to livestock, or have spoiled on the way to market or while awaiting processing.[8]

To stem the great wastage of agricultural raw materials, a new supraministerial body may soon be established to coordinate the work of related branches. To the extent that investment resources are committed to making marked improvements in the care and marketing of farm products, a reduction in losses and an increase in resource productivity can be expected. Otherwise, new organizational forms by themselves will not provide the desired result. For example, the recent creation of a republic level network of ministries of fruits and vegetables will only provide another layer of bureaucratic control unless it is accompanied by an expansion of modern storage and marketing facilities and an enhanced transportation priority for perishable products.

Private Agriculture. Private agriculture in the USSR consists almost exclusively of individual holdings up to 0.5 hectares, frequently combined with the ownership of one or two head of livestock and a small flock of poultry. Although the share of total farm output produced in the private sector has declined during the 1970s, the sector has provided roughly one-fourth of production in recent years. The private sector has specialized in potatoes, of which it contributes about 60 percent of total output; other vegetables, 30 percent of total output; meat and milk, 30 percent of total output; and eggs, 35 percent of total output.

Although the basic official policy toward private activity can be characterized as one of repression, campaigns to suppress private activity have alternated with periods of relaxation. The dismal performance of agriculture in recent years, coupled with a widening gap between retail supplies and consumer demand for meat and other livestock products, has once again spurred official interest in encouraging the private sector. After a rather low-key effort in 1977 to tolerate some expansion in the private sector failed to elicit more activity, a new and more positive set of measures was adopted in January 1981. The new decree combines several approaches used in the past with some innovative tactics. The measures that have been used before include:

1 Increasing the volume of credit advanced to individuals for developing private plots and improving the repayment terms.
2 Urging state and collective farm managers to supply more feed, make available more land for grazing, and provide more assistance to individuals in marketing their produce.

The following measures in the decree are new:

1 Contracts are to be negotiated between state and collective farms and individuals on a case-by-case basis. The farms are to provide young animals, feed, and veterinary and other services and are to buy back some of the mature livestock.[9]
2 If an individual promises to deliver his livestock above the current ceilings to the socialized sector, restrictions on the number of livestock are eased.
3 Newly formed households are to be granted young livestock free of charge.

Whatever the response of individual households to these official initiatives, expansion in private sector livestock holdings depends heavily upon the socialized sector's success in providing the required feed base.[10] The 8 million hectares of arable land (1.5 percent of the total) directly under the control of individuals can supply only a small share of the feedstuffs used by the private sector. Private livestock holders, however, are able to use certain land in the socialized sector for pasturing livestock and harvesting hay—roughly 103 million hectares of pasture and 29 million hectares of hayland.

If all of the area in the socialized sector that directly or indirectly produces feedstuffs for the private sector is added to the relatively small area directly held by households, the total area given over to supporting private farming comes to about 140 million hectares, or about 23 percent of all the arable land in the USSR. In addition, feedstuffs (grain, straw, silage, hay) may be received as payment in kind for participating in work on collective or state farms.[11] Theft or "misappropriation" of feedstuffs is also not uncommon. Approximately 70 percent of total feed used by the private sector (in terms of feed units) is supplied by the socialized sector. Overall, the available evidence suggests that there is no marked difference between the private and socialized sectors in livestock feeding efficiency.[12] Hence, to the extent that expansion of private sector livestock output relies on more feed from the socialized sector, there will be less feed for increasing livestock output on state and collective farms.

As a result, even if the new Soviet policies are successful in encouraging private sector output, they probably will not lead to overall efficiency gains. On the other hand, a relaxation of constraints on private agriculture could increase inputs of labor into agriculture during 1981–85 by inducing individual households to extend their workweek on private plots at the sacrifice of leisure.[13]

Outlook for Grain and Meat

Unless weather conditions are unusually favorable during the 11th Five-Year Plan period, there is no persuasive evidence to suggest that—with the currently planned allocations of resources to agriculture—the overall output goal for agriculture will be achieved. In particular, the all-important grain target seems clearly too ambitious.

Weather conditions are likely to continue to be less favorable than they were in the 1963–74 period. Accordingly, grain yields will not advance at a pace faster than that indicated by recent trends. We therefore estimate that average grain output during 1981–85, with no reduction in area sown to grain, will be roughly 15 million tons below the announced target of 240.5 million tons (midpoint of range 238–43 million tons).[14] This level of grain production, coupled with a continued high level of imports, will probably be enough to support the relatively modest meat target of 17 to 17.5 million tons per year set for 1981–85.[15] Assuming household incomes grow by at least half the past rate and the regime holds to its promise not to increase meat prices, the planned growth of meat production will result in an ever widening gap between supply and demand. Even if the output goals for other quality foods (for example, sugar and vegetable oils) are met, recent very high levels of meat imports will likely continue.

Because of the surge in imports of farm products in recent years, the share of total hard currency outlays accounted for by purchases of grain, meat, vegetable oil, sugar, and other agricultural products rose from an average of 18 percent in 1971–75 to an average of 29 percent in 1979–80. Even if the recent rapid growth in net imports of farm products slows and eventually levels off, shortages of hard currency could force the leadership to make hard choices between keeping consumer grumbling in a tolerable range and maintaining current levels of nonfood imports.

Notes

1. Of the 10.5 billion ruble annual net increase in domestic supply of farm products between 1971–75 and 1976–80, 4.3 billion rubles was attributable to an increase in net imports. Both production and trade values are expressed in 1970 average realized prices received by all producers. (For details concerning the construction of the index of farm output in 1970 prices, see Dave W. Carey, "Recent Performance and Future Plans" in JEC, *Soviet Economy in a New Perspective*. Washington, D.C., U.S. Government Printing Office, 1976.)
2. About half of the increase in Soviet grain production between 1963 and 1974 was due to a favorable climatic deviation that may have ended with the severe drought of 1975. CIA, ER-76-10577, *USSR: The Impact of Recent Climate Change on Grain Production*, October 1976.
3. "Normal" weather is taken to reflect average conditions over, say, a thirty-year period.
4. The categories of inputs considered are labor, fixed capital (building, structures, and machinery and equipment), land, materials purchased from outside agriculture (fuels and lubricants, electric power, fertilizer, some individually processed feeds and current repairs of machinery and building) and livestock herds. The several inputs considered are aggregated into a geometric production function of the Cobb-Douglass type where each input is weighted with its relative share or contribution to total output in the period. See Douglas B. Diamond and Lee W.

Davis, "Comparative Growth in Output and Productivity in U.S. and U.S.S.R. Agriculture." In JEC, *Soviet Economy in Time of Change*, Washington, D.C.: U.S. Government Printing Office, 1979.

5   Data from indicated annual editions of *Narodnoye khozyaystvo SSR*. These are Soviet measures of cost and hence *exclude* a return to land and interest charges on capital. Because of the rapid growth of the value of plant and equipment associated with the livestock sector, if full costs (including interest charges) were reflected, the rise between the two periods would have been larger. The cost comparisons are given for two-year periods to reflect a blend of good and poor weather years.

6   The provisions of the 1955 decree to decentralize farm management were often violated, and continued to be sent by district (*rayon*) and regional (*oblast*) authorities to state and collective farms. *Pravda* 25 December 1961, and *Planovoye khozyaystvo*, No. 5, 1962, p.1.

7   See Everett M. Jacobs, "Some Recent Changes in Soviet Agricultural Planning and Management." April 1981. (Processed.)

8   For example, in recent years nearly 3 million tons of vegetables, or 15 percent of the total produced by collective and state farms, was returned to farms for "reprocessing" or for feeding livestock. (Based on data for the RSFSR in *Planovoye khozyaystvo*, No. 7, 1978, p. 49). Roughly one-fourth of fruit and berries are lost from poor harvesting, storage and transport practices (*Ekonomika Selskogo khozyaystvo* No. 2, 1973, p. 15). In addition, much sugar from sugar beets is lost because of delays in processing: from the harvest in September to the following March, the sugar content of beets awaiting processing falls by some 50 percent. Similarly, according to the stream of evidence in the Soviet press, lack of adequate slaughtering and processing facilities results in losses in meat production, either from weight losses of animals backed up en route between farms and processing plants or from overexpenditure of feed due to retention of animals for months beyond the appropriate age and weight for slaughter. (See, for example, *Voprosy ekonomiki*, No. 6, 1979, pp. 83–91 and *Sovetskaya rossya*, 25 April 1981.)

9   Although a contractual system had been promulgated earlier, it had not been widely employed. The contract system is voluntary and therefore depends upon the interest of individuals and the proclivities of farm managers. State and collective farms are allowed to include products obtained under contract towards their own plan fulfillment targets.

10 Since acreage allocations per household are not to be increased, the aggregate amount of land directly under the control of individuals will not expand substantially. Under the proposed incentive arrangements, it is doubtful if many households currently without acreage allotments will be attracted.

11 For example, many socialized agricultural enterprises permit the work force participating in the annual hay harvest to retain 10 percent of the hay cut; the balance goes to feeding herds on collective and state farms.

12 In the sense that the number of feed units required per unit of meat, milk, and other livestock products differs among sectors.

13 To the extent that additional labor input (persons or added hours per person) is forthcoming the overall indicator of planned inputs for 1981–85 given on p. 110 above is understated.

14 CIA, ER 79-10057, *USSR: Long Term Outlook for Grain Imports*, January 1979.

15 For purposes of projecting grain requirements for 1981–85, we have assumed that the share of grain and other concentrates in total feed rations will be maintained at roughly one-third of total feed units. If Soviet plans for expansion of production of nonconcentrated feeds (silage, hay, coarse feeds, fodder roots, pasture, and other minor feedstuffs) are not fulfilled, grain and other concentrates may rise as a share of total feed units. In that event, we have underestimated the required concentrates and hence the required level of imports of grain. If grain import capacity is also a constraining factor, then we have also overestimated the level of meat output.

6
Soviet Energy Policy: From Big Coal to Big Gas

Thane Gustafson

For Soviet energy the 26th Party Congress stands out as an important occasion. After a decade of growing official attention energy now appears to have displaced agriculture as the top civilian concern of the Brezhnev leadership, and the delegates to the Congress witnessed the unveiling of a new energy strategy: instead of the heavily coal-oriented approach announced in 1976 and the shift toward oil that took place two years later, the official strategy adopted in February 1981 wagers chiefly on gas. The aim of this chapter is to describe the main features of the new policy, its evolution over the last five years, and the implications of the changes, both for the Soviet economy and for the West.

Since the early 1970s, as the urgency and complexity of the energy problem have grown more apparent, the response of the Soviet leaders has often appeared erratic and uncertain. Several times in the last ten years they have shifted their basic strategy. In view of this pattern, the most important question about the latest policy is whether it has a more realistic chance of success than its predecessors. We shall attempt to approach that question in two ways: first, by looking at the technical and financial requirements of the gas-centered strategy and comparing them to those of earlier strategies; and secondly, by inferring what we can of the decision making that lies behind the recent twists and turns of Soviet energy policy. Why was the coal-oriented strategy changed? Are the leaders better equipped now than they were five or ten years ago to approach the energy problem as a unified whole and to carry out an integrated policy?

For advice and comments on earlier drafts of this paper the author is indebted to Dr Grey Hodnett.

Answers to these questions may help us to understand whether, after a decade of debate and trial and error, something like a solid consensus on energy has developed, or whether we are likely to see further uncertainty and vacillation in the future.

For the West, one of the most important questions is whether the Soviets can execute the gas-oriented strategy on their own, or whether they will need Western help. That question was not an issue in the coal-oriented strategy of 1976, because it was seen by the Soviet leaders (rightly or wrongly) as essentially an autarkic strategy. Indeed, that is undoubtedly one of the reasons it was adopted in the first place.[1] The gas strategy, in contrast, is likely to require a major contribution from Western industry, and European firms are already heavily involved in it. Consequently, the shift toward gas may require at the same time a shift toward greater Soviet participation in world trade and possible dependence upon it. But have the Soviet leaders faced up to this fact and to the possible constraints it may impose on them? Later in the paper we shall try to glimpse the answer.

Main Points of the Energy Program Announced at the 26th Party Congress

Overall Increase in the Priority of Energy Issues

Energy issues were noticeably more prominent at the 26th Party Congress than at the 25th Congress. In both Brezhnev's and Tikhonov's speeches energy was listed ahead of any other industrial sector and well ahead of agriculture. In contrast, five years earlier Kosygin had given top billing to machinery rather than energy, and Brezhnev had hardly mentioned energy at all, preferring to concentrate on agriculture instead.

Unfortunately, no investment figures for the energy sector were announced at the Congress or in the Main Guidelines for the 11th Five-Year Plan, so it is not possible to verify the impression of higher priority with a more concrete measure. The sole exception was gas, which according to the late Gas Minister S. A. Orudzhev[2] is scheduled to receive a total of nearly 22 billion rubles over the next five years, well over double the level of the 10th Five-Year Plan.[3] Table 6.1 shows the output targets for 1985.[4]

Eclipse of the Coal Strategy

The most remarkable difference between the leaders' state-

Table 6.1 Soviet Energy Output Targets for 1985

	1985 Targets	1980 Output
Oil (inc. gas condensate) (million metric tons)	620–45	603
Coal (m.m.t.)	770–800	716
Gas (billion cubic meters)	600–640	435
Electricity (billion kwh)	1550–1600	1295
of which Nuclear (b.kwh.)	220–25	65
and Hydropower (b.kwh.)	230–35	180
Related items:		
Rolled steel (million tons)	117–20	103
Cement (m.t.)	140–42	125

SOURCES: 1. Figures for 1980 are taken from *Pravda*, 24 January 1981.
2. Figures for 1985 are taken from the Main Guidelines of the 11th Five-Year Plan, *Pravda*, 5 March 1981.

ments in 1976 and in 1981 is the greatly reduced role assigned to coal. In 1976, long-range development of coal appeared to the leaders to be the best hope for rationalizing the Soviet fuel balance. Oil and gas, Kosygin declared then, were to be reserved as much as possible for nonfuel uses. Large coal-fired power plants would be built in the Volga and Ural regions. Most important of all, the vast brown coal reserves of Kazakhstan and Siberia would be converted to electricity by complexes of mine-mouth plants located nearby, and the power would flow to points of demand in the European USSR over the world's longest high-voltage transmission lines. To begin this long-term shift toward coal, the Guidelines for the 10th Plan called for an increase in coal output of 14 to 16 percent over five years.

Instead, the coal industry in 1980 came in a phenomenal 74 million tons short of the low end of the initial 10th Plan target; very few new coal-fired power plants were actually built (and no oil-fired ones were converted to coal); and the preliminary groundwork for the high-voltage transmission lines had barely begun by the time the 26th Party Congress opened. We shall examine the reasons for this failure below, in order to establish the mixture of political and technical reasons involved; but at any rate it became clear less than two years after the 25th Party Congress that progress in coal would be slower and considerably more expensive than had been originally anticipated.

As a result, the role assigned to coal in the 11th Plan is considerably more modest; indeed, the target assigned for the end of the 11th Plan is actually lower than the one originally set in 1976 for the end of the 10th Plan. Even that much may be overambitious, for coal output has actually declined for the last two years.

Oil too failed to meet the ambitious heights set for it in 1976; while production continues to grow slowly, the level announced for the 11th Plan is essentially the one that the Soviet leaders had hoped to reach by the end of the 10th Plan.[5]

The New Line: A Big-Gas Strategy

Gas, in contrast, was the star performer of the 10th Plan. It was the only major energy source actually to achieve the five-year targets set for it in 1976. Gas is rapidly overtaking oil as a money-earner abroad; and at home it is the easiest substitute for fuel oil as an energy source in boiler uses. It is hardly surprising, therefore, that gas has become the main hope of the Soviet leadership for getting through the energy bottleneck of the 1980s. In a five-year plan that is noteworthy for its very modest increase in overall capital investment, the gas industry is scheduled to receive a sizable share of the increment: out of a total of 77 to 106 billion rubles to be added to the investment budget over the next five years, gas will get nearly 12 billion.[6]

Nevertheless, the demands placed on the gas industry over the next five to ten years will be nothing short of phenomenal: 50,000 kilometers of new major pipeline, 25 megawatts of new compressor capacity, and 102 billion cubic meters of additional gas-treatment capacity are to be installed.[7] Total gas production is slated to rise from 435 billion cubic meters in 1980 to between 600 and 640 b.c.m. in 1985, which means average annual increments of between 33 and 41 b.c.m. West Siberia's Tiumen' province alone is expected to produce between 330 and 370 b.c.m. by 1985, an increment over the 1980 level of 174 to 214 b.c.m. In other words, West Siberia is expected to provide virtually the entire net increase. Within Tiumen', the crucial battlefield is Urengoi, which if all goes according to plan will provide 250 b.c.m. alone by 1985.

The new energy priorities are intended to hold for at least the next ten years. "I consider it necessary," Brezhnev stated in his report to the Congress, "to single out the rapid increase in extraction of Siberian gas as a task of first-class economic and political importance. The deposits of the West Siberian region are unique. The largest of them—Urengoi—has such a gigantic amount that it could, for many years, meet the internal needs of the country as well as its export needs—including exports to capitalist countries."

To implement the allocation of top priority to Tiumen' gas and oil, special administrative bodies are being created: according to Brezhnev, a special commission of the USSR Council of Ministers was recently established to deal with the development of the West Siberian gas and oil complex. In addition, an interagency commission under the authority of Gosplan has been created in Tiumen' to oversee coordination of the work of the many industrial ministries working there.[8]

Substitution and Conservation

The new emphasis on gas in Soviet policy sheds some indirect light on the leaders' views on energy substitution and conservation. One constant theme in Soviet energy policy is that a substitute must be found to replace oil as the chief Soviet boiler fuel. But what substitute? One part of the answer remains the same as five years ago: maximum development of nuclear power and hydropower. If anything, that policy has been stepped up in the 11th Five-Year Plan. Whereas nuclear power and hydropower were supposed to provide 40 percent of net additions to electrical capacity during the 10th Plan, their share for the next five years has now been raised to 70 percent. The first five-year target for hydropower (12.3 megawatts) seems realistic, but that for nuclear power seems overambitious: the goal is to add 24,000 to 25,000 megawatts of nuclear-generated capacity by 1985, an extraordinary undertaking when one considers the fact that during the entire 10th Plan Minenergo's builders managed no more than 8,000 megawatts.

The other major substitute for oil, as envisioned by the 25th Congress, was to have been coal. Gas was to be limited as much as possible to nonfuel uses. Indeed, during the 10th Plan regulations were adopted in a number of agencies to limit the use of natural gas as fuel,[9] and that policy was one of the most constant themes of official speeches during the last plan. Now all that has changed. In the next ten years, gas will be widely substituted for oil in boiler uses, even though there have been some expressions of reluctance in the speeches of people like Gas Minister S. A. Orudzhev and Central Committee Secretary V. I. Dolgikh.[10] There is even a revival of talk of a major expansion of gas-fired electrical generation, a policy long advocated by gas enthusiasts.[11]

As for conservation, although it was frequently mentioned at the Congress and has been discussed abundantly by the Soviet press in recent years,[12] the stress in the current energy policy seems to be on developing new energy resources rather than making better use of them. By 1985, according to the Main Guidelines, conservation polices are supposed to produce a saving of 160 to 170 million tons of standard fuel a year, compared to what would be consumed otherwise. However, that is the only specific number to be found for conservation; while there are references to the need to develop more energy-saving technology and more centralized heat supply, to make better use of waste heat, to cut losses of oil and to increase the output of light oil fractions, no specific targets are assigned to these programs.

Brezhnev's report is similarly imprecise about conservation. After pointing out to the delegates that "in comparison with the best world indicators we use more energy and raw materials per unit of output," the measures he advocates are more exhortation than plan: raising the efficiency of extractive industries, making more efficient use of equipment, and developing energy-saving technological designs. The only specific items Brezhnev chooses to mention are increases in the recovery rate from oil fields and conversion of automobiles to diesel and gas-derived fuels.[13] Lastly, Tikhonov in his speech to the Congress calls attention to the fact that because of the rapidly rising production costs of new energy, the economic attractiveness of conservation measures is growing too. But he too avoids specific conservation targets other than the global one. The only numbers he gives refer to conservation of metals, such as the target to economize 10 to 12 percent on metal used in pipelines, a saving that would have obvious consequences for energy policy, both directly and indirectly.[14]

Energy Policy and Competition for Investment Resources

The energy policy outlined at the Congress is certain to cause the competition for scarce investment resources to tighten drastically. To demonstrate this, we begin with some rough projections: for oil, electricity, and coal, let us assume for the 11th Plan a continuation of the trends of the 10th Plan—that is, modest growth for coal and electricity and rapid growth for oil. We obtain five-year investment totals of 38, 26, and 8 billion rubles for oil, electricity, and coal respectively. Add to that the figure hinted at by Orudzhev for gas investment—roughly 22 billion rubles. That yields a total of 94 billion rubles for energy

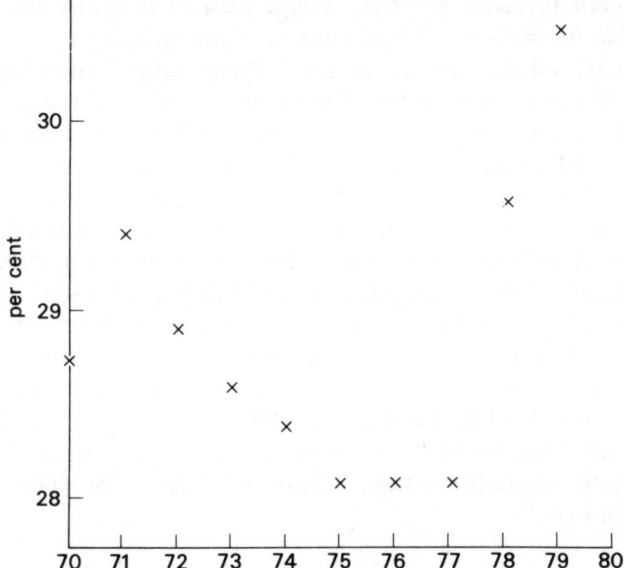

Figure 6.1 *Energy as a percentage of total industrial investment, 1970–79*

during the 11th Plan, compared to 66 billion in the 10th Plan. Now, what share of the industrial investment budget will that represent?

During the 11th Plan, overall investment will be 711 to 730 billion rubles. If industry's share remains the same as in the last plan (roughly 222 billion rubles out of 634, or 35 percent), industrial investment will be 250–56 billion. Our projection for energy investment represents 36.7 to 37.6 percent of that sum. Is that likely? As Figure 6.1 shows, the share of energy investment (as a percentage of industrial investment) started climbing sharply in 1978, gaining 2.4 percentage points in two years. In other words, the energy sector is well on its way to reoccupying the 40 percent share it routinely held in the 1950s, before the Soviet economy shifted to cheaper hydrocarbons. Still, our projection requires the energy sector to reach the 40 percent range by 1985; to put it mildly, that will mean no small jostling of other investment sectors. How much jostling? We can get an idea if we look at the figures from another angle: industrial investment of 250–56 billion rubles during 1981–85 means an increment of 28 to 34 billion over the 10th Plan. But 28 billion happens to be the increment called for by our energy projection. In other words, *a simple continuation of recent investment trends in oil, coal, and electric power, combined with the targeted investment increase for gas, would absorb virtually the entire available increase in capital resources for industry.*

Clearly, something has to give. Presumably it will be some corner of the energy sector other than gas, most likely coal. But even if we assume no investment growth for coal at all, we are still left with an increase of some 20 billion rubles for the energy sector. There is no getting around it: if the Soviet leaders really mean business about energy, they are going to have to pay for it with a very sizable share of their capital increment for at least the next decade. And for all that, what will they get? A mobilization of gas resources and a grim holding action for oil, together with a postponement of longer-term solutions for lack of funds. In any emergency program, there is the danger that the needs of the near term will displace those of the longer term. This danger is already causing some concern among high Soviet officials, notably the president of the USSR Academy of Sciences, A. P. Aleksandrov.[15]

Soviet Decision Making in Energy

Structure and Recent Evolution of Decision Making

Soviet decision making in energy over the last decade has been erratic and uncertain. From an emphasis on oil in the early 1970s, the Soviet leaders have moved to gas, then to a mix of energy sources with particular emphasis on coal, then back to oil, and finally to gas again. How should one interpret such apparent vacillation? Is it the result of pulling and hauling by various institutional groups and regional spokesmen? Have the leaders been divided, with policy disagreements complicated by jockeying for political position? Or is the central leadership simply struggling to come to grips, by successive and not necessarily coherent stages, with the full implications of a complex and fast-moving problem that has no easy solutions?

Undoubtedly none of these possibilities is completely false; however, as we try to understand how the Soviet leaders may react to the energy problem in the future, it would be helpful if we could be more precise. Therefore, the aim of the next section is to examine how these diverse answers may plausibly fit together.

First of all, what is the basic structure for decision making on energy questions? A recently published organization chart gives as complete a picture as is available in the West, including, for the first time, mention of a *referentura* attached to the Council of

Ministers, apparently a body of technical advisers which presumably includes some experts on energy.[16] The point that stands out immediately from the chart is that a large number of bodies have a role in energy, not just in implementation and technical advice, but apparently also in policy formation. Each of the principal energy sources has its own ministry, complete with facilities for planning and research. Further technical advice comes from a multitude of institutes in the USSR Academy of Sciences, and Gosplan itself has two research groups, the Council for the Study of Productive Forces and the Institute of Complex Fuel Energy Resources. The Council of Ministers has—along with its *referentura*—a recently formed Special Commission for West Siberian Energy. Lastly, the State Committee on Science and Technology and the State Committee for the Utilization of Atomic Energy, though they have no energy-related research institutes of their own, have specialized departments and directorates that are additional sources of information and advice.

What had not been clearly present until recently was a central decision-making body to form and oversee energy policy overall. While the Central Committee apparatus has sectors for coal, oil, and geology in the Department of Heavy Industry, and sectors specializing in power in the Departments of Machine Building and Construction, no single high-ranking official in the Secretariat appears to have extensive career experience in energy affairs or to have crosscutting jurisdiction over the entire field.[17] The senior Central Committee secretary with authority for general supervision of the economy, A. P. Kirilenko, has addressed the subject of energy frequently in his public speeches, but his interest has focused mainly on atomic power, power transmission, and general problems of electricity, and much less on oil and gas.[18]

Until late 1977, Brezhnev's own role in energy policy seemed remote; at the 25th Party Congress, as we noted above, his report contained only a few generalities about energy, and the task of spelling out the coal-oriented policy announced then was left to Kosygin, who over the years had played a more visible role in energy affairs than any other top official of the Soviet government. Another top official with clear authority in energy matters was Gosplan Chairman N. K. Baibakov, whose career began in the oil industry and who was deputy minister of the oil industry from 1940 to 1955.[19] The implication seemed to be that the party leadership was not playing the top role in energy decision making at the time.

This broad allocation of responsibilities changed abruptly in late 1977, when the policy established at the 25th Party Congress was set aside in favor of a crash effort to accelerate West Siberian oil and gas, especially oil. The shift was due above all to Brezhnev, who in a speech to the December 1977 plenum of the Central Committee stressed the decisive importance of Tiumen'.[20] In the months following there was a good deal of discussion over the course to take, during which officials with links to Tiumen' lobbied vigorously for Siberian oil.[21] The new line was apparently consolidated after Brezhnev's trip to Siberia in the spring of 1978,[22] and by a strongly worded speech to the 13th Komsomol Congress in April 1978.

Over the next three years Brezhnev's role in energy policy has grown even more prominent. The latest shift toward gas, far from detracting from Brezhnev's luster, was described by Prime Minister Tikhonov as Brezhnev's initiative. At the same time, the apparent role of the Central Committee staff has grown also. V. I. Dolgikh, the Central Committee secretary in charge of heavy industry, has played a more visible role in energy matters.[23] The impression that the Central Committee Secretariat and Brezhnev's own staff have taken active control of energy policy in the last three years is further suggested by G. P. Bogomiakov, who in his speech to the 26th Party Congress stressed the role of the Central Committee in concentrating resources and supervising performance in the oil and gas industry of Tiumen' province. "The questions connected with this," Bogomiakov observed, "have been discussed more than once at Central Committee plenums, in the Politburo, and in the Secretariat. The secretaries and departments of the Central Committee have systematically and exactingly overseen the fulfillment of their instructions."[24]

For all that, there still exists no apparent "czar" for energy policy, either in the party apparatus or elsewhere, although there have been occasional calls for the appointment of one.[25] The role of the staff of the Presidium of the Council of Ministers presumably declined during 1979 and 1980, first as Kosygin gradually fell out of step with the evolution of policy (see below), and then as he fell ill and was replaced. Though V. E. Dymshits remains prominently involved in energy affairs, there has been such turnover in the last year among the deputy chairmen of the Council of Ministers that it is plausible to assume that the energy role of the Presidium of the Council of Ministers has been reduced for the time being. Perhaps the creation of a Special Commission for Western Siberia in the Presidium is a model for a broader commission along the lines of the VPK.[26]

Are the Soviets well or badly served by the system of decision making for energy that has evolved in the last three years? If there exists no powerful and specialized state body for energy policy, and decisions are made instead through high-level, ad hoc interventions by the party leadership, will the Soviets be able to develop a balanced, long-term policy? Will the result instead be a series of lurches? Or is a long-term policy even appropriate, in view of the rapid and unexpected changes that have characterized the energy "environment" in the last decade, both within the Soviet Union and outside? The lesson of the last five years may be that Soviet leaders coped more effectively with the energy problem in the second half of the 10th Plan period, when Brezhnev took personal charge, than they did in the first half. We shall return to this question below.

A related question is whether the Soviet leaders are now any closer to a consensus on energy policy than they were a few years ago. It is instructive to see that Brezhnev's launching of a West Siberian strategy did not put an end to what Bogomiakov had referred to in early 1978 as "contradictory judgments in views on the future." In 1978 and 1979 top officials appeared reluctant to line up behind the crash shift to Tiumen', and those who did line up had gas in mind more than oil.[27] By the end of 1979 the formula of a "balanced" mix of energy sources had begun to appear in Soviet writings, foreshadowing a partial retreat from the previous two years' all-out emphasis on oil. Yet this did not necessarily mean unanimity behind gas, as events in 1980 showed, for in that year one could find in the Soviet press no less wide a variety of high-level public views than two years before.[28] The "preemption" of the energy issue by Brezhnev in the last three years may mask a continuing lack of agreement among the other officials, one that will emerge again in a few years.

What Happened to the Coal Strategy?

The most spectacular development in Soviet energy policy in the last five years is the eclipse of the coal-based strategy adopted at the 25th Party Congress. Why was that strategy rejected? But first, what exactly happened? It is important to bear in mind that the coal-based strategy of 1976 was not intended to pay off in the short term; it was a long-term program. Indeed, the 10th Plan Guidelines projected a decline in the share of coal in the total energy balance for the 10th Five-Year Plan, from 30 percent in 1975 to 26 percent in 1980.[29] The investment data reinforce this impression: on the one hand, it is true, during the three years in which the coal strategy enjoyed official favor capital investment in the coal industry grew at an accelerating pace (by 2.2 percent in 1976, 5.6 percent in 1977, and 10 percent in 1978);[30] but these were years of steady growth in investment for other energy sources too, and as a result the share of coal actually declined, from 15.6 percent of total energy investment in 1975 to 15.2 percent in 1978.[31]

If one were to infer from the investment statistics which energy source had the leaders' actual favor during the first half of the 10th Plan, the answer would be oil and gas, not coal. From 1975 through 1977, their share in total energy investment increased from 51 to 54.6 percent. In other words, the *perelom* of 1978 was not a radical departure from the pattern of earlier years; rather, it reinforced the preference already being given to oil (particularly Western Siberian oil), chiefly at the expense of gas, whose share of investment for the rest of the 10th Plan stopped growing.

In sum, the eclipse of the coal strategy, upon examination, appears to be less a rejection of one energy source for another (although it was undoubtedly also that, as we shall see) than an implicit increase in the urgency with which the energy problem was viewed, followed by a deliberate shortening of the decision-making horizon.

Some such interpretation is required if we are to make sense of Kosygin's public behavior from 1976 through early 1980. In all his speeches during that period he stuck doggedly to the pro-coal formula he had used at the 25th Party Congress.[32] Only in one of his very last addresses, at the 34th session of the Council for Mutual Economic Assistance in Prague, did Kosygin shift his public stance: he dropped all mention of coal and omitted as well another theme that had assumed ritual status in his speeches—the need to cut down on the use of gas as fuel.[33] Meanwhile, since the beginning of 1979 coal output had actually been declining, and it would have taken a very optimistic man to continue—as Kosygin did—to advocate coal as the solution to the nation's energy problems, unless Kosygin simply continued to view the energy problem as long-term, *or* unless he and Brezhnev were locked in a political struggle in which the substantive aspects of the energy issue were merely incidental.

The latter possibility does not seem plausible. The days when Brezhnev and Kosygin were rivals and did open battle over agricultural policy ended in 1970. Indeed, the measure of the difference is that in 1967–68, when the Kosygin line on agriculture briefly held the field, its impact on investment was sharp. As we have seen, however, there was no such impact on coal investment in 1976–77. The evidence points instead to a difference of viewpoint over the seriousness of the energy problem and the extent to which immediate and drastic action was needed.

Summary: Major Implications of the New Energy Strategy

The energy policy outlined at the 26th Party Congress appears designed above all to cope in the near term with an energy situation that is increasingly perceived as urgent. Avenues that would require major administrative or technological innovations to yield results, such as conservation or coal, are apparently being relegated to a more remote and hence vaguer future. One implication of the new policy is that the leaders have acknowledged an unpleasant truth that they were apparently not willing to accept in 1976—that the energy problem is going to require a massive and rapid increase in capital spending, at a time when capital is particularly short. Whereas the Soviet leaders held back investment in gas in 1976–77, thus implicitly rejecting the big-gas strategy at that time, they are now going full steam ahead.[34]

By failing to respond to the urgency of the energy problem five years ago and by delaying a full-scale commitment to natural gas at that time, the Soviet leaders may have placed themselves in a vulnerable position. That would be an ironic result, because their intention at the 25th Party Congress seems to have been to preserve national independence by stressing energy sources that could be developed without foreign help and hence without foreign constraints. Instead, the Soviet leaders have now opted for a crash strategy that will most likely require the extensive participation of both Eastern and Western Europe.

Yet here we must add a word of caution: we cannot be entirely confident that the latest official energy policy actually means what it appears to. As we have seen, the shift in emphasis to gas, just like the shift that preceded it, came suddenly and without clear warning. We cannot be sure that the policy was fully hammered out by the time of the 26th Party Congress. In particular, the investment figures for gas may represent more wishful thinking than fully worked-out positions. Indeed, as several of the authors in the present collection point out, the 26th Party Congress represented a postponement of hard choices on all the major issues facing the Kremlin. Energy policy, despite the appearance of movement, may be yet another instance of that. If so, then it is entirely possible that the Soviet leaders themselves have not yet faced up to the fact that their new energy policy requires more elaborate Western help than previous energy policies.

Moreover, there have been clear indications over the years that Soviet leaders are not settled in their own minds on the question of how safe it is to rely on the West for key technology and resources. It is no easy step for a country with a long history of economic autarky to rid itself of long-held habits of mind. To be sure, in recent years the Soviets have steadily increased the share and importance of foreign trade in their economy, even to the point of allowing themselves to depend on foreign suppliers for so strategic a commodity as bauxite.[35] And their experience has not been unfavorable, especially since during the 1970s the Soviets enjoyed an unexpected $30-billion windfall, due to lucky shifts in the terms of trade, especially in the prices of oil and gold.[36] Yet at the same time the Soviets have shown great caution in their foreign-trade policy, even cutting back major development projects in order to prevent their foreign debt from exceeding what the leaders regarded as safe bounds.[37] The leaders' major speeches over the years indicate uneasiness over the dangers of excessive dependence on Western technology,[38] and their more recent unpleasant experience with the American embargo on grain and high-technology exports has presumably strengthened their doubts.[39]

Where Soviet exports of gas and oil are concerned, there is the additional element of national pride. Among the many reasons for the collapse of the North Star negotiations in the mid-1970s was discomfort on the part of some Soviet leaders over the idea of selling away to the West an irreplaceable natural resource. To be sure, at that time gas appeared scarcer and other energy resources more abundant; yet even as the Soviets negotiate with Western firms over the largest gas deal ever, one continues to find signs of ambivalence in official Soviet writings.

In sum, there is still much that is uncertain about Soviet energy policy. The course adopted at the 26th Party Congress suggests that the Soviet leaders are coming to grips with its urgency. But they appear confident that they will make it through the present squeeze and that over the next two decades they will be the only major industrial country to enjoy true energy independence. Whether or not this turns out to be right, the important thing is that the Soviet leaders appear to believe it is, and are addressing the problem through essentially traditional methods, which include occasional reliance on large-scale Western help. In that sense the energy field does not differ from the others discussed in this volume. The next few years will tell a great deal about whether the problems facing the Soviet Union will require more drastic solutions.

Notes

1 As Kosygin observed in his report to the 25th Party Congress, "The Soviet Union is the sole large industrial state in the world that bases its economic development on its own fuel-energy resources. This is a serious advantage of our economy and a quite important precondition of its steady growth. But in order to turn this advantage fully into reality, it is essential to attain rational and economic development of our resources." Source: *XXVyi. s"ezd KPSS*, (Moscow: "Politizdat," 1976), volume 2, p. 35.
2 S. A. Orudzhev died on 20 April 1981. He has been replaced as minister by Iu. V. Zaitsev, the more senior of the ministry's two first deputy ministers. Zaitsev's appointment thus continues the recent pattern in technical ministries of appointing a first deputy minister to succeed a minister who has retired or died. (For interesting speculation on the possible political implications of this pattern, see T. H. Rigby, "The Soviet Government since Khrushchev," *Politics*, vol. XII, No. 1 (May 1977), pp. 5–22) However, in this case Zaitsev's appointment presumably also symbolizes the leaders' determination to maintain Orudzhev's gas policy.
3 Speech of S. A. Orudzhev, *Pravda*, 2 March 1981. Orudzhev's actual words were, "During the 11th Five-Year Plan it will be necessary to assimilate as much capital investment as in the last three five-year plans combined."
4 In addition to the material presented at the 26th Party Congress, further information on energy plans for the next five years can be found in *Ekonomicheskaia gazeta*, Nos. 12–15 (1981), page 2 of each.
5 Initial targets for the 10th Five-Year Plan are taken from the text of the Main Guidelines, as reprinted in *XXVyi. s"ezd Kommunistcheskoi partii Sovetskogo Soiuza* (stenograficheskii otchet), volume 2 (Moscow: Izdatel'stvo politicheskoi literatury, 1976), pp. 226 ff.
6 The data on overall investment growth are given in the report by L. I. Brezhnev, *Pravda*, 24 February 1981. For further discussion of the investment implications, see below, pp. 126–8.
7 *Ekonomicheskaia gazeta*, No. 13 (March 1981), p. 2; and "Ratsional'noe ispol'zovanie material'nykh i trudovykh resursov na stroitel'stve magistral'nykh nefte- i gazotruboprovodov," *Planovoe khoziaistvo*, No. 4, 1981, p. 50. The latter source adds that the delivery of West Siberian gas to the western and central regions of the country will require 16,000 kilometers of pipeline 1420 millimeters in diameter. For some idea of the quantities of rolled steel entailed, the following is a conservative estimate: if we assume that we are talking about 48- and 56-inch pipe, 50,000 kilometers represents something on the order of 30 million tons of rolled steel, or 25 million tons if one assumes an average diameter of 40 inches. For comparison, the 1985 Soviet target for rolled steel of all types is 117 to 120 million tons. I am indebted to Professors Leslie Dienes and Edward Hewett for these estimates.
8 Brezhnev report, op. cit. This appears to be a relatively recent move: in an account of a meeting at Central Committee headquarters in April 1980, at which increases in capital investment for oil and gas in Western Siberia were discussed, no mention was made of any major administrative changes. See "Soveshchanie v TsK," *Sotsialisticheskaia industriia*, 15 April 1980.

9   USSR Gosstroi, for example, adopted rules barring the use of gas in new institutional-food facilities, such as school canteens; and the USSR Ministry of Trade rejected gas as the fuel of choice in residential and municipal uses. I. L. Shmuel'son, "Gaz ili elektrichestvo—diskussiia prodolzhaetsia," *Gazovaia promyshlennost'* No. 12, 1980, pp. 26–27.

10 V. I. Dolgikh, "Povyshat' uroven' rukovodstva predpriiatiiami toplivno-energeticheskogo kompleksa," *Partiinaia zhizn'*, No. 1, 1980, p. 23.

11 One of them is G. P. Bogomiakov, first secretary of the Tiumen' Regional Committee (*obkom*), whose speech before the Congress contained a reference to gas-fired electrical power. See *Pravda*, 27 February 1981.

12 For a review of Soviet energy conservation, see the essay by Leslie Dienes in U.S. Congress, Joint Economic Committee, *Energy in Soviet Policy* (Washington, D.C.: forthcoming). See also Thane Gustafson, "Soviet Energy Conservation and Substitution: Their Implications for East-West Technology Transfer," one of a collection of papers to be published by the Office of Technology Assessment in late 1981.

13 The theme of increasing attention to diesel engines has been a frequent one in recent Soviet writings. See for example A. Chulkov, "Puti ekonomii toplivno-energeticheskikh resursov na transporte," *Planovoe khoziaistvo*, No. 5, 1979, p. 45. According to R. M. Musin, first secretary of the Tatar regional committee, the Kamaz plant plans to turn out 600,000 diesel-powered cars by the end of 1985. See *Pravda*, 27 February 1981.

14 The latest official document on the subject is a decree of the party Central Committee and the Council of Ministers, "Ob usilenii raboty po ekonomii i ratsional' nomu ispol'zovaniiu syr'evykh, toplivno-energeticheskikh, i drugikh material'nykh resursov," *Pravda*, 4 July 1981. It is equally imprecise about quantitative targets.

15 See A. P. Aleksandrov, "Energoobespechenie strany," *Kommunist*, No. 4, 1981 (March), pp. 84–90. In this article Aleksandrov manages to avoid any reference to natural gas.

16 Central Intelligence Agency, National Foreign Assessment Center, *Energy Decision Making in the Soviet Union*, CR 80-10623 (Washington, D.C.: August, 1980).

17 The three Central Committee sector chiefs who appear on the energy organization chart have, if nothing else, longevity in their specialties: V. I. Sorokoletov was first mentioned as head of a heavy-industry sector (presumably for coal) in 1966 (*Moskovskaia pravda*, 27 July 1966); N. M. Eronin was identified as an instructor specializing in oil in the same year (*Moskovskaia pravda*, 31 May 1966); and the head of the geology sector, A. A. Yamnov, has been in that position since at least as early as 1965 (*Kazakhstanskaia pravda*, 26 August 1965).

18 To take a recent example that seems to fit the general pattern, in early June 1980 Kirilenko delivered the keynote address at a major Central Committee gathering on problems of electrical power (for a detailed account and a summary of Kirilenko's speech see *Energeticheskoe stroitel'stvo*, No. 8, 1980, pp. 2–12); but at another Central Committee meeting two weeks before, devoted to the problem of additional funding for West Siberian gas and oil, Kirilenko was not present (*Sotsialisticheskaia industriia*, 15 April 1980). For information about Kirilenko's public statements on energy I am indebted to Eric Jones (Department of Political Science, University of Michigan), who has recently analyzed the speeches and writings of the major Politburo members, in order to establish their public views on energy policy. A condensed version of his work will be published shortly by the Office of Technology Assessment, as part of a study of Soviet energy policy and technology transfer.

19 *Deputaty Verkhovnogo Soveta SSSR*, 10yi. sozyv (Moscow: "Politizdat," 1979), p. 45.

20 Brezhnev's speech has not yet been reprinted in its entirety. A paraphrase appeared in an editorial in *Pravda*, 18 December 1977. Eric Jones' study of the leaders' speeches (referred to above) confirms that December 1977 was indeed a turning point in Brezhnev's public views on energy.

21 See in particular an article by G. P. Bogomiakov, Tiumen' Regional Committee first secretary, in *Literaturnaia gazeta*, 18 January 1978, in which he states that the

December 1977 plenum had determined precisely the place of the Tiumen' complex in satisfying the needs of the country for oil and gas, thus settling what Bogomiakov described as "not just a few contradictory judgments in views on the future."

22 Brezhnev's 1978 trip to Siberia is treated by Tiumen' "patriots" as a highly symbolic event, as one may see from the words of G. P. Bogomiakov at the 26th Party Congress: "Of fundamental importance have been the instructions of L. I. Brezhnev on the future development of the fuel and power sector, the advice and comments made by him in the course of his trip to the regions of Siberia and the Far East." (*Pravda*, 27 February 1981). At the time, the fundamental importance was far from plain, since Brezhnev's trip occurred right on the heels of a similar trip by Kosygin, and the energy aspects of both trips received modest treatment in the press.

23 In January 1980, for the first time, an article on energy policy appeared under Dolgikh's byline, in *Partiinaia zhizn'*. In addition, in the last two years Dolgikh's name has appeared regularly in Soviet accounts of major official meetings on energy.

24 Bogomiakov, op.cit. The authority of the party apparatus is reinforced by the traditional method of moving officials with experience in the party apparatus to top positions in industry and vice-versa; in the case of gas and oil this device seems to have been used unusually often. Recent examples include the first deputy minister of the oil industry, V. I. Kremnev (formerly head of the oil-industry sector in the Central Committee Department of Heavy Industry), and many officials associated with energy development in Tiumen': B. Ye. Shcherbina (formerly first secretary of the Tiumen' Regional Committee, now minister of oil and gas construction), G. P. Bogomiakov (deputy director of an oil exploration research institute until 1967, now first secretary of Tiumen' Regional Committee), and Ye. G. Altunin (recently head of V/O Tiumen' gazprom, now secretary for gas of the Tiumen' Regional Committee).

25 In July 1980, an article by the director of Gosplan's Institute for Complex Fuel and Power Problems, S. N. Iatrov, described as a "task of the first importance" the creation of a "single economic organism" in charge of the entire fuel and power sector. See "Toplivno-energeticheskii kompleks," *Ekonomicheskaia gazeta*, No. 10 (March, 1980), p. 10.

26 Recent changes in the Presidium of the Council of Ministers include the replacement of V. A. Kirillin by G. I. Marchuk as head of the State Committee for Science and Technology; of T. Ia. Kiselev, V. N. Novikov, and M. A. Lesechko by V. N. Makeev, L. A. Kostandov, N. V. Talyzin, A. K. Antonov, and I. I. Bodiul. Several of these changes have been interpreted in the West as a replacement of Kosygin-connected officials with Brezhnev-connected ones (although the Kirillin/Marchuk case is another matter). Since many of these changes affect energy policy, one may say that they are still another element in Brezhnev's apparently growing role in this sphere. It is interesting to note the personnel listed at a meeting held at the Central Committee in April 1980. The subject was West Siberian energy development, and the meeting was presided over by Dolgikh, but there were no top figures from the USSR Council of Ministers such as V. Dymshits or V. Novikov (who did not retire until December of that year, when several changes were made in the wake of Kosygin's death). Since Novikov's retirement, his duties in the energy area may have been assumed by A. K. Antonov, who had been minister of electrical equipment before being named deputy chairman of the Council of Ministers in December 1980. Antonov was present at a major meeting of the collegium of Minenergo in February 1981 (*Pravda*, 11 February 1981), and was listed in second place among the signers of the obituary of A. P. Aleksandrov, long-time deputy minister of Minenergo for hydropower (*Izvestiia*, 11 March 1981).

27 In the months following the December 1977 plenum, there was evidence of some discomfort within Gosplan about Brezhnev's new policy. Articles by Baibakov and Iatrov, for example, underplayed West Siberian oil and gas, while restating some of the main themes of the 25th Party Congress. Officials who had previously favored coal and nuclear power, such as Kosygin and the president of the Academy of Sciences, A. P. Aleksandrov, continued to do so. On the other hand, Siberia-minded officials such as B. Ye. Shcherbina and G. P. Bogomiakov reacted quickly to the

December 1977 plenum with enthusiastic language, while going on to restate the case for West Siberian gas. How to interpret shades of wording in the various public statements of those months is a difficult problem, however, since it was apparently not "against the rules" to dwell on the practical difficulties of Tiumen' development. An illustration is the series of articles about Tiumen' that appeared in the fall of 1978 and the winter of 1979 in *Voprosy filosofii* (No. 9, 1978), *Planovoe khoziaistvo* (No. 9, 1978), and *Ekonomika i organizatsiia promyshlennogo proizvodstva* (No. 3, 1979). These articles dealt in frank detail with the problems of Tiumen' and might be taken as evidence of covert opposition to the Brezhnev policy, but for the fact that they grew out of a common round table held in Tiumen' in the summer of 1978, which was summoned (as the EKO article describes it) at the initiative of the Propaganda Department of the Central Committee and the Tiumen' Regional Committee. Thus, regardless of their realism, such articles should probably be considered part of an orchestrated pro-Tiumen' campaign conducted during the spring and summer of 1978, serving the same promotional purpose as, for example, the article "K severu ot Tiumeni," in *Kommunist*, No. 8, 1978, pp. 33–42

28   A few examples will give some of the flavor of this discussion: V. Iu. Filanovskii, chief of the Oil and Gas Department of Gosplan, calls attention to serious problems in future oil production in West Siberia, underscores the potential of gas in northern Tiumen', and advocates the creation of a central authority and a central plan for gas and oil in Tiumen'. ("Zapadno-Sibirskii neftegazovyi kompleks: rezul'taty i perspektivy," *Planovoe khoziaistvo*, No. 3, 1980, pp. 19–26.) At about the same time Party Secretary V. I. Dolgikh asserts that in the future the share of both oil *and* gas will drop, and cautions against the use of gas as a fuel, pointing out that gas brings almost ten times as much *ekonomiia* when used as a chemical feedstock than when used as a fuel. At the same time, he appears to argue in favor of giving greater priority to older oil-producing areas, on the grounds that in those places the necessary infrastructure for enhanced recovery is already in place. (Dolgikh, *Partiinaia zhizn'*, op. cit.) Also at the same time, Gas Minister S. A. Orudzhev (who has been consistently less than enthusiastic about a big-gas strategy), signs his name to a catalog of horror stories about gas development at Urengoi, criticizing serious problems in drilling, pipeline reliability, development of operating wells, etc., while simultaneously stressing the importance of gas conservation. ("Zadachi rabotnikov gazovoi promyshlennosti na 1980 god," *Gazovaia promyshlennost'*, No. 2, 1980, pp. 4–9.) On the other hand, still fighting for the "coal by wire" concept, the president of the Academy of Sciences, A. P. Aleksandrov, openly attacks the Fuels Department of Gosplan in the presence of Gosplan Chairman Baibakov, for delaying funding and resources for the 1500 kv DC line from Ekibastuz to the center. ("Vstupitel'noe slovo Prezidenta Akademii nauk SSSR A. P. Aleksandrova," *Vestnik Akademii Nauk*, No. 5, 1980, p. 12.)

29   See A. M. Nekrasov and M. G. Pervukhin, eds., *Energetika SSSR v 1976–1980 godakh* (Moscow, "Energiia," 1977), p. 149. I am indebted to Grey Hodnett for calling my attention to this point.

30   *Narodnoe khoziaistvo*, relevant years. For the three years prior to the 25th Congress, the rate of investment in coal had remained virtually the same.

31   *Narodnoe khoziaistvo*, relevant years.

32   The last collection of Kosygin's selected speeches, *K velikoi tseli* (Moscow: "Politizdat," 1979) covers the period through November 1978, including particularly his address on the occasion of the 61st anniversary of the October Revolution (4 November 1978). Two later speeches with significant material about energy were published in *Pravda*, 2 March 1979 and 24 May 1979.

33   *Pravda*, 18 June 1981.

34   From 1974 through 1979, annual investment in gas grew by less than 300 million rubles, whereas from 1971 through 1974 annual investment in gas had increased by twice that amount in half the time. *Narodnoe khoziaistvo*, relevant years.

35   Theodore Shabad, "Raw Material Problems of the Soviet Aluminum Industry," in U.S. Congress, Joint Economic Committee, *Soviet Economy in a New Perspective* (Washington, D.C.: USGPO, 1976), pp. 661–76.

36   Edward A. Hewett, "On the Probable Impact of Deteriorating Soviet Economic

Performance on the Organization of its Foreign Sector." (Unpublished paper presented at the Study Group on Domestic Sources of Soviet Foreign Policy, Council on Foreign Relations, February 1980).

37 For statistics on trends during the last decade, see Central Intelligence Agency, National Foreign Assessment Center, *Estimating Soviet and East European Hard Currency Debt*, Er 80-10327 (Washington, D.C.: June, 1980).

38 See the forthcoming book by Bruce Parrott, MIT Press, 1981. The whole question of imports of high-technology equipment has evidently been the subject of several high-level reviews. Brezhnev, in his speech before the June 1980 plenum of the Central Committee, referred to memoranda he had written to the Central Committee on foreign imports. *Pravda*, 24 June 1980.

39 Witness the strong remarks of the president of the USSR Academy of Sciences, A. P. Aleksandrov, at a meeting devoted to the subject of compensating for the effects of the American embargo on certain types of scientific instrumentation. *Vestnik Akademii Nauk SSSR*, No. 11, 1980, pp. 32–37.

For example, a recent article by A. Lalaiants, the deputy chairman of Gosplan with responsibility for the energy sector, stresses that Soviet energy exports must be reserved above all to the USSR's Comecon partners. ("Problemy ekonomii toplivno-energeticheskikh resursov v narodnom khoziaistve," *Planovoe khoziaistvo*, No. 1, 1981, p. 34.) Brezhnev himself, in his report to the 26th Party Congress in February 1981, used noticeably defensive language in arguing that accelerated gas development would enable the Soviet Union to continue energy exports, "—including exports to capitalist countries" (*v tom chisle i v kapitalisticheskie strany*).

7
Reform and Technological Innovation in the 11th Five-Year Plan

Nancy Nimitz

Soviet dissatisfaction with technological innovation in industry emerged as a major public issue about twenty-five years ago, at a meeting of the party Central Committee in July 1955. Today, after many more party meetings and several decrees on R and D (research and design) and the abortive effort at economic reform in the second half of the 1960s, persistently unsatisfactory technological advance has become a central concern of Soviet leaders, since it translates into increasingly expensive and slow growth.

A new reform program, outlined in a decree of 12 July 1979, is to be introduced over the 11th Five-Year Plan.[1] Initial reactions to it from Western students of the Soviet economy have been skeptical. Common impressions are that the proposed changes are either so superficial that they will have little effect, or so distasteful to one or another element of the planning and administrative bureaucracies that they will not be carried out.[2] Even within the Soviet Union the 1979 decree has received muted treatment compared with the enthusiasm that attended the launching of the 1965 reform.[3] Editorial comment has emphasized that its execution will require extraordinary effort to overcome psychological barriers at every level from central planners to blue-collar workers; the implication is that the beneficial effects may come rather slowly. The decree embodies compromises and contradictions distressing to both theorists and practical men;[4] and there are already complaints that the broad directives of the decree have been weakened or distorted in the process of converting them into operational instructions.[5]

Given the long history of the problem, the repeated efforts to deal with it, and the reservations expressed both outside and inside the Soviet Union about the coherence or enforceability of the new program, it is not surprising that many Western specialists on the USSR have dismissed in advance the possibility that it will do much good. But even if this turns out to be true, the program deserves consideration for two reasons. First, it sheds light on the relative weights now attached by Soviet leaders to indigenous technological proficiency on the one hand, and on the other hand such traditional socialist values as job security and equal pay for equal work and such traditional bureaucratic values as hierarchical authority and predictability in the decision-making environment. Secondly, its rationale involves issues relevant to the general theory of innovation, which so far has developed almost entirely on the basis of Western experience. If Soviet approaches to innovation, successful or unsuccessful, can add to our understanding of Western problems in the same area, it would be a pity to neglect them.

The judgment of this chapter will be that the 1979 decree is a respectable third-best reform in a world where the first-best never comes and the second-best comes too late.[6] It is conservative, intended to rationalize rather than fundamentally alter the system. It is uneven in texture, with reinforcing redundancies denser in some areas than others. But it does address the ultimate cause of unsatisfactory technological advance in the crucial producer-goods industries—namely, *buyers* of intermediate and capital goods who are not motivated to reject uneconomical technologies. The first section of the paper presents the diagnosis of systemic problems that underlies this interpretation. The second describes the main thrust of the new measures.

Systemic Obstacles to Beneficial Innovation

The basic proposition here is that Soviet diagnosis of the obstacles to beneficial innovation has improved greatly over time, and necessarily through trial and error. Reliable guidance was lacking because the systematic study of industrial innovation (as distinguished from the dynamics of science, or the rules for economic efficiency in an imaginary static world without technological change) is relatively new and inconclusive.[7] As of the late 1970s, Western students of innovation could offer little useful advice to government policy-makers because there was still no consensus on the variables that explain differences in innovative performance across branches of industry within a single country.[8]

This last puzzle—uneven technological advance across sectors of industry—was the main one facing Soviet leaders when they first began to look around in 1955. The weapons sector was doing reasonably well; even the Americans expressed alarm at its progress. But most civilian producer goods branches shunned new technology and turned out a lot of obsolete output. Initially it could have seemed—particularly to leaders who hoped to correct civilian technological lag on the cheap—that the difference came from the differing guidelines given to producers of military and civilian hardware over the postwar recovery period. Military producers were consciously competing with a much more advanced rival, while prevailing economic doctrine with respect to civilian capital goods was that obsolescence did not matter within a noncompetitive socialist economy.

So the first response was to declare that obsolescence *did* matter, and that civilian managers should do something about it. When they didn't, they were blamed for being conservative, uninformed, or lazy. The first Russian to say bluntly that the problem lay deeper was not an academic economist, much less a member of the planning and administrative bureaucracy, but the aircraft designer Antonov. In a 1957 essay he argued that the real obstacles to new and improved output were overly centralized planning and performance indicators that stressed quantitative plan fulfillment over qualitative characteristics of value to *users*.[9]

The reform that finally emerged in 1965 after lengthy discussion reintroduced industrial ministries as vehicles of branch planning, but otherwise left the philosophy and practice of central planning essentially untouched. In particular, it did nothing to improve the stability of plans. Large hopes were pinned upon new performance indicators stressing sales and profits, for which economists offered very plausible arguments. But in combination with cost-plus prices that continued to be set on the basis of information supplied by producers (without input from users), the new indicators turned out to be disastrous. The adverse effect of the reform on the *rate* of innovation was immediately evident. Enterprises boosted profits by avoiding the high cost of introducing new products; in nine civilian machinery ministries the proportion of products in manufacture for not more than three years declined as follows (percentage of total output): 1965—13.8, 1966—10.4, 1967—9.3, 1968—8.2.[10] The *tendency* of such innovation as occurred was wasteful:

the cost (and prices) of new producer goods rose more rapidly than their productivity. By the end of 1969 disillusion with the 1965 reform was total, and party opinion was divided on whether to move forward or backward.[11]

Over the 1970s the divisions in party opinion were reflected in three streams of measures. The first was a variety of experiments with new economic arrangements in selected groups of enterprises or individual ministries. Soviet leaders had learned that discussion of proposed measures was no substitute for actually testing them. Even sophisticated types of analysis, such as mathematical modeling, do not shed light on the psychological effects of new arrangements on enterprise management, if only because such models disregard the behavior of superior and local authorities with whom enterprises interact in an intricate combination of adversary and collusive relations. However, the drawback of such experiments is that it is hard to test novel arrangements in the small when the rest of the economy—including planners, suppliers, and customers—continues to operate on old principles. It is also hard to interpret results when each experiment involves not just one change but a cluster of changes whose relative importance is disputable. Nevertheless, experiments are invaluable in one respect: they flush out the opposition to proposed changes (which fully emerges only after their potential has been demonstrated) and show where compromises to appease potent opposition may be unavoidable. All of the 1979 reform except the changes in planning rests on such experiments.

The second stream of measures included organizational changes of an ambivalent or neutral character, adaptable to either novel or traditional purposes. The most prominent was the accelerated formation of production associations (*proizvodstvennye ob"edineniia*) merging several vertically or horizontally related enterprises with one or more formerly independent R-and-D organizations. Conservatives liked them because they seemed to simplify the transmission of central commands. Liberals liked them because they were large enough to become truly autonomous and responsible entities (able to finance their own investment and bear sanctions for poor performance) should conditions for greater autonomy be established in the future. Another ambivalent measure was the quiet expansion of employment offices, which had been experimentally revived in the late 1960s after a hiatus which had lasted over three decades (ever since unemployment officially disappeared in the early 1930s). Conservatives could approve of their potential for exerting more compulsion in the comparatively free labor market. Liberals could value them as a precondition for reform that increased labor mobility, either by encouraging enterprises to lay off redundant labor, or by reducing the subsidies to inefficient enterprises that allow them to pay "equal" wages.

The third stream of measures involved traditional administrative methods of exerting greater pressure on producers to seek out new technology instead of "dodging away from it the way the devil does from incense," as Brezhnev put it at the 24th Party Congress in 1971.[12] Ministries were instructed to classify the output of subordinate enterprises into three grades defined by technical level, to increase the share of the highest (world-level) grade, and to phase out the lowest (obsolete). Enterprise bonus funds began to be determined in part by the share of new products in total sales. The predictable and illusory result of such pressures was that the number of new machinery products introduced into series production over the 1971–75 period was double the 1966–70 level.[13] But as Brezhnev reported to the 25th Party Congress in 1976, many were "new only in their date of manufacture, not in their technical level."[14] And many were produced in merely token quantities;[15] as a result their contribution to efficiency was slight even if they were economically more effective than the models they replaced.

The problem that came to the fore over the 1971–75 period was that many new machines were *less* effective than old ones; as in the 1960s, their prices continued to rise faster than their productivity in use. By the mid-1970s Soviet sources were referring to this tendency as typical—a mass phenomenon. It was increasingly identified as the main cause of declining capital productivity. It was finally recognized as a critical problem by the party in the 1976–80 plan, which made lower prices per unit of effectiveness of new machinery an explicit goal.[16]

The trend toward higher prices per unit of effectiveness is critical because it violates the primary function of technological change, which is to yield a surplus.[17] The trend is deeply rooted and not amenable to reversal by increasing inputs to civilian innovation or by importing more technology from abroad. In other words, the causes are not lack of resources or technical knowledge (reasons often advanced for the deficiencies of civilian technology in the USSR). There is now abundant evidence that new Soviet machinery is uneconomical because producers deliberately use materials and add features that cost more than they are worth to the user. In the West this style is commonly called goldplating. It is explained not by technical incompetence but by strong incentives to producers to make new products more expensive than they have to be, *and* by the weak incentives of buyers to resist goldplating. Of these complementary faults, the latter is more fundamental, because the responsibility for screening new technology and rejecting what costs more than it is worth falls inescapably on the users.[18] It is the singular misfortune of the USSR that its least exacting customers are concentrated in the market for producer goods—those branches of industry whose performance most affects productivity throughout the economy.[19]

Producer incentives to goldplate derive from the performance indicators that most affect bonus funds: sales, labor productivity, and profits. In an economy where administered prices are intended to cover costs plus normal profit, all of these indicators impel machinery producers in the direction of larger, heavier, more complex, and more expensive output. The higher the price that can be justified for a new product, the easier it is to meet sales targets in rubles. The higher material costs are relative to labor costs, the easier it is to meet labor productivity targets in rubles per man. For any given amount of labor and given rate of profit (expressed as a percentage markup over labor costs plus material costs), total profits increase with material costs.

Weak incentives of buyers to resist goldplating derive from taut and unstable plans and from the way most investment is financed. Plan pressures create pervasive demand for excess capacity. The demand is indifferent to cost because most investment is financed by nonrepayable grants from above rather than from the buyer's own resources or from repayable loans. The imperatives are to get the grants and spend them by the end of the year (thus fulfilling one's investment plan), rather than to care whether the new plant or replacement equipment is economical. Gosplan *should* care about such things, but it lacks the expertise to second-guess ministerial proposals. The proposals typically and deliberately understate costs in order to obtain Gosplan approval. The resulting built-in cost overruns cause stretchouts in construction schedules, the freezing of enormous resources in uncompleted construction, and more plan instability due to reassignment of production targets to existing plant.

From the perspective of Soviet leaders, the most ominous result of systemic deficiencies is the declining effectiveness of new investment, because investment planning is the main instrument of socialist growth planning. By 1976 it was evident that "further improvement of the economic mechanism" was

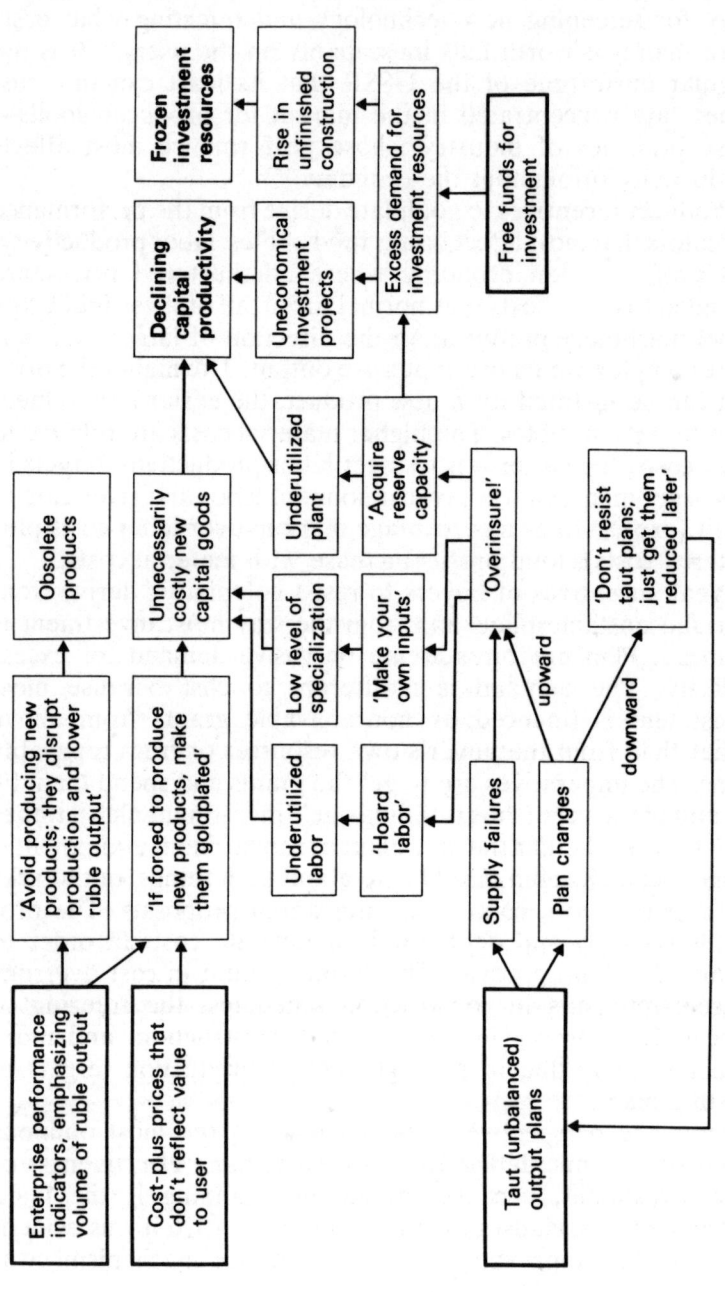

Figure 7.1 *Systemic origins of the declining effectiveness of new investment*

unavoidable, and the top levels of economic managers and advisers were instructed to draft a reform program. It took them three years to arrive at the compromises embodied in the 1979 decree.[20]

The argument is summarized in Figure 7.1. The problems that precipitated reform (declining capital productivity and frozen investment resources) appear in the northeast corner, while their systemic origins (misleading indicators, producer-dominated prices, unstable plans, and free funds for investment) are in the more heavily framed boxes on the west and south margins. Intermediate boxes show chains of causality; inscriptions in quotation marks are managerial rules of thumb.

The Thrust of Reform

The 1979 decree introduces or extends the application of measures affecting planning in general, the planning and financing of investment projects in particular, and the incentives of enterprises to meet production plans efficiently. Its main goals are to: (1) make plans more stable over the five-year-plan period; (2) cut excess demand for investment and shift the structure of investment away from new plant and toward the modernization of old plant; (3) reduce for both producers and buyers the incentives that foster goldplating; and (4) reduce producer incentives to hoard labor. These goals are interrelated. There is little hope of stabilizing production plans unless investment planning (a major function of the five-year plan) can be brought under control.[21] So long as production plans are incessantly changed, there is little hope of cutting excess demand for production capacity (at any price) and labor.

One tendency of the 1979 reform contributes directly or indirectly to all four goals. This is the cautious movement in the direction of full self-financing (*samofinansirovanie*), which means that producers cover not just current operating costs but also capital costs out of their own retained incomes. Collective farms have always operated on this basis. In its purest form it requires that the penalties for wasteful choices (and also unfavorable production conditions) be borne by individual enterprises and their employees, through reduced profits and wages, rather than by society as a whole, through operating and investment subsidies to the extravagant or unlucky.

The extension of self-financing to the state sector is a delicate matter for four reasons, three partly ideological and one wholly practical. The ideological obstacles are the party commitments to zero unemployment, equal pay for equal work (especially with respect to blue-collar workers), and a free labor market (as distinguished from compulsory assignment of workers to jobs). Zero unemployment has protected workers from job loss due to technological change; it also inhibits the firing of incompetent or indifferent workers. The equal-pay doctrine allows differentials between industries but implies near uniformity of basic pay scales within an industry. If all enterprises had to meet uniform wage rates out of their own income or go out of business, equal pay might stimulate efficiency. But because state enterprises are not allowed to fail (if only because this would reflect poorly on the responsible ministries), deficits of inefficient as well as unlucky enterprises have been covered by transfer of resources from the efficient or lucky. It is the freedom to change jobs that makes equal pay a matter of practical as well as ideological concern to planners. When workers are legally free to leave jobs, pronounced inequalities in pay encourage unplanned—by definition, undesirable—labor mobility. Yet such inequalities are inevitable with pure self-financing, as is demonstrated by the record of collective farms. That is why the party commitments to zero unemployment, equal pay, and freedom to change jobs have never extended to collectives.[22]

The collective farm record also illustrates the fourth reason (wholly practical) why central and ministerial planners are apprehensive about self-financing. Planners' mistakes are not accepted philosophically by producers who are not going to be bailed out when things go wrong. Compared with state farms, who have always done pretty much what they are told to do (however silly), collective farms are *intractable*. They tend to resist or feign compliance with commands that affect them adversely. They are sensitive to economic opportunity, and therefore do things they were not commanded to do (like shipping grapes to Moscow by air to take advantage of favorable collective farm market prices). They react strongly to flaws in the structure of relative prices; it is because they have been loath to feed high-priced grain to underpriced livestock that the state has had to raise livestock prices repeatedly until they are now well above the retail prices paid by consumers in stores. Budget subsidies to cover this gap now amount to 25 billion rubles a year.[23] They have been reluctant to buy overpriced manufactured inputs; as producer-goods prices have risen, the budget has had to subsidize price discounts to farms that currently amount to over 4 billion rubles a year.[24]

It is precisely because self-financing makes producers less tractable that it can contribute to the elusive first goal of reform—more stable plans. The goal is elusive not just because it is technically difficult, but because planners are not automatically penalized for plans that are worse than they have to be—that are deliberately unrealistic, or sloppy, or unfair.[25] Bad plans must be consciously protested and resisted, and not just by academic economists who find them "nonoptimal" but by producers whom they tangibly hurt. Self-financing stimulates resistance by concentrating the hurt on specific producers.[26]

The experience of the Ministry of Instruments and Means of Automation (Minpribor), which has been operating experimentally on pure self-financing at the ministerial level since 1970, sheds light on the effects of self-financing—particularly on the first and second goals of reform. Minpribor spokesmen have been conspicuously active critics of unstable and unfair plans; presumably it is because of their criticism that the 1979 reform recognizes (at least as an ideal) that self-financing requires stable financial plans and the immunity to confiscation by the budget of retained enterprise profits not spent by the end of the fiscal year. As for the second goal, Minpribor, unlike other ministries whose investment was financed largely by the budget, began almost immediately to estimate investment costs honestly.[27] For this reason, and also because it was motivated to accelerate the returns from investment outlays, it has followed methods of designing and implementing construction projects that sharply reduced construction schedules.[28]

The Minpribor experience sheds less light on the third and fourth targets of reform—goldplating and labor hoarding—for two reasons. First, while self-financing was brought down to the Minpribor subbranch level by 1976, ministry officials were reluctant to introduce it at the enterprise level—that is, to guarantee the share of profits that enterprises could retain—so long as the branch's share of profits was not guaranteed by higher planning organs.[29] It is at the enterprise level that self-financing should most strongly affect incentives to resist goldplating and conserve labor.[30] Secondly, since Minpribor faced customers who were not self-financed, it undoubtedly goldplated its own products as vigorously as it could (except for items destined for export to the competitive Western market, such as watches and cameras).

The reform version of self-financing that is to be extended in industry and construction over the 11th Five-Year Plan is unhurried and also impure. Ministries not now on self-financing[31] will adopt it at the ministry level from 1981 on "as they become ready"; there is no published deadline. Similarly, self-financing at the enterprise level is to be introduced "as experience is acquired." The reluctance to specify deadlines could reflect the desire of higher-level economic bodies to delay change indefinitely,[32] or could be merely prudent. The reform version of self-financing is impure (less than full) because it allows for some budget financing of investment in industries with below-average levels of profitability or above-average need for new plant (such as branches expanding in eastern regions).[33]

Figure 7.2 summarizes the new measures that bear partly or wholly on the first two reform goals. The northeast corner shows the instruments that allow (but do not force) planners to arrive at more balanced plans. The southeast corner shows the crucial objective condition for overall stability of five-year plans—a stable capital investment plan, which at least for the next few years means a smaller one, since recent plans have overestimated the country's physical capacity to produce investment goods and build. The north, west, and south margins show the measures calculated to promote the managerial rules of thumb given in quotation marks in the center. If these subjective rules can be established, there will be increased pressure on planners to avoid deliberately overoptimistic plans that immediately start to unravel. Even a modest increase in plan stability should operate, in turn, to improve the quality of information from below, which will remain false or slanted until enterprise managers are convinced that plans are binding on planners as well as producers.

The new measures intended to reduce the incentives of producers to goldplate—the third goal of reform—seem promising. Sales are no longer a directive indicator. The output measure for calculating labor productivity (normalized net output) omits material costs. The profit margin on each product will be proportional to its wage content; this means that producers will be less motivated to boost total profits by emphasizing products with high material costs. Nor will they be penalized (as now) by lower profit margins on new products with lower material costs than the old analogue. The incentives of customers to resist goldplating depend critically on the achievement of more stable plans; given stability, the demand for excess capacity should gradually decline. It remains to be seen whether enterprises will actively resist uneconomical equipment, but self-financing both increases the pressure to resist and makes it more feasible: assuming that the profit allocation formula is

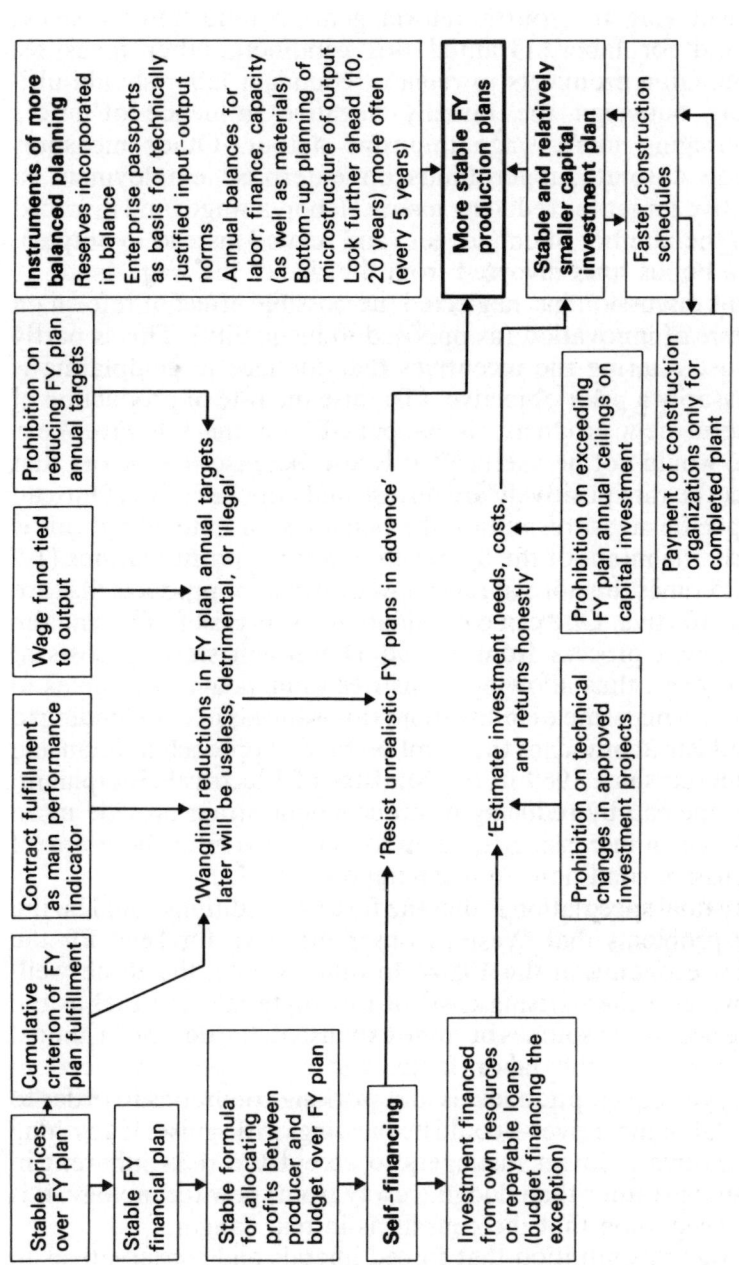

Figure 7.2 *Reform measures contributing to more stable five-year (FY) plans*

observed, enterprise resources for investment will not be confiscated by the budget, and the spend-it-or-lose-it psychology should decline.

Again, the achievement of plan stability is a critical condition for achieving the fourth reform goal—a reduction in excess demand for labor. Granted this condition, other measures encouraging producers to release redundant labor should ultimately outweigh the initially negative influence of prices encouraging more wage intensive output. Other measures include absolute upper limits on enterprise employment, a directive target for reducing manual labor, a wage fund divorced from the number of employees (and related instead to output), and a bonus fund divorced from the size of the wage fund.

This discussion has neglected the possible effect of reform on the *rate* of innovation (as opposed to its quality). This is partly because altering the incentives that conduce to goldplating is necessarily a prior objective. (To raise the rate of production of wasteful new products, as happened over the 9th Five-Year Plan, would not be useful.)[34] It is also because the factors that affect the rate positively are diffuse and imponderable. One can by specific measures reduce the penalties for innovating; this is clearly the intent of the higher-than-normal profit margins (1.5 to 2.25 times the normal rate) now possible for products that are truly effective. One can consolidate the sources of financing the production process from R and D through start-up costs at enterprises, thus allowing ministries to maneuver resources to achieve a high rate of innovation; this is the point of extending to all industrial branches the "unified fund" approach to financing pioneered since 1969 in the Ministry of Electrical Equipment. And one can by reducing macroeconomic strain provide more slack, again increasing freedom to maneuver. But these are all permissive conditions, not forcing ones.

My final speculation is that the forcing conditions could be the very problems that Western observers have foreseen for the Soviet economy in the 1980s. In other words, the three well-known crunches—rising costs of raw materials and fuel as the more accessible sources become exhausted, the decline in annual increments to the labor force, and the imperative need to improve consumption levels and working conditions in order to raise labor incentives—could be blessings in disguise. If anything can motivate Soviet managers to accept the risks inherent in pursuing (rather than dodging away from) new technology, it is the recognition that the country is in real danger.

It was this intuition that forced liberals and conservatives to arrive at the sometimes awkward compromises of the reform program. It could impel them to make a third-best reform work better than we expect.

Notes

1 "Ob uluchshenii planirovaniia i usilenii vozdeistviia khoziaistvennogo mekhanizma na povyshenie effektivnosti proizvodstva i kachestva raboty," *Sobranie postanovlenii pravitel'stva SSSR*, 1979 no. 18, pp. 390–431. An abbreviated version of the decree first appeared in the daily press on 29 July 1979, two weeks after it was adopted. A virtually complete version, omitting only the final paragraph, appeared in the weekly *Ekonomicheskaia gazeta* in August (1979 no. 32, pp. 9–16). The omitted paragraph (no. 64) directs the Ministry of Justice to prepare proposals for amending existing legislation to bring it into conformity with the decree.

For a translation of the complete decree, see Foreign Broadcast Information Service, *USSR Report: Economic Affairs*, no. 902 (JPRS 74717, 5 Dec. 1979).

Instructions amplifying the broad guidelines of the July 1979 decree appeared in *Ekonomicheskaia gazeta* throughout the rest of 1979 and 1980.

2 Keith Bush, *Soviet Economic Growth Slows*, RL 347/79, Radio Liberty, 16 Nov. 1979; Hans-Hermann Hoehmann and Gertraud Seidenstecher, "Soviet Economic Policy: Reform Measures But No Reform," *Osteuropa*, 1979 no. 11, pp. 936–42; Julian Cooper, "Scientific and Technical Change in the USSR," *Futures*, v.11 no. 6 (1979), pp. 471–81; Central Intelligence Agency, National Foreign Assessment Center, The *Soviet Economy in 1978—79 and Prospects for 1980*, ER 80–10328, June 1980, p.18.

3 Officially, the July 1979 program is not called a reform but a "further improvement of the economic mechanism." See, for example, the reports to the 26th Party Congress by Brezhnev and by Tikhonov, Kosygin's successor as chairman of the Council of Ministers (*Pravda*, 24 February 1981, p. 6; 28 February 1981, p. 4).

4 One pervasive contradiction is between the ultimate goal of increasing the initiative and responsibility of enterprises, and the transitional strategy of leaving numerous loopholes for ministerial intervention in the affairs of subordinate enterprises. In the past such intervention has usually operated to redistribute financial resources from successful plants to unsuccessful ones, thus reducing for both the incentives to be smart and frugal.

The new indicator of output growth in fabricating industries, normalized net output (*normativno-chistaia produktsiia*), introduces a specific contradiction between the aim of restraining material costs per unit of output and the need to economize on labor in the 1980s. For any product, normalized net output is proportional to the wage component in price. Initially, at least, it is bound to encourage production of goods with a higher-than-average wage content.

5 Bunich, a distinguished academic proponent of reform, notes that the instructions on establishing enterprise norms for wage costs per unit of normalized net output allow ministries to vary norms by individual plant, when the original intent was that such norms apply uniformly across a branch or subbranch (*Sotsialisticheskaia industriia*, 12 March 1981). See also comments by Shkabardnia, head of the Ministry of Instruments and Means of Automation (*Pravda*, 9 March 1981).

6 The terminology is borrowed from Watson-Watt, the British inventor of radar.

7 "There is very little reliable knowledge concerning the factors which tend either to facilitate or to retard technological innovation. What is known is highly tentative. In general, the findings of economists and others tell us what pitfalls to avoid rather than what should be done." Robert Gilpin, *Technology, Economic Growth, and International Competitiveness*, Washington, D.C., GPO, 1975, p. 35.

This uncertainty is illustrated by the widely divergent judgements of why U.S. industrial innovation seems to have lost some of its vigor in the 1970s. Prime importance has been variously ascribed to each of the following: underinvestment in R and D; the increasing bureaucratization or overmanagement of R and D (even in the private sector); overcomplacence about U.S. technological prowess, leading to neglect of foreign developments; declining rivalry among industrial firms; government regulations tending to inhibit or distort the direction of innovation; tax policies that make it harder to finance new ventures; inflation, which discourages projects with a distant pay-off; public misgivings about the social or environmental consequences of new technologies.

8   Richard Nelson and Sidney Winter, "In Search of Useful Theory of Innovation," *Research Policy*, v. 6 no. 1 (1977), pp. 36–76.
9   Oleg Antonov, "Pochemu novaia tekhnika vnedriaetsia s boem," *Znamia*, 1957 no. 2, pp. 148–62.
10 L. Gatovskii, *Ekonomicheskie problemy nauchno-tekhnicheskogo progressa*, Moscow, Nauka, 1971, pp. 110, 113.
11 See Brezhnev's report to the December 1969 meeting of the Central Committee, excerpts from which were not published until 1976 (L. Brezhnev, *Voprosy upravleniia ekonomikoi razvitogo sotsialisticheskogo obshchestva; rechi, doklady, vystupleniia*, Moscow, Politizdat, 1976, pp. 207–8, 215–16.
12 Brezhnev, *op. cit.*, p. 294.
13 *Narodnoe khoziaistvo SSSR v 1978 g.*, pp. 94–95.
14 Brezhnev, *op. cit.*, p. 529.
15 V. Pokrovskii, "Povyshenie effektivnosti ispol'zovaniia nauchno-tekhnicheskogo potentsiala," *Planovoe khoziaistvo*, 1977 no. 3, pp. 20–21.
16 *Osnovnye napravleniia razvitiia narodnogo khoziaistva SSSR na 1976–1980 gody*, Moscow, Politizdat, 1976, p.19.
17 A country's proficiency at innovation is sometimes equated with its ability to employ a technology before other nations do, or to make large technological leaps instead of small ones, or to excel in sophisticated areas of technology. These are all impressive, but it is the characteristic of yielding a surplus that increases economic productivity, consumer welfare, and military potential over the long haul.
18 There are segments of the market in Western economies where producers would do anything to please the customer, and where goldplating flourishes because the customer prefers it.
19 This is in marked contrast to market economies where the customers for producer goods tend to be better informed and more economizing than buyers of either consumer goods or government services (K. Pavitt and W. Walker, "Government Policies Toward Industrial Innovation," *Research Policy*, v. 5 (1976), pp. 42–43.
20 A. Birman, "New Economic Approaches," *Soviet Life*, December 1979, p. 38.
21 A deputy head of Gosplan's Department of Long-Term Planning emphasizes that "...the new approach to the five-year plan resides in the stability of the plan for capital investment, not in specifying five years in advance who makes what down to the last nail" (V. Kossov, "Novyi oblik planirovaniia," *Ekonomika i organizatsiia promyshlennogo proizvodstva*, 1980 no. 2, p. 22).
22 Seasonal unemployment on farms is still severe, and earnings differentials between farms wide. But because collective farmers have not been as free to change jobs as state workers, their unplanned labor mobility has been kept within more or less tolerable bounds.
23 N. Glushkov, "O razrabotke novykh optovykh tsen," *Ekonomicheskaia gazeta*, 1980 no. 17, p. 8.
24 Ibid.
25 Gosplan deliberately approves unrealistic capital investment projects in order to preserve the illusion that the interests of all ministries can be met (see "Stroiteliam—real'nye plany," *Pravda*, 1 November 1980).

    Both Gosplan and ministerial planners have been reluctant to develop technically justifiable input-output norms because this would constrain their freedom to set and change plans at will (V. Sominskii, "Normativnye osnovy planirovaniia: novye zadachi," *Ekonomika i organizatsiia promyshlennogo proizvodstva*, 1978 no. 6, p. 108).
26 The need for producers to resist bad plans is a delicate subject in a solidary society that espouses directive planning and denies conflicting economic interests. For a

rare aknowledgment that (only?) such resistance will force planners to try harder, see V. Starodubrovskii's remarks in a round table discussion in *Voprosy ekonomiki*, 1977 no. 1, p. 24.
27 V. Seliunin, "Proekt s dvoinym dnom," *Sotsialisticheskaia industriia*, 4 Sept. 1973.
28 V. Cherniavskii, "Faktor vremeni v stroitel'nom dele," *Kommunist*, 1980 no. 1, p. 36.
29 V. Seliunin, "Khozraschet v podotrasli," *Sotsialisticheskaia industriia*, 4 August 1977. Over the 9th Five-Year Plan, the budget confiscated about 100 million rubles to which Minpribor was entitled by the profit-sharing formula.
30 Nine Minpribor enterprises were experimentally shifted to full self-financing in July 1980.
31 By 1980 self-financing had already been introduced in four all-union machinery ministries besides Minpribor (agricultural machinery, heavy and transportation machinery, power machinery, electrical equipment), as well as in a number of republican construction ministries and republican ministries of motor transport.
32 The Ministry of Finance may be even less enthusiastic about self-financing than Gosplan. However, both bodies contain some enthusiasts, and their top administrators have expressed approval of it "in principle."
33 In another sense it is impure because the formula for allocating planned total profits between the producer and the budget bases the producer's share on his planned need for resources; in other words, crybabies who convincingly plead greater need may keep more than efficient producers who might make better use of retained resources. However, since the budget gets its absolute planned amount even if actual total profits are below plan, the inefficient will ultimately be penalized by below-plan retained resources.
34 See p. 144.

8
The 26th Party Congress and Soviet Foreign Policy

Robert Legvold

Leonid Brezhnev is not someone who appears particularly amused by irony, so maybe he sees no irony in the way certain issues dealt with in his reports to earlier party congresses haunt this latest congress. When he laments the fate of détente—destroyed, he would argue, by U.S. leaders who let their indignation over Soviet involvement in local crises from Angola to Afghanistan take precedence over SALT and other opportunities to ease the risk of nuclear war—chances are he is not remembering his first Central Committee report to a party congress in 1966, in which he condemned the Vietnam war as a great blight on U.S.-Soviet relations. "We are prepared to develop our relations with the U.S.A.," he had said at the time, "but for these relations to develop the U.S.A. must drop its policy of aggression."[1] "The good fruit of political cooperation cannot be grown on the poisonous soil of aggression and violence," words that doubtless sound different to him today when quoted back by American leaders.

Then there is Brezhnev at the latest congress somberly warning of the peril to socialism in Poland, and Brezhnev exactly ten years earlier explaining to another congress the mortal danger socialism had just survived in Czechoslovakia. "Opponents of socialism supported by outside forces are, by stirring up anarchy, seeking to channel events into a counter-revolutionary course," said he in February 1981.[2] "Internal anti-socialist forces" had "become active" and had even mounted "direct counter-revolutionary action in the hope of support from outside, from imperialism, which, for its part, is always prepared to form blocs of such forces," said he in March 1971.[3] But, again, Brezhnev more than likely sees little irony in the parallel, and almost certainly spends little time wondering whether his successor at the 28th Party Congress in 1991 will be railing at comparable counterrevolutionaries from some other part of the empire and threatening fraternal assistance to save the situation.

The most ironic aspect of Brezhnev's recent foreign-policy report, however, is how different it turned out to be from the one he originally thought he would be giving. In the five years since the 25th Party Congress, things have not worked out as expected. At the 1976 congress, Brezhnev's perfunctory exhortation on behalf of SALT was delivered without an inkling that five years later a SALT II treaty would languish unratified, while the process of negotiating arms limitations threatened to disintegrate. When he talked about making détente "irreversible" at the 25th Party Congress, he could not have dreamed that five years later détente—at least between his country and the United States—would be dead. When he groused about "rightist forces" in West Germany who "cling to revenge-seeking positions" and "influential circles" in the United States who refuse to "shake off a cold-war psychology"—in an otherwise distinctly optimistic assessment of East-West relations—he clearly had no notion of how radically the political climate would change in the next five years and how much these "forces" would turn out to be harbingers, rather than cast-offs, of the future. At the 25th Party Congress, when he reviewed the successes of a quiescent Eastern Europe and dutifully outlined the tasks ahead, the Polish labor strikes of *1976* had not yet occurred.

Brezhnev's opening line to the earlier 25th Party Congress, "the world is changing before our very eyes, and changing for the better"—a line that set the tone for the remainder of the report—was a line he presumably expected to embroider on five years later.[4] But that, doubtless to Brezhnev's mild surprise, was not to be. His latest report starts quite differently: "On the international plane," he says, "the period under review has been rough and complicated," marked by a resurgent struggle between the ways of cold war and the hopes of détente. He talks about "thunderclouds gathering on the international horizon" and about other "difficult times, and critical situations" that the "world of socialism" has always before survived. Gone are the buoyant phrases celebrating the "turn from explosive tensions to détente and normal mutually beneficial cooperation"; gone is the preening of Soviet foreign policy on having anticipated "the main practical tasks of consolidating international security" and for having deftly "accustomed" the other side "to the thought that not brinkmanship but negotiation of disputed questions, not confrontation but peaceful cooperation, is the natural state of things."[5] In their place a point made early in the report to the 26th Party Congress echoes gently but insistently throughout: "On the whole, comrades," Brezhnev says, "the period since the 25th Congress has not been a simple one. There have been no few difficulties in the country's economic development and in international affairs."

Disappointed expectations, of course, are not the same as policy failures, and the dour mood of Brezhnev and most contemporary Soviet foreign-policy commentators hardly represents a surge of Soviet self-doubt. Events have not unfolded as the Soviet leadership wished or expected, but the results are far from dissatisfying. The deterioration in U.S.-Soviet relations, after all, is partly offset by (admittedly also partly the consequence of) Soviet-abetted changes in strategically significant regions, from southern Africa to Southeast Asia. Regimes close to the United States, even without Soviet complicity, have crumbled, sometimes—as in the case of Iran—utterly transforming the strategic equation in an area, in other cases—like Nicaragua—opening an area to further far-reaching shifts. The Soviets tend to lump these changes together, claiming credit for themselves, and to parade the list as a measure of deep flowing trends. The tally since the 1976 congress—Afghanistan, Iran, Kampuchea, Nicaragua, and Zimbabwe—is a handsome sequel to the triumphs of Ethiopia, Mozambique, Vietnam, and Angola.

The Soviet leaders know, of course, that these changes are often widely disparate events, different in their origins, accessibility to Soviet influence, revolutionary orthodoxy, historic significance, and durability. They also are keenly aware of events that have gone the other way, as in Somalia, Egypt, Jamaica, and now potentially Iraq.[6] But the larger pattern is what counts, and by this standard, despite the headaches ahead in Afghanistan, the dangers in Iran, and the imperfect outcome in Zimbabwe, these last five years offer Soviet leaders comforting evidence that beneath the storm and stress of superpower relations the world is advancing in the right direction.

In much the same way they do not let ruined hopes for Soviet-American relations obscure the progress of Soviet power in that relationship—that is, obscure the relative improvement in the Soviet military position, the growing reach of Soviet power (again, particularly in military respects), and the increasing gap in the security burdens each side faces. The last involves a distinction between the intensity of threats facing the two sides and the range of objectives on which their national security is based. The Soviet leaders undoubtedly see the Americans, or the Americans in collusion with the Chinese, as a more intense threat, but they also realize that oil, distant allies, far-flung economic interests, and vulnerable lines of communication present the other side with a security challenge exceeding its means by a wider margin than the dramatic but simpler challenge of defending a Eurasian empire exceeds Soviet means. Poland is suddenly evening the balance, but, to extend the point, the Soviets seem to regard it as a success that the Americans, more than themselves, take on more than they can handle.

As a general matter, despite shortcomings at home and disquieting developments abroad, the Soviet leaders, if we take them at their word, believe that their country has not fared badly over the last five years. The weight of the Soviet Union in international politics has grown. (Gromyko on the eve of the 26th Congress repeated his celebrated comment to the 24th Party Congress in 1971 that "no major international problem is being settled or can be settled today without Soviet participation."[7]) U.S. fortunes, an important standard for Soviet leaders, have suffered relatively more than their own. If not all of the hoped-for benefits of cooperation with the Japanese have been theirs, a considerable proportion have. The Soviet Union has managed to use its power more actively without producing direct confrontations with the Americans—thus far, at least. Despite rattling setbacks in Egypt and Somalia, on balance the pace and thrust of change in the contestable parts of the world have reinforced a basic Soviet optimism.

There is, however, another more crucial side to Brezhnev's report which in my view contains the central dilemma of current Soviet foreign policy. If Soviet policy has a surpassing concern—aside from Poland, which short-circuits all else—it is to keep East-West relations from unraveling entirely. Brezhnev and a phalanx of Soviet commentators plead constantly the cause of détente, for the good reason that détente as Brezhnev and his colleagues have always conceived it offers them the cheapest, safest, and handiest framework for managing most of the toughest problems on their foreign-policy agenda. But—and this is the source of the Soviet dilemma—détente, the favored framework, freshly reaffirmed at the 26th Party Congress, rests on premises whose soundness diminishes by the day.

When Soviet leaders grew enthusiastic about détente in the early 1970s, beyond their saintly professions they had four hardheaded objectives in mind. First, the process of détente—for the Soviets, unlike many Americans, viewed détente as a process, not a state of mind or an international regime—was to help pare from the arms competition any developments likely to leave them at a disadvantage. Negotiated agreements, the mechanism of the process in this instance, were accepted as at last feasible—indeed, as a better way to affect U.S. and NATO military programs and the only way to avoid needless or counterproductive excursions in the larger arms competition.

Secondly, the Soviet leaders counted on détente to stimulate a steady, expanding infusion of goods, capital, and skills into the Soviet and allied economies. The basic decision to get more deeply involved with the other side stemmed from the economic weaknesses revealed during the 8th Five-Year Plan (1964–69), and, thus, the Soviet leadership would probably have sought a larger trade in any event. But without the prospect of better East-West relations, trade with the industrialized market economies, as Soviet analysts wrote at the time, would remain small and irregular.

Thirdly, the Soviet leaders viewed détente with the United States as the most effective way to influence the course of the newly launched U.S.-Chinese relationship. They understood that Kissinger and Nixon, for their part, and the Chinese leadership, for its, meant to use Sino-American ties to Soviet disadvantage—and even if this were not so, Soviet leaders would have assumed it to be so. But when they began the "normalization" of U.S.-Soviet relations (their phrase) in the early 1970s, they also seemed confident that in the triangle their country was and would remain the United States' primary and preferred adversary-partner. The superpowers, they like to think, have business to do transcending the concerns of all other (lesser) powers. Détente was in their eyes the necessary precondition permitting this "logical" state of affairs to float forward.

Finally, by easing the generalized tension with the United States, they assumed, they could assure that changes like those in Vietnam and other tumultuous parts might flourish without reflexive American intervention. Détente was to be a constraint on the role the United States felt it must or could play in the unstable regions of the world. It was also meant to enlarge the Soviet role—where the United States would otherwise alone try to mediate outcomes, as in the Middle East—by inducing American leaders to make the Soviet Union a partner.

Détente, the source of these aspirations or hopes, in turn rested on five critical premises, some of which were conscious and even explicit, others unspoken and perhaps unrecognized. What went under the stylized ideological label of "a shifting correlation of forces" was the first and clearest of these. The concept—though it is unduly generous to call it such—amounts to the battle report of an age, to a balance sheet of an era's basic trends. It embraces nearly all that is happening, from the overthrow of a disapproved regime somewhere in Africa to a good harvest in the Soviet Union. Such a shapeless and measureless notion has severe limitations as a tool for understanding anything, including the underlying logic of recent international trends, but Soviet analysts are bound to use it, with a wholly appropriate imprecision; and, in the early 1970s, the correlation of forces, according to their accounting, underwent an unusual acceleration. (By definition, the correlation of forces moves in only one direction.)

No doubt much of the "acceleration" was due to the growth of Soviet military power, leading in particular to the elimination of the U.S. strategic nuclear advantage; but other developments were also featured, such as the gathering strength of the "national liberation struggle" (a billboard claim that had most to do with the nearing defeat of American power in Vietnam), and the intensification of "interimperialist contradictions"—ideologese for the real tensions generated among the Japanese, West Europeans, and Americans by a collapsing Bretton-Woods economic order. Thrust forward by these three primary currents, the correlation of forces, Soviet speakers seemed to be saying, had reached a turning point.

Even when reduced to these few critical dimensions, the shifting correlation of forces remained an obviously unquantifiable slogan, but enough was changing, as Soviet observers viewed contemporary international politics, to persuade them that the context of East-West relations that had prevailed for the last twenty years no longer had to be accepted as given. By all indications, the Soviet leaders did not regard the warmer relations between East and West emerging at the close of the 1960s as only the latest in the cycle of postwar thaws and freezes. Rather, they apparently let themselves believe in the possibility of a far-reaching remaking of the external order, or at least that part of it shaping the East-West contest. Hence the readiness to go beyond the claim of a "world balance of forces changing in favor of socialism" to the proposition that conditions now permitted a "restructuring of the entire postwar system of international relations."

Soviet leaders hardly had in mind liquidating the underlying contest between socialism and imperialism, and they were not in some mad-hatter fashion predicting a sudden revolution in the character of international relations. Least of all were they announcing a retreat from their traditional view of history and its inevitable outcome. But they were evidently tempted to conclude that the shifting military balance, the chastening U.S. experience in Vietnam, producing what they took to be a long-term retrenchment in U.S. globalism, and the tangle of concerns breaking down neatly divided alignments on both sides were creating a durable new basis for East-West relations. In effect, they were mostly assuming a critical constricting of U.S. possibilities and a realistic adjustment on the part of American leaders. True, the Soviet leaders never meant that only the United States and its allies would make the concessions in détente, but they were taking it for granted that détente itself arose out of a fundamental change in the international position of only one side. The ultimate point, however, is that détente, in their eyes, flowed from a major structural change, not merely a fleeting shift in atmosphere, and they expected this change to last and develop.

The second premise underpinning the Soviet approach to détente concerned the relationship of détente to developments in the third world and the so-called national liberation struggle. Committed to both, the Soviets simply assumed that they could insulate their efforts on behalf of détente from those on behalf of the national liberation struggle and vice versa. At the outset they worried more about disaffected friends in the third world who—egged on by the Chinese—saw détente as a sellout. The Soviets presented détente to these friends as a subtle rear-guard action against U.S. imperialism, Portuguese colonialism, and South African apartheid (isolated among nations seeking to reduce the sources of tension). Soon, however, the Soviet leaders also faced discontented Americans with a minimum tolerance for Soviet revolution making in troubled quarters, whatever the Soviet theory. These Americans were reminded that détente was a transcendent opportunity, too precious to clutter with lesser grievances, and that they should follow the Soviet example of receiving Nixon in May 1972 and getting on with SALT I despite the U.S. bombing of Hanoi and mining of Haiphong harbor. Besides, there was nothing the Soviet Union could do to stem the tide of history, and, thus, nothing was served by making détente hostage to a natural course of events.

Thirdly, the Soviets assumed that improved Soviet-American relations would be at the center of a widening and deepening East-West détente. The acceleration of détente, as Soviet writers often noted, began in Europe late in the 1960s, but from the beginning it was the future American role to which the Soviets attached preeminence. The Americans would turn limited economic cooperation into something of scale. The Americans would count noses among the Western powers, bring obstreperous allies into line, and cut through the confusion of alliance politics when it came time to move forward on Berlin, the Conference on Security and Cooperation in Europe (CSCE), force-reduction negotiations, and the other enterprises of détente. The Americans would be the Soviet Union's primary interlocutor in the process, joining with it to define détente's agenda, negotiate SALT—the centerpiece of détente—and protect détente from the nay-saying and disruptions of the Chinese and other troublemakers.

Fourthly, the Soviet leadership assumed a stable Eastern Europe—indeed, an Eastern Europe made more stable by the fruits of détente. To Soviet leaders, their intervention in Czechoslovakia in 1968 both reinforced the need for a European settlement and made such a settlement safe. Détente's decisive first task was to buttress a periodically vulnerable East European status quo by achieving what Soviet speakers referred to as recognition of Europe's "postwar territorial reality." Involvement with the West, Soviet leaders knew, meant the risk of exposing their dominions to contaminating influences, a danger that grew when the West's determination to make human rights an issue of the Helsinki process became apparent. But these were manageable risks, in the Soviet Union's estimation, and no fundamental threat to the basic assumption that détente could count on, and would contribute to, a stable Eastern Europe.

Finally, the fifth premise underlying the Soviet approach to détente was that all the negotiations which started in the early 1970s—the German accords, SALT, CSCE, the mutual force reduction talks, and so on—would take on an internal momentum, gradually acquiring a cumulative force and helping to overcome residual pockets of opposition within the key Western countries. Precisely because the American turn toward détente was not a matter of good will, argued the Soviet proponents of détente, but imposed on the United States by a changed context, the process was thought to be relatively self-sustaining.[8] When trouble struck in late 1973–74, Soviet analysts introduced a worried exhortation to make détente "irreversible," but it is important to recall how much the original Soviet notion trusted the basic momentum of events.

Not one of these five premises remains intact. The progression of détente, far from creating its own momentum, or even maintaining an irregular momentum, has collapsed everywhere but in Europe. Eastern Europe's stability is no more, disrupted not by superficial risks of détente, but by the failings of a system accentuated by exactly the rewards the Soviet Union and its partners had sought from détente. The United States, rather than becoming détente's central source, has become the Soviet Union's central problem. Détente ultimately could not be insulated from Soviet loyalty to the national liberation struggle, and the Soviet Union's inability or unwillingness to understand this, more than any other factor, dealt détente a mortal blow. And the international setting, whose structural alterations had justified the Soviet commitment to détente shows serious signs of reverting to old forms.

Events have ravaged the assumptions behind the policy formally inaugurated in 1971 at the 24th Party Congress, and on their ruins left the outlines of a radically different future. Three dimensions of the change must concern Soviet leaders. First, the thrust of basic trends—the shifting correlation of forces—has suddenly weakened and begun wobbling in unpredictable directions. American globalism is not contracting, but reviving. The military balance seems likely not to continue its favorable evolution but to halt and in some respects reverse itself over the next decade. If the United States is constrained by the correlation of forces to move over and make room for the Soviet Union, it appears not to realize it and instead seems to be gearing up for another attempt to put the Soviet Union in its place.

Secondly, the inherent flaw in the Soviet Union's security system has resurfaced. For the Soviet security system is based not merely on an alliance, but on an empire, and on an empire that depends not only on the sinews of power but on the orthodoxy of local political orders. In Poland, once again, only this time more gravely than ever before, a challenge to orthodoxy threatens the whole edifice.

And, thirdly, the benign or even constructive interaction that Soviet leaders a decade ago counted on between foreign and domestic affairs has turned into the opposite. Rather than relief on the international front as the Soviet Union heads into a hard decade at home, the Soviet leadership must now look forward to serious pressures, distractions, and threats from outside. If the Soviet leaders thought they had broken the cycle of the Civil War, the first five-year plans, and the postwar reconstruction—times when foreign-policy preoccupations added to domestic-policy preoccupations—the period between now and the next party congress is likely to disappoint them.

At a certain level of abstraction, therefore, the wonder of Brezhnev's report to the 26th Party Congress is not the conciliatory line he took in response to the new American administration, but his reaffirmation of a détente whose original premises have disintegrated, a détente designed for a world bearing faint resemblance to the one emerging. The incongruity must also have occurred to the Soviet leadership. Gromyko, in an important *Kommunist* article preceding the congress, takes unusual care to make the case for the last decade of Soviet policy. Reading his painstakingly detailed accounting of the achievements under détente, stage by stage, Peace Program by Peace Program, one gets the impression that he and his colleagues are trying to persuade someone—perhaps themselves—that they have been on the right track.[9] But having made the case for past policy and then rededicated the Soviet Union to continuing it, Gromyko might be expected to justify his confidence in the future. Instead he in effect gives a string of reasons why this policy is in jeopardy, starting with the overall deterioration of the international context and proceeding through the shift in U.S. policy, the rapprochement of "imperialism with Chinese hegemonism," and the risk of conflict in unstable regions.

A moment ago, I used the phrase, "at a certain level of abstraction," because in reality the old ones in the Kremlin are not interested in the fundamental condition of their policies nor in the contradictions often surrounding these policies. In the circumstance, it would have been unrealistic to expect of the 26th Party Congress a profound foreign-policy review, let alone dramatic measures either to save or to displace détente. Unable to choose at a fundamental level, the current leaders have, in their reaffirmation of détente, settled for a tactical response to what they hope will be a short-lived deterioration in East-West relations.

Their tendency to temporize, to respond tactically, to deal with opportunities as a matter of short-run expediency and with deep-seated problems in narrow damage-limiting terms dominates contemporary Soviet policy. The Soviets are not so much grappling with basic choices as attempting to survive on half-choices.

I am not saying that surviving on half-choices is an uncommon or totally untenable proposition. Brezhnev and his colleagues would not be the first leadership to disregard the deeper, longer-term dilemmas of its foreign policy and to concentrate instead on the exigencies and openings of the moment. As a matter of fact, the Soviet leaders' approach to the short run spares them the need to reflect on the deep-seated limitations of current policy. This is an important qualification that deserves a word more before I go on to analyze the kinds of basic choices that are not being made.

For now, U.S. policy remains the Soviet Union's preoccupying concern—the policy by which the Soviet leaders orient their own. The response they have chosen to the Reagan administration dramatizes the way the short run now obscures and constrains the long run in Soviet policy.

Rather than consider the reasons U.S.-Soviet relations have reached their current pass, the Soviet leadership is evidently content not to ask why, but to take things as they are. By all indications, it is not interested in what went wrong with détente, not if it involves examining both sides' actions. Even the policy intellectuals from the foreign affairs institutes rarely venture beyond one-sided explanations limited to the pathology of contemporary capitalism and the peculiar insecurities and illusions of its leading representative. The interaction of Soviet and American ambitions, hopes, fears, frustrations over the last half-decade apparently does not figure at any level of Soviet deliberation. Policy, as a result, has a distinctly shallow, circumscribed quality.

Soviet policy has gone through two stages since Reagan's election in November. Initially the Soviet stance was to wait and see whether the new administration's actions would bear out its campaign rhetoric. Although the election outcome caused a certain nervousness, particularly when viewed alongside the sharp change in the Senate, Soviet observers seemed genuinely inclined to believe that the new people would soften in office. As Valentin Zorin was reported to have said on the morning after the election, "American Presidents, including this new one, cannot indulge their personal preferences, but must be guided by the realities of the modern world, such as the balance of forces."[10] In rather short order, however, most Soviet analysts came to recognize that Reagan and his people meant what they had been saying. Not only did they continue to talk about the Soviet Union and the challenge it posed in the harshest terms, but they then followed their talk with deed. Haig's sharp admonition on Iran, Afghanistan, and Poland in his first letter to Gromyko, the storm over Soviet and Cuban involvement in El Salvador, the massive defense commitment, Haig's March trip to the Middle East and June trip to China—all of these persuaded Soviet observers that they were facing the hardest-line administration they had seen in decades.

As was the fashion among many Western commentators and some leaders through the spring and summer of 1981, various Soviet analysts did note how slow the administration was to articulate the concrete lines of its policy, and lectured on the difference between pose and policy. Sometimes these commentaries came with the hope-filled observation that the administration's policy course was not yet determined. But at the same time, Soviet analysts could see that Reagan and his men had strong predispositions and were determined to follow through. Any expectation that the administration would quickly trade its campaign rhetoric for a pragmatic approach soon ended, and Soviet policy—though the word *policy* hardly seems appropriate—entered a second stage.

Satisfied that the Reagan administration took its rhetoric seriously and intended to do something about it, Soviet analysts fell back on a second calculation: would the administration be able to pull it off? From all appearances, the essence of Soviet policy became the gamble that it could not. Soviet accounts began to dwell on the obstacles to the reassertion of U.S. power. Whatever the new leadership's instincts and preferences, Arbatov grumbled in one piece, it will iscover that "politics remains the art of the possible."[11] Or, as he put it on a later occasion, "These people in Washington may yet discover that they must build a bridge between their gut feelings and reality."[12]

Behind this not-altogether-confident claim, Soviet analysts appeared to be wagering that the administration would run into trouble with both its domestic and foreign programs. As the spring months passed, most people in Moscow seemed to be gambling that the Reagan gamble would not work. They acknowledged that the administration might get its first budget, along with a sizable increase in defense spending but they doubted that it would get any of its next three annual budgets. They doubted that it would be able to sustain the defense effort for the full four years, let alone beyond. They doubted that the administration would be able to rally the NATO Alliance behind its super-charged notion of the East-West contest or have its way on El Salvador if the Canadians, Mexicans, and Venezuelans weighed in. They assumed that the transcendent (Soviet) focus that Haig and others attempted to give the Middle East would crack apart on the rocks of local conflict, and that the new African policy would run afoul of both Black African states and major European allies.

Perhaps this response was a natural retreat for Soviet observers taken by surprise by the vigor and depth of the new administration's conservatism. Perhaps it was a gamble with some merit. It *was* a reaction that provided a certain cushion in U.S.-Soviet relations, though this was not overstated because of the edginess with which each side regarded the other. It was also a reaction—to return to the theme of this essay—that prevented the Soviet leadership from facing the limitations of its own policy.

If the Soviet leadership were of a mind or in a condition to look hard at its own policy, its basic alternatives would fall into three categories. Two of these dominate Western assumptions, but inappropriately, in my judgment. The first of these juxtaposes militancy to détente and is sometimes inaptly expressed as a choice between cold war and détente. It is not a realistic choice, and not one that the Soviet leadership would likely make, but as a framework of analysis it does illustrate critical features of policy. Thus, in theory, the Soviet Union could cast aside the rhetoric and paraphernalia of détente—could stop worrying about the fluctuations in American, German, or Japanese mood, scrap the nuisance of arms control, save the energy that now goes into Helsinki review conferences, peace campaigns, and summits—and simply go about its business. With sufficient military power, on which it has a good head start, the Soviet Union could theoretically take care of its own problems, make its own opportunities, and insist on an appropriate level of deference. Apart from the fact that Soviet leaders have never thought in these terms, this alternative is simply beyond Soviet means, and nothing even the most hidebound of Brezhnev's colleagues say suggests that they think otherwise.

On the other hand—again, in theory—the Soviet leadership could choose to make détente a reality, or at a minimum to give it a chance. But to do so it would have to come to grips with the untenability of its own original premises. If the Soviet Union were to choose to deal with its problems and ambitions within a more carefully managed East-West competition, it could not expect the change to come only from Americans accommodating a shifting correlation of forces. Real détente between the superpowers requires an equal adjustment to the limits of power, equal restraint in the face of change, and equal sacrifices for international stability and peace. Nor could the Soviet Union expect to exempt from the process what it pleases, such as its role in support of the national liberation struggle. Were the Soviets to embrace a genuinely meaningful détente, they would have to reconcile themselves to the comprehensive nature of the process.

The second way of thinking about basic Soviet choices juxtaposes retrenchment to accelerated expansionism. This seems to be the category with which the Reagan administration and many American commentators work. If the United States is strong and demonstrates its determination to end Soviet aggressive behavior, these Americans assume, the Soviet leadership will choose to retreat. Conversely, if no force appears to check Soviet misbehavior or counterbalance its power, then the Soviet leadership will only grow bolder. The sway this categorization has over so much Western analysis is reinforced by the perception that severe problems at home and within their empire will compel Soviet leaders either to draw back from foreign-policy adventures and concentrate on an economic and political rejuvenation of the socialist core, or to strike out in some desperate Samson-like fashion to distract the Russian people from their discontent and give the Soviet system a substitute external momentum. Again, however, this would not likely be the frame of reference within which a Soviet leadership would make basic choices were it of a mind to make them.

The most pertinent category, it seems to me, is a third choice between a U.S.-centered policy and a decentralized policy. The first emphasis, a U.S.-centered policy, now prevails. Regarded earlier as the best hope of détente and more recently as the primary problem, the United States remains the overriding preoccupation of the Soviet leadership. The most striking thing about Brezhnev's international report to the 26th Party Congress is how thoroughly dominated it is by the U.S. factor. (Poland no doubt has an urgency and priority that neither the report nor most open Soviet commentary conveys.) Directly or indirectly the United States figures in nearly every problem. It is the cause of the disintegration of détente, the impetus behind a new eruption of the arms race, the instigator of anti-Soviet collusion from East Asia to northern Europe, the catalyst of instability and interventionism in the third world, the foil of the Chinese, and the principal sponsor and beneficiary of trouble in Eastern Europe. As I will discuss in a moment, it also appears to be the primary target of the foreign-policy strategy emerging from the 26th Party Congress.

But instead of perceiving the Americans this way, the Soviet Union could have chosen to downgrade its preoccupation with the Americans. The central importance of U.S. outlook and actions cannot be blinked away, but the Soviets have alternative ways of dealing with the problem. They could follow a second strategy focusing on all other critical relationships, rather than—as I think is now the case—tying all other relationships to their relationship with the United States. Instead of concentrating on coaxing or pressuring the United States to return to détente or, alternatively, on directly defeating an American policy of global confrontation, the Soviet leaders could concentrate on repairing their position with the remaining major power centers. Rather than treating the Sino-Soviet conflict largely as an extension of its increasingly hostile relationship with the United States, the Soviet leadership could attempt to isolate the conflict and to tamp it down separately. Rather than lumping the Japanese with the Americans, as Soviet analysis does increasingly these days, it could attempt to deal more seriously with the special issues that prejudice Soviet-Japanese relations. Rather than approaching the West Europeans as cat's-paws within a U.S.-dominated Atlantic alliance, it could begin treating the West Europeans as genuinely equal alternative partners to the United States.

By deemphasizing the importance of the United States to its own policy, the Soviet Union would be reducing the multiplier effect that a high-tension relationship with the United States has on all other important relationships. This, however, would require making substantial concessions—particularly to the Chinese, but also to the Japanese and (on a lesser scale) to the West Europeans. For the moment such an option gestates only in the musings of frustrated (or disingenuous) Soviet foreign-policy intellectuals. Nothing about the 26th Congress—neither the parts of the report devoted to China nor Dimitri Polyansky's barren exchanges with the Japanese foreign minister immediately after—suggests any interest on the part of the current leaders in this option. Should they be wrong about the fate awaiting the Reagan foreign policy, should Reagan's gamble turn out to be more effective and enduring than they expect—in short, should they be forced to face basic choices of their own—then I think this is likely to be the frame of reference within which they do so.

For the moment, however, either the Soviet leadership does not believe in the inevitable prolongation of the current tension in U.S.-Soviet relations, or else it does not know what else it can do. For the target of Soviet foreign policy is still preeminently the United States. The proposals in the general secretary's report, in my view, are directed as much to, as against, the United States; the approach to others is intended as much to influence, as to isolate, the United States; and Soviet hopes are as dependent upon, as independent of the United States.

It is often argued by Western analysts that a major objective of current Soviet policy is to split the allies, primarily the West Europeans, from the Americans, and that the conciliatory tone, the talk of dialogue, and the arms control appeals in settings such as the 26th Party Congress are designed to further this objective. On the contrary, whatever long-term interest the Soviet Union has in divorcing Europe from the United States, I think the Soviets at the moment are more interested in using the Europeans to moderate American policy—in getting the West Germans and the French to persuade the new administration of the need for SALT, for restraint in the Persian Gulf, for East-West economic cooperation, and for limited arms building.

If I am right about Soviet intentions, then Brezhnev's report to the Congress emerges as a still more U.S.-focused document. Obviously the Soviet Union has other objectives in mind than merely influencing U.S. behavior, but the preoccupation with the United States gives focus and coherence to Soviet strategy.

Viewed in this light, the Soviet leadership for the moment appears to have settled on a strategy with three elements. First, they are making a major effort to relax the mounting, general atmosphere of tension. Without addressing the sources of the current tension, they mean to dull its impact, to work at soothing public alarm, and to offer an image of Soviet steadiness and restraint. It is largely a matter of atmospherics, as Soviet writers frankly confess, but considered important nonetheless, not only because they sense that a tense atmosphere advances a hard-line American posture, but also because they appear genuinely worried about the dangers in the present level of tension.

Secondly, as already suggested, the Soviets are counting on the West Europeans and, to a lesser extent, the Japanese to limit the general deterioration in East-West relations. They want, in this respect, not merely to preserve what they can of détente in Europe, but to rebuild a more general détente around this regional core. This, of course, is what they set out to do in the early 1970s, only then they put their money on the Americans. Now, when Brezhnev talks of giving détente "a second wind," he is relying on the West Europeans—not an ideal arrangement from the Soviet perspective.

To reach the West Europeans, the Soviets are pursuing two tracks. On the one hand they seek to influence the popular political climate in key countries by mobilizing the peace movement, appealing to sympathetic political leaders, and encouraging the prodétente aspects of the "Euro-left's" strategy (the strategy of the Socialist International and its Eurocommunist allies). On the other hand, they seek to galvanize Schmidt, Mitterrand, and other national leaders around a set of negotiating opportunities (e.g., Theater Nuclear Forces (TNF), a conference on military détente in Europe, an energy conference, talks on the Persian Gulf, and an undulating array of other ideas). By these two paths they evidently hope at a minimum to make it more difficult for the Europeans to go forward with TNF modernization and a major strengthening of NATO, but also to reinforce the stake the West Europeans feel they have in détente not only in Europe but in U.S.-Soviet relations.

The third element is addressed directly to the United States. While unhappy with the apparent direction of its policy, the Soviet leadership has seemingly decided not to write the Reagan administration off. Given the leadership's preoccupations, it can hardly afford to. Given its tentative assumptions about the likely outcome of the Reagan policy, it hardly needs to. Thus, Brezhnev's proposals at the 26th Party Congress may have been intended as much to keep options open as to throw the new administration off guard or to isolate it from Western public opinion. It would be a mistake, therefore, to interpret the urging of a dialogue or the possibility of a summit as mere atmospherics; to dismiss the concession on SALT II ratification (as a precondition for further negotiations) as an empty ploy; or to discount the vaguer commitment to negotiate confidence-building measures for more of Europe, to explore the possibility of negotiating CBMs in Asia, or even to open discussions on the Persian Gulf region (including the external dimension of the Afghanistan problem) as tricks intended only to take the wind out of sentiment for a larger Western defense effort. The Soviet leadership is surely not interested in negotiating its way out of Afghanistan and these last proposals signaled no readiness to seek a political settlement on any terms but its own, as the Soviet Union's later response to West European initiatives underscored. For the rest, however, the Soviet Union well may be prepared to engage in substantive exchanges—exchanges they still hope will include American participation.

If in the main this is the strategy of Soviet *Westpolitik* blessed by the 26th Party Congress, then it is a pygmy of a response to the fundamental problems that lurk behind the current to-and-fro in Soviet-American relations. Were the Soviet leadership to think more profoundly about the 1980s and the underlying limitations on East-West relations, then superficial, tactical responses to the flourishes of a new U.S. administration would not seem to be enough. For ultimately, no matter what happens to the Reagan foreign policy, durably constructive, stable relations between the superpowers cannot be developed until this or some other Soviet leadership grapples with the long-term dilemmas of its own policy.

The first, and in many ways the central, dilemma of Soviet policy grows out of the misjudgment that the Soviet Union can pursue its vision of the world and the enlargement of its own role in relatively unrestrained ways and at the same time achieve détente with the West. To some extent, the Soviet leadership misled itself by assuming that the combination of dwindling Western influence over international trends and of growing Soviet power left Western leaders with no alternative but to accept unpalatable Soviet-abetted change while welcoming various forms of bilateral cooperation with the Soviet Union. In fact, however, the West had a choice and will continue to have one, in turn leaving the Soviet Union with a choice of its own: it can either subordinate its global aspirations to the requirements of a managed East-West rivalry or pursue untrammeled aspirations in an unregulated competition with an equally unconstrained United States. The Soviet Union cannot be expected to exercise restraint refused by the other superpower, but they must be ready to moderate and limit the use of all forms of power, especially military power.

Much of this critical choice centers on the way the Soviet Union approaches superpower rivalry in third areas, particularly areas of instability. For most of the 1970s, the Soviet leadership placed this rivalry outside the bounds of détente, in part no doubt because it suspected or hoped that a wearied United States would be a less determined rival. But even now, when the Soviets no longer make that assumption, they are still inclined to let the competition unfold freely.

A few Soviet analysts have begun to write about the need for mutual restraint. Thus, according to one, the two sides need to adopt "a sharply negative attitude to the 'export of revolution' and the 'export of counterrevolution' [he includes both in the same breath] and to the utilization of inter-state conflicts in the interests of global confrontation."[13] Such an attitude, he continues, "could form the foundation for mutually acceptable 'rules of behavior.'" And Brezhnev's report to the 26th Party Congress conspicuously downplays the Soviet commitment to the national liberation struggle, reducing the issue to the Soviet Union's security ties with a particular set of established third-world regimes. The phrase itself is used only once in the report, and the related notion of the "world revolutionary process" for the first time in a quarter of a century appears nowhere. The section of Brezhnev's report to the 25th Party Congress entitled "The CPSU and the World Revolutionary Process" included a reference to Soviet involvement in Angola which stressed that "détente does not in the slightest abolish, and cannot abolish or alter, the laws of class struggle"; the analogous section in the 1981 report is called "The Soviet Union and the World Communist Movement" and primarily contains a discussion of Soviet relations with the Eurocommunist parties.[14] But these, again, are tactical adjustments, reflecting no clear readiness to deal squarely with the essence of the problem.

"It seems obvious that the growing desire of peoples for national liberation, independence, economic and social progress," writes a Soviet spokesman on the op ed page of *The New York Times*, "is an inevitable and natural process that one can neither 'repeal' nor 'ban' no matter how much some people may wish it."[15] Since the issue is not "repealing" or "banning" change in the third world, but constraining superpower interference, the statement is either a subterfuge or a reflection of the distance the Soviet Union has to travel before the two countries can begin containing the effects of local instability on their relationship.

The second dilemma derives from the historic and deeply imbedded Russian tradition of equating increased power, principally military power, with increased security. As other nations are also learning, this is not always so. More is involved than the fateful commonplace that in the nuclear age the perfection of arms menaces as much as it adds to each side's security. And more is involved than the obvious point that the great growth of Soviet military power often leads adversaries to band together, producing the very encirclement of the Soviet Union that Soviet leaders arm against. (The first point the Soviets understand; the second they may never understand.) Nor can Soviet security be successfully pursued by increasing proportionately the insecurity of everybody nearby. At the heart of each of these antinomies is the Soviet Union's exaggerated determination to maintain its security only by its own effort, disdaining or, at best, indulging those who through arms control and confidence-building measures seek greater reciprocal security. The Soviets have various stakes in arms control and a relaxation of tensions in the surrounding strategic theaters of Europe and Asia, but shaping military balances and security relationships in ways allowing them to achieve increased security less unilaterally does not appear to be one of their priorities.

To the degree that the Soviet Union's unilateral defense efforts increasingly stir apprehensions and counterefforts that undermine normal and productive relations between the Soviet Union and most of its neighbors, as well as the other superpower, its leaders need to consider alternative routes to national security. The question is what compromises are they prepared to risk to achieve arms control arrangements that make a difference, and what regional arrangements—including a restructuring of military balances—will they dare accept, thereby forfeiting control for a more widely based security.

The third dilemma is an involved one and can only be touched on in passing. Over the last decade the Soviet Union has accepted and, in important respects, sought a larger role in the outside world, particularly in the international economy, a development reendorsed by Soviet leaders at the 26th Party Congress. The evolution of Soviet attitudes and behavior in many of these less salient dimensions of the international order is an important, unnoticed new reality. This participation, however, is critically constrained by a still more powerful Soviet determination to insulate the Soviet system from the effects of participation. The Soviet Union seeks to be a "free rider" in the international economy and in settings where the so-called global issues are confronted, looking for benefits but avoiding the burden of helping to shape and improve the system. There is, however, a sharp limit to how far the Soviets can go in participating without actually engaging themselves—that is, without assuming burdens and without altering their domestic system in limited ways to accommodate the larger international economic systems. For the moment, the return of economic warfare to East-West relations and the limited trading resources of the socialist countries have obscured the issue. But, in the longer run, neither side can avoid either the more thorough integration of the centrally planned economies into the world economy or the adjustments this will require of both.

Finally, the Soviet leadership is already squarely caught up in the dilemmas of change within its own camp. The issue is how much orthodoxy and control the Soviet leadership is prepared to sacrifice for increased vitality and stability in Eastern Europe. To preserve a measure of residual authority with nationalist Communist leaders like Tito, with revisionist Communist parties like the Spanish and Italian, and with third-world countries of a "socialist orientation" like Mozambique, Algeria, and South Yemen, the Soviet Union learned long ago how to swallow heresies originally considered intolerable. Now the question is whether it can do so where it regards change and antiorthodoxy as most threatening, indeed where the essence of the Soviet system is at last at stake.

In the past, the challenges have been to authority as the Soviet leaders conceive it—political revolutions bestowed from above by restless East European party leaders and reformers. Poland, in breathtaking fashion, has opened an era of systemic crisis rooted in the failure of orthodox institutions and policies, and produced a revolution swelling from the grass roots to engulf the entire society. The antidote of intervention worked passably in Czechoslovakia, but the Soviet leaders grasp that it offers no relief in the Polish case. Aside from rescuing the party from a complete collapse of authority, a Soviet military intervention would do nothing to solve the problems with which Poland now seethes. Whether the Polish "renewal" as it evolves produces solutions or not, the Soviet Union must live with the process in some fashion or else undertake to impose a second and still more difficult Soviet revolution on Poland. Sending its armies will not suffice. To be spared a similar choice elsewhere in Eastern Europe, the Soviet leadership will have to tolerate a great deal of unnerving and often disorderly innovation. It may also have to tolerate a period of time when feared change runs deeper and faster within its own camp than within the West, a factor that will add to the psychological burden.

Whether the Soviet Union cares to or not, it is now forced to deal with the last of these four basic dilemmas. The question is not whether it will, but how well it will. With the other three, the Soviet Union can, if it closes its mind, avoid facing up to basic choices. If so, however, it will find the strategy of détente reaffirmed at the last party congress in constant jeopardy and, more seriously, the prospects of actually achieving a substantial détente with the United States heavily mortgaged.

Notes

1 "Report of the Central Committee of the Communist Party of the Soviet Union to the 23rd Congress of the CPSU," Delivered by Leonid Brezhnev, *23rd Congress of the Communist Party of the Soviet Union, 1966* (Moscow: Novosti Press Agency Publishing House, 1966), p. 45.
2 See his report to the 26th Party Congress, *Pravda*, 24 February 1981, p. 2.
3 See stenographic report to *Twenty-Fourth Congress of the CPSU*, 20 March–9 April 1971 (Moscow: Novosti Press Agency, 1971), p. 17.
4 See stenographic report to 25th Congress of the CPSU, *XXV S'ezd Kommunisticheskoi partii Sovetskogo Soyuza, Stenograficheskii otchët* (Moscow: Politizdat, 1976), p. 26.
5 Ibid., pp. 27 and 39.

6 A risk that has not been diminished by the attack Aziz Muhammed, the Iraqi Communist party leader, was permitted, or encouraged, to make at the 26th Party Congress on Iraq's war against Iran. See *Pravda*, 2 March 1981, p. 4.
7 A. Gromyko, "Leninskaya vneshnyaya politika v sovremennom mire," *Kommunist*, No. 1 (January, 1981), p. 1.
8 G. Arbatov, "O Sovetsko-amerikanskikh otnosheniyakh" ("On Soviet-American Relations"), *Kommunist*, No. 3 (February 1973), pp. 101–113.
9 Gromyko, "Leninskaya vneshnyaya politika," pp. 14–17.
10 *The New York Times*, 6 November 1980.
11 *Pravda*, 4 May 1981.
12 Interview with Strobe Talbott in *Time*, 6 July 1981, p. 9.
13 E. M. Primakov, "The USSR and the Developing Countries," *Journal of International Affairs*, Vol. 34, No. 2 (Fall/Winter 1980).
14 Soon after the Congress, Vadim Zagladin, the deputy head of the Central Committee's International Department, published an article conspicuously devoted to the "26th Congress of the CPSU and the World Revolutionary Process" (in *Mirovaya Ekonomika i Mezhdunarodnye Otnosheniya*, No. 4 [April 1981], pp. 3–19). Even more conspicuously, Zagladin's few militant references to the national liberation struggle are of necessity drawn from the speeches of third-world guests at the Party Congress.
15 Yuri Kornilov, "Which Road, U.S.?" *The New York Times*, 3 February 1981.

9

The Soviet Stake in Eastern Europe

Charles Gati

> One Pole is the Pope of Rome,
> Another helps run Carter's show
> Some kneel in homage to Uncle Brezhnev
> The rest queue in sunshine, rain or snow.[1]

I

By the time the 26th Party Congress was being held in Moscow, one Pole was still the Pope of Rome and many Poles continued to line up for food and other necessities throughout Poland. But Zbigniew Brzezinski was no longer the President's national security adviser, nor did Poles come to Moscow to pay homage to "Uncle" Brezhnev. Indeed, of the six East European leaders speaking at the CPSU Congress, only Stanislaw Kania, head of the Polish United Workers' Party (PUWP), failed to single out Leonid Brezhnev for praise. Conversely, while Brezhnev did praise the leader of the other beleaguered Communist Party, Babrak Kamal of Afghanistan, he failed to endorse or express confidence in the leadership of Poland's Kania. Another omission was equally ominous. Brezhnev dropped earlier assurances—which he had repeatedly stressed as late as December 1980—that the present leadership of PUWP could resolve Poland's "critical situation" on its own.

Such tidbits of news notwithstanding, the several speeches made at the Congress offered few if any significant new insights into Soviet thinking either about Soviet–East European rela-

---

Research and writing for this chapter was completed on 1 June 1981. Generous assistance by Columbia University's Research Institute on International Change, particularly by Mr. Richard Coffman, is gratefully acknowledged.

tions in general or about the Polish crisis of 1980–81 in particular. The speeches were meant to indicate, as they had in the past, that the bonds between the Soviet Union and its East European allies were stronger than ever; that the spirit of internationalism permeated the "socialist commonwealth;" that economic relations, multilateral within Comecon as well as bilateral, were both equal and mutually beneficial; that Soviet military power, combined with that of the East Europeans, represented a mighty force for peace and security in Europe; and, indeed, that the experience of the past few years (since the 25th Party Congress) had affirmed both the essential correctness of the present course of Soviet–East European relations and the utility of proceeding along the same path in the decade ahead.

Thus, Brezhnev's main address began with an assessment of Soviet foreign policy, and that assessment in turn began with a discussion entitled "Development of the World Socialist System and the Cooperation of the Socialist Countries."[2] As he did not seek "to paint the picture of the present-day socialist world in exclusively radiant colors," Brezhnev spoke of some of the "complications" as well, one of which was "the visible sharpening of the ideological struggle." The West, he stated, employed "a whole system of means designed to subvert or soften up the socialist world," including some which were "increasingly refined and treacherous."[3] Thus, his *description* of what was happening in Poland ("Opponents of socialism supported by outside forces are, by stirring up anarchy, seeking to channel events into a counterrevolutionary course ... the pillars of the socialist state in Poland are in jeopardy") fit logically with his *explanation* of what was being done to redress the situation ("At present, the Polish comrades ... are striving to enhance the Party's capacity for action and to tighten links with the working class and the other working people, and are preparing a concrete program to restore a sound Polish economy"). No one was therefore surprised by his *warning* that "the Polish Communists, the Polish working class and the working people of that country can firmly rely on their friends and allies; we will not abandon fraternal, socialist Poland in its hour of need, we will stand by it."[4]

Of all the East European leaders who addressed the Congress, only the Hungarian Janos Kadar and Kania joined Brezhnev even in raising the subject of Poland. Affirming Brezhnev's warning about Western subversion ("Our enemies would like to see the positions of socialism weakened"), Kadar nonetheless expressed the hope that "under the guidance of the PUWP, the

Polish people will find a socialist answer to cope with the present difficult situation."[5] Thus Kadar was still suggesting that while the PUWP's leading role in Polish society must be reestablished, in his view it ought to be done by the Polish people and by political means rather than as a result of military intervention. As for Kania, he was more explicit on this point. Although he alluded to the "Brezhnev Doctrine" by noting that the defense of the "socialist links of friendship" was "the concern of each state and of the entire socialist coalition," Kania went on to declare that "our party chose the road of political solution to the social conflict, the road of restoring society's trust in the people's authority, and this is the fundamental direction of our activity."[6] In their own ways, then, both Kania and Kadar still pleaded for more time in order to settle the crisis without Soviet military intervention.

At the Congress itself, none of the other East European leaders echoed their plea. Erich Honecker of the German Democratic Republic (GDR), Gustav Husak of Czechoslovakia, Todor Zhivkov of Bulgaria, and Nicolae Ceausescu of Romania uttered not a single word about Poland, although, after he returned to Bucharest, Ceausescu assured the Poles that "we are convinced that the PUWP, the government, the working class, and the people of Poland are able, closely united, to solve all problems facing them at present."[7] Not incidentally, such assurances were notably absent from the speeches and press reports published after the Congress in Czechoslovakia, the GDR, and Bulgaria. As if to confirm their differences on the Polish issue, by the way, such a code-word as "proletarian internationalism" was specifically mentioned only by Honecker, Husak, and Zhivkov (but not by Kania, Kadar, and Ceausescu), and the United States was singled out for general criticism also by Honecker, Husak, and Zhivkov (but not by Kania, Kadar, and Ceausescu).

That such differences could still openly emerge among the East European parties suggested that *the Soviet leadership itself had not yet decided on the particular course it would follow*. Indeed, the day after the Congress had concluded its deliberations, the Soviet leaders met their Polish counterparts[8] for still another session to evaluate the situation. The communiqué issued after this Soviet-Polish summit confirmed what Moscow wanted: "Reverse the course of events" and "eliminate the peril looming over the Socialist achievements of the Polish nation." However, the Soviet position still reflected a degree of ambivalence about *how* to accomplish this task. By calling the meeting with the Polish leaders "friendly" and by alluding to the "common approach" of the two delegations, Moscow did not exclude the possibility of letting the Poles "reverse the course of events." Yet the communiqué left no doubt about what the Soviet Union would have to do in the absence of a Polish solution: "The Soviet leaders declared that the USSR, together with other fraternal nations, has rendered and will render every necessary support to socialist Poland and to the Polish Communists in their strenuous effort to bring about the fundamental normalization of the situation in the country."[9]

All in all, neither the 26th Party Congress nor the post-Congress Soviet-Polish summit marked a dramatic turning point in the Soviet view of the Polish crisis. True, there were ominous signs that the Soviet leaders had begun to lose their earlier confidence in the PUWP's ability to reestablish its role in Polish society, to contain the national euphoria in Poland, and to roll back at least some of the workers' political gains. Yet the CPSU was not yet ready to cross the Rubicon, perhaps partly because of the reluctance of the Polish, Hungarian, and Romanian parties to favor a Soviet-led military intervention and mainly because of the obvious costs to the Soviet Union of such an intervention.

II

The Soviet dilemma is illustrative of new problems inherent in the making of Soviet foreign policy today. The Soviet Union has come to face the global power's classical problem of concurrently trying to appeal to as many diverse states, groups, and political audiences as possible—something it cannot always do so effectively. Simply put, Moscow has found that it cannot have all the benefits of "détente" and at the same time keep invading other countries; that it cannot befriend the "moderate" Arab states and at the same time support the "confrontationists"; and, indeed, that it cannot easily reconcile the goal of stability in Eastern Europe with its concurrent demand for strict East European adherence to Soviet policies and norms. Like other global powers with diverse interests, then, the Soviet Union must make agonizing choices, and in some cases the expected gains may not outweigh the expected costs.

At the heart of the current dilemma in Eastern Europe is the painful choice between (*a*) continuing a policy of relative tolerance towards the region (in order to encourage the several regimes' stability and viability) and (*b*) returning to a policy of coercion and repression (in order to assure uniformity and to secure Poland's place in the "socialist commonwealth").

To appreciate the Soviet dilemma, it is useful to recall that only certain aspects of the Soviet interest in Eastern Europe have remained constant since the end of World War II.[10] Under Stalin, Khrushchev, and Brezhnev, Eastern Europe has been regarded as a military buffer zone, protecting the Soviet homeland against any potential Western attack. The area has been considered important for ideological reasons, too, in that it has provided Moscow the opportunity to proclaim, at home and abroad, the increasing appeal of Soviet-style communism. Finally, control over the region has given the Soviet Union geopolitical proximity to the rest of Europe, with all the claims and advantages associated with being the dominant European power.

Although such military, ideological, and geopolitical goals are permanent in the Soviet political mind, they are no longer the only determinants of Soviet policy. At least five additional considerations growing out of recent experiences, developments, and pressures have produced a somewhat broader definition of the Soviet interest in Eastern Europe, one that may be briefly identified as a mixture of *hegemonical habits* and slowly evolving, if unevenly applied, *pragmatic flexibility*.

First, in response to expressions of nationalism and the region's chronic political instability, the Soviet leaders have recognized some of the particular needs and distinctive features of the several East European party-states. Whereas Stalin, who, between 1948 and 1953, could subordinate Eastern Europe to Soviet foreign-policy interests and to his own personal and ideological inclinations, his successors—on encountering open and persistent anti-Sovietism—have seemed willing to accommodate adaptations fostered by local conditions, traditions, and customs. The dilemma was obvious: if they were to follow a Stalinist approach, the expected result might be real or perceived ideological cohesion—but political instability. Conversely, should they adopt a more circumspect course and allow for national peculiarities, the East European regimes might be more viable—but also more difficult to control. As there was a price to be paid in either case, Moscow has rather grudgingly tended to acquiesce in *controlled change* away from Soviet patterns, especially when an East European country could make the threat of instability credible. (For example, the hard-earned Romanian, Polish and Hungarian reputations for national self-assertiveness have certainly helped these countries obtain more elbow-room in recent years.)

The *second* factor affecting Soviet policies has been the deteriorating economies of Eastern Europe. Though there was a time when Moscow, overlooking local needs, could impose its will and exploit these countries for short-term gain, such a Soviet approach now would only exacerbate economic problems and ignite political explosions. Today, the Soviet Union has a genuine, vested interest in the viability and prosperity of the East European economies—because its trade with Eastern Europe is essential to the Soviet economy, because Moscow needs increased East European military contributions to the modernization and general upgrading of the Warsaw Pact, and because serious East European economic problems create political tensions which, in turn, necessitate either costly economic rescue operations or military interventions, or both. As the Soviet Union has learned several times, the actual cost of sustaining an ineffective or near-bankrupt East European regime can be exorbitant.

Although it might appear that the Soviet Union would best serve its interests by actively encouraging gradual and controlled economic reforms throughout the area, this has not been its practice, perhaps because of political inertia, or a conviction that economic reforms, however carefully guided, would inevitably erode the region's political "superstructures." Whatever the cause, Soviet policy, while tolerating a measure of reform and experiment in some countries, has continued to rely on the old formula: fewer new investments, combined with Soviet aid and the enticement of future benefits accruing from regional integration. Inadequate as such an old formula may be to meet present and future needs, it still constitutes a more circumspect and indeed more accommodating Soviet approach to Eastern Europe than the economic exploitation of earlier times.

Thirdly, Soviet relations with the region have become complicated by new pressures within the world Communist movement. During the last decade, both China and the Eurocommunist parties have vocally opposed Soviet "hegemony" in Eastern Europe. As Hua Kuo-feng's 1977 visit to Romania and Yugoslavia illustrated, China plays its "East European card" rather actively in order to draw Moscow's attention away from the Sino-Soviet border, while the two Balkan countries want to maintain the Chinese connection in order to keep the Russians off balance. The piquancy of this international power game notwithstanding, it is unclear what specific security or economic benefits Peking can actually offer; after all, as the late Chou En-lai himself observed in 1971, "We will never betray our friends. We sympathize with small and medium-sized countries ... and we shall extend as much support as possible. But we are far away from Europe, and as one of our popular proverbs says, 'Distant water cannot quench fire.'" Even though China's fire brigade is as far away now as it was in 1971—something Peking, Belgrade, Bucharest, and even Moscow must realize—it is symptomatic of the Soviet political mind that Moscow still feels so very deeply threatened by the prospect of such an anti-Soviet Communist coalition, however remote and illusory that possibility may be.

As for the Eurocommunists,[11] while they can offer neither security nor economic benefits to Eastern Europe, their call for the easing of Soviet controls and for the limited expansion of civil liberties in the region has struck a responsive chord among their East European comrades. In contrast to China's exclusive stress on the principle of national autonomy and hence on pure anti-Sovietism, the Eurocommunists' appeal for gradual change in both foreign and domestic matters can build on what all the autonomists *and* reformers of Eastern Europe have sought for three decades. Given the Eurocommunists' advocacy of evolution rather than confrontation and the essentially European character of their platform they can offer something which is quite appropriate and constructive to the region's less orthodox elites and also less immediately threatening to Moscow. Significantly, too, the Eurocommunists—again unlike the Chinese—still belong to, and thus speak from within, an international movement of which the Soviet Union is the nominal leader; therefore, to the extent that Moscow still regards them as comrades rather than renegades, their electoral needs may militate against the resurgence of Soviet interventionism in Eastern Europe.

A seldom recognized *fourth* factor affecting Moscow's East European policies has been the Soviet leaders' preoccupation with the struggle for power in the Kremlin. For during both the "thaw" of 1953–56 and the reformist era of 1964–68 there was a coincident succession crisis in Moscow. In the first instance, Khrushchev extended the processes of domestic de-Stalinization to Eastern Europe, partly in order to discredit political opponents (principally Molotov) and partly in order to release regional tension pent-up during Stalin's last years. In the second instance, several of the East European regimes exploited the opportunity for maneuver afforded by the Soviet leaders' absorption in internal political matters. When released from these concerns, the Soviet leaders could once again clarify—and implement—policies which culminated in interventions in Hungary (1956) and Czechoslovakia (1968). It is possible, therefore, that the current succession crisis may erode, if only temporarily, Soviet dominance over Eastern Europe and thereby hasten existing tendencies toward autonomy and reform. Indeed, this eventuality might be prevented only if a new Soviet leader quickly becomes *primus inter pares*, obtaining almost at once the kind of authority Khrushchev was denied until 1957 and Brezhnev until 1968.[12]

Finally, the *fifth* factor influencing Soviet policies toward Eastern Europe has been Soviet relations with the West. Although the Soviet Union has not accommodated itself to the prospect of any East European country denying the leading role of its Communist party[13] or removing itself from the Warsaw Pact for the sake of Western trade and whatever else "détente" denotes, Moscow has nonetheless remained sensitive to the damage its East European policies could cause to the fabric of East-West relations. In other words, while the West has not deterred the Soviet Union from protecting its real or perceived interest in Eastern Europe, it can make the ultimate option of military intervention somewhat more difficult to adopt. After all, Moscow intervened in Hungary in 1956 when the West was deeply involved with the concurrent Suez crisis, in Czechoslovakia in 1968 when the United States was thoroughly preoccupied with the Vietnam war, and in Afghanistan in 1979 when Washington's attention was focused on the American hostages in Iran. In all three instances, the Soviet Union could, and probably did, assume that a firm or concerted Western response to Soviet military intervention was highly unlikely. In short, Moscow's perception of Western negligence, apparent indifference, or preoccupation elsewhere in the world has influenced Soviet choices in dealing with its East European dependencies.

On the whole, the five factors discussed above suggest that the changes that have taken place in Soviet–East European relations in recent years are important enough to temper Moscow's interventionist urge. The evolution of Soviet policy towards Eastern Europe points to tolerance for controlled change, economic experimentation, and even political liberalization. Indeed, the very fact that there is as much diversity in the region as there is indicates that decisions of considerable magnitude are locally made; the Soviet empire has been decentralized.

III

These no doubt hopeful tendencies may or may not continue towards Poland (or, for that matter, towards the rest of Eastern Europe). The Polish crisis is unique, and hence no simple tendency-analysis can explain current Soviet thinking. Put another way, the Polish crisis has presented the Soviet leaders with an experience substantially different from what they had to confront in the past in Eastern Europe.

First, the enormous significance of Poland for the Soviet Union cannot be compared to the importance Moscow has attached to any other East European country. Historically, Russia or the USSR has played a role in the partitions of Poland in 1772, 1793, 1795, and 1939; and it has been invaded by or through Poland in 1610, 1709, 1812, and in 1941. Towards the end of World War II, Stalin told the leaders of the Communist parties of Hungary and Czechoslovakia to seize power in "no less than ten to fifteen years" in order to draw Western attention away from the more rapid takeover of Poland; gradualism in those countries between 1944 and late 1947 was quietly explained to party cadres as Stalin's "Polish trade-off."[14] Poland's future was absolutely nonnegotiable because, aside from Germany's defeat, its capture constituted the most meaningful postwar gain for the Soviet Union. And that perception of Poland's significance remains, because of the country's location as well as the size of its population and its armed forces. It is a vital and necessary nexus between the USSR and Germany.

Secondly, unlike Hungary in 1956 or Czechoslovakia in 1968, the Polish movement for "renewal" is unique because it is organized and led by the industrial working class, the presumed mainstay of Communist regimes.[15] The Soviet Union may call these leaders misguided, antisocialist, anti-Communist, or anti-Soviet, but it cannot dismiss them as troublesome intellectuals demanding mainly "bourgeois freedoms." Instead, they are the very people the Communist regime was supposed to serve. Moreover, the workers' movement is national in scope, embracing at least one-third of the country's population and equipped with rather modern means of communications. Thus, not only is the Soviet Union forced to wrestle with the ideological dilemma of how to deal with another Communist state's proletariat, but it must also devise ways to curtail the activities of a huge, national movement which has had an opportunity to organize itself and which can, if necessary, defend itself. While the intellectual leaders of the Hungarian revolution and of the Prague Spring could be, and were, rather easily subdued,[16] the same thing cannot be expected to take place in Poland. Far more likely is the possibility of extensive fighting, particularly in the Baltic region, combined with passive resistance—political and economic—for a long time to come.

A *third* peculiarity of the Polish crisis is the economic condition of Poland—and of the Soviet Union. By aiding Hungary after 1956 and Czechoslovakia after 1968, Moscow was able to provide the necessary economic assistance to Kadar and Husak; in neither case did the aid package put an extensive or unbearable burden on the Soviet economy. Obviously, this is not the case now. The Polish economy cannot be compared to Czechoslovakia's in 1968 or 1969 or even to Hungary's in 1956–57, nor is the Soviet economy known to be endowed with surplus resources. If Solidarity is to be suppressed—with all the economic and political consequences that can be predicted— who is to pay for Poland's foreign debt? Who will feed the population? What will be the effect of the expected suspension of East-West trade on the Soviet Union and its East European dependencies?

Fourthly, in contrast to its preoccupation with other problems in '56 or '68, the West—and particularly the United States—is now paying close attention to the Polish crisis. Both in early December 1980 and during the tense days of late March and early April 1981, the United States made an unparalleled effort to publicize Soviet military preparations and to formulate a united NATO position. Despite the apparent temptation to focus exclusively on the Iranian hostage crisis in December and on El Salvador in 1981, Washington found enough political energy both to caution Moscow and to advise restraint to the leadership of Solidarity. By keeping the issue alive instead of quietly observing Soviet preparations—and then being confronted with a *fait accompli*—the United States has probably exacerbated divisions in the Kremlin and helped at least postpone any ultimate Soviet decision to intervene.

These four factors identify the uniqueness of the Polish dilemma, but they offer no easy conclusion for the Soviet leaders. The very significance of Poland probably argues for intervention of some kind; the fact that the movement for "renewal" is led by the industrial proletariat probably argues against it; the economic situation in both Poland and the Soviet Union suggests caution, as does the apparent interest of the West. All in all, the relative restraint displayed by the Soviet leaders so far implies their acute awareness of the costs of intervention.[17] They seem to know that, diplomatically, it would drive the Western Europeans closer to the United States and thus negate long-term Soviet diplomatic efforts to weaken the Atlantic alliance. Militarily, an invasion would entail the concurrent engagement of Soviet armed forces on two fronts (in Afghanistan and Poland) and hence the possible overextension of Soviet power. Economically, a Soviet intervention would prompt not only the termination of Western credits to Poland and of Western technology to the Soviet Union, but also a very expensive program of Soviet assistance to the struggling Polish economy. Ideologically, it would further erode Soviet prestige among workers and Communist parties everywhere. Politically, an invasion would effectively end Brezhnev's career in a Polish quagmire.

On the other hand, by allowing the PUWP to work out Poland's domestic problems by political means and without Soviet intervention, the Soviet leaders would show that they have become as confident about their political skills as they are self-assured about their military power. By refraining from the use of force, they would make it possible for the West to return to the conference table to discuss arms control and indeed arms reduction. By confirming that their notion of "different roads to socialism" signifies a serious commitment to noninterference, they would modify Western perceptions of their role in Eastern Europe. By staying out of Poland, the Soviet leaders would make a tangible contribution to the universal—including Soviet—goals of European security and global détente at a crucial time in East-West relations.

Which aspect of this balance sheet proves to be crucial in determining the ultimate Soviet decision may have been revealed by the time this chapter is published. As of now, it seems likely that events in Poland itself rather than broader, global considerations will ultimately influence the Soviet outlook. Thus, if the present Polish leadership (or the one that may replace it) is either unwilling or unable to regain authority, to stifle new, ever-increasing demands for "renewal", and especially to curtail democratization of the PUWP, then the introduction of some form of expanded military presence in Poland is all but inevitable. Yet, that fateful decision, as the Soviet and some of the East European leaders know only too well, will mark not an ending but the beginning of an extremely dangerous and even explosive decade in the Soviet empire.

IV

As far as the future evolution of Eastern Europe and Soviet–East European relations is concerned, one lesson of the Polish crisis of 1980–81 is that the Soviet Union is still prepared to accept economic reforms and even limited political liberalization. Departure from the Soviet norm is acceptable so long as it doesn't challenge party hegemony, so long as it constitutes controlled change, and so long as it is not accompanied by open anti-Sovietism. Indeed, in his speech at the 26th Party Congress, Brezhnev explicitly endorsed diverse economic experiments in Eastern Europe. He praised the way agricultural cooperatives and enterprises are organized in Hungary, the way the GDR has rationalized production and saved energy, and the way the "social maintenance system" works in Czechoslovakia. Such experimentation should be studied "more closely" and even utilized "more broadly," Brezhnev stressed, presumably by Soviet leaders and experts.

The promise of incremental change in Eastern Europe notwithstanding, the other lesson of the Polish crisis is that the region's Communist leaders find it excruciatingly difficult to pursue controlled, gradual change and to steer a course between what the people want and what Moscow accepts. With the notable exception of Janos Kadar in Hungary, they do not possess the political finesse the 1980s seem to demand of them. They are unnecessarily servile to the Soviet Union and rigid at home, and they make small concessions when it is too late to resist popular pressure for more. If they know what their people want and what Moscow can tolerate, they do not act accordingly. In short, they seem to lack both strategic thinking and tactical flexibility. Thus, "faithful" as the Honeckers, Zhivkovs, and Husaks may be to the Soviet Union, they are not serving Moscow's long-term interest in the stability of this volatile region.

In the absence of skillful, astute leadership, the future of much of Eastern Europe is therefore very uncertain in the 1980s. Unless the base of political and economic participation is expanded, there will be demands for fundamental change of the type the Soviet Union will find unacceptable. Under the circumstances, and given their preoccupation with succession and other matters of deep concern, will the Soviet leaders resort to military intervention or will they still encourage gradual reform to prevent sudden explosions? That choice, which is inherent in the Polish crisis, is a major item on the Soviet foreign policy agenda in the 1980s. If the Soviet leaders opt for gradual change, the emergence of a new type of political order in Eastern Europe—one that may be identified as "socialist pluralism in the Soviet sphere"—will become a new and promising reality rather than a Western pipe dream; it will be, indeed, the likely consequence of the Polish drama that has been played before anxious audiences everywhere in Eastern Europe.

Notes

1. This was heard in Poland in the fall of 1980. The Polish original went like this:
    Jeden Polak jest Papiezem,
    drugi wazny przy Carterze,
    kilku przed Brezniewem kleczy,
    reszta sie w kolejkach meczy.
2. "Report of the Central Committee of the CPSU to the XXVI Congress of the Communist Party of the Soviet Union and the Immediate Tasks of the Party in Home and Foreign Policy," Delivered by L. I. Brezhnev, General Secretary of the CPSU Central Committee, 23 February 1981 (Moscow: Novosti Press Agency, 1981).
3. *Ibid*, p. 7.
4. *Ibid*, pp. 7–8.
5. *FBIS Daily Report*, (Soviet Union), Vol. III, No. 37, Supp. 002 (25 February 1981), p. 41. Italics added.
6. *Ibid*, p. 25.
7. Agerpress, March 3, 1981.
8. The composition of the Soviet delegation suggested that since the same seven Soviet leaders had represented the Soviet side at the 5 December 1980 summit meeting of the Warsaw Pact as well (which also dealt with Poland), they constituted a decision-making committee or working group chosen to formulate Soviet policy toward Poland. The seven Soviet participants were L. I. Brezhnev; Yuri Andropov, chairman of the Committee for State Security (KGB); Foreign Minister Andrei Gromyko; Mikhail Suslov, secretary of the Central Committee; Nikolai Tikhonov, chairman of the Council of Ministers; Defense Minister Dmitri Ustinov; and Konstantin Rusakov, another secretary of the Central Committee. Six of the seven leaders are Politburo members, while Rusakov is in charge of relations with ruling Communist parties. See Bruce Porter, "Soviet and Polish Leaders Meet in Moscow," *Radio Liberty Research* (RL 102/81), 5 March 1981.
9. *Pravda*, 5 March 1981.
10. This section draws extensively on my contribution to *Perceptions: Relations Between the United States and the Soviet Union* (Washington, D.C.: GPO, 1979), pp. 147–52.
11. Cf. Charles Gati, "The 'Europeanization' of Communism?" *Foreign Affairs*, Vol. 55, No. 3 (April 1977), pp. 539–53.
12. Cf. Seweryn Bailer, *Stalin's Successors: Leadership, Stability and Change in the Soviet Union* (New York: Cambridge University Press, 1980)
13. Cf. Christopher D. Jones, "Soviet Hegemony in Eastern Europe: The Dynamics of Political Autonomy and Military Intervention," *World Politics*, Vol. 29, No. 2 (January 1977), pp. 216–41.
14. For evidence, see my forthcoming *The Gradual Road to Power: Stalin and the Hungarian Communist Party, 1944–1947* (1982). The study also identifies the reasons why the Soviet Union subsequently discarded the gradualist approach just prior to the founding meeting of the Cominform in September 1947.
15. For a comprehensive account and analysis of the status and condition of the industrial working class in Eastern Europe, including Poland, see Jan F. Triska and

Charles Gati, eds., *Blue-Collar Workers in Eastern Europe* (London: Allen & Unwin, 1981).
16 Cf. Ferenc A. Vali, *Rift and Revolt in Hungary: Nationalism Versus Communism* (Cambridge: Harvard University Press, 1961) and Jiri Valenta, *Soviet Intervention in Czechoslovakia, 1968: Anatomy of a Decision* (Baltimore: Johns Hopkins University Press, 1979).
17 This discussion has benefited from conversations with Seweryn Bialer, Abraham Brumberg, Ross Johnson, and Jiri Valenta. See also my letter to *The New York Times*, "A Balance Sheet for Moscow on the Poland Issue," 4 December 1980.

10

The 26th Party Congress Conference: The Soviet Union in a Time of Uncertainty

Richard Coffman and Michael Klecheski

The 26th Congress convened at a time of emerging changes in the Soviet Union's domestic and international situation. Some Western observers believe that these changes have engendered immobilism in the Soviet Union's domestic politics and disarray in its foreign policy. Others contend that such an evaluation is exaggerated, and insist that the impact of these changes has not been so pronounced. Assessments of the Congress vary according to interpretations of the gravity of these changes and the appropriateness of the policies selected by the leadership.

Discussions at the Rand-Columbia Conference, while revealing a general recognition of mounting problems confronting the Soviet Union, centered on two equally important sets of questions. First, have these problems become so severe as to place the Soviet Union at a crossroads requiring immediate and drastic action, or can they continue to be managed by the gradualist approaches of the past? A second set of questions concerned the perspectives of the Soviet leaders and the political context within which they act: Do the Soviet leaders perceive their problems as urgent? What is the range of responses that they find appropriate and politically feasible?

Drawing upon the discussions at the conference, this essay traces differing interpretations of Soviet domestic and foreign policies to contrasting reponses to these two dominant sets of questions. The relevance of these questions is magnified by the increasingly uncertain contexts within which Soviet domestic and foreign policies are formulated. These uncertainties complicate both the conduct of Soviet policy making and its analysis in the West. Domestic uncertainties are reflected in appraisals of the problems confronting the Soviet economy, the prospects for the 11th Five-Year Plan, and the urgency and political feasibility of Soviet reformism, and are reinforced by the approaching leadership succession. Diverging views of Soviet foreign policy are apparent in evaluations of the appropriateness of the decisions taken at the 26th Congress, the prospects for Soviet foreign policy in the 1980s, and the status of the East-West military balance. Thus we offer a thematic synthesis intended to supplement the analyses presented in the preceding chapters.

Domestic Policy

The Soviet Union in the late 1970s

While uncertainties have always characterized the study of Soviet politics, those posed by recent developments are particularly challenging to the Western observer. During the late 1970s, potentially threatening changes in the context of Soviet domestic policies became apparent, yet their full impact on the long-standing social and political stability identified in the Bialer paper remained unclear. For example, the precipitous decline of economic indicators for the years 1979 and 1980 sharply contrasts with the previously gradual downward trend in Soviet economic performance, but it does not necessarily signal a permanent disruption of that trend. Participants at the conference offered two competing assessments of these economic problems and of the appropriateness of the Soviet leaders' policy responses to them. These differences can be traced to alternative time-perspectives and conflicting evaluations of the years 1979 and 1980.

Some analysts emphasize that the sharp downturn in Soviet economic performance has occurred only during the last two years and is reversible. Focusing on the immediate situation, they point out that the adverse consequences of this downturn have, at the present time, been fairly limited; they therefore see little reason for grave concern about the economy's future performance. They also observe that the forces of change in the context of Soviet domestic policies have been developing for more than a decade, and will not be a feature unique to the 1980s. The sharp downturn in 1979-80 is understood to be an aberration from the pattern of gradual economic downturn characteristic of the entire post-Stalin period, a pattern which is expected to resume during the 1980s. Viewed from this perspective, the problems facing the Soviet leaders are qualitatively unchanged. These analysts conclude that the gradualist responses of the past will be sufficient to manage these problems until the demographic and resource constraints of the 1980s are reversed in the 1990s.

Other analysts insist on the importance of examining the situation from a longer-term perspective. While conceding that the impact of economic difficulties remains limited as of the 26th Congress, they stress that these difficulties will be magnified during the 1980s. They also regard the years 1979 and 1980 as marking the beginning of a new, more severe economic downturn. Economic problems continue to result from declining rates of growth of both inputs and productivity. However, these analysts argue, it is precisely the cumulative impact of these gradually worsening problems which has qualitatively transformed the problems confronting the Soviet Union. Advocates of this perspective conclude that new and dramatic measures are required to reverse these trends and revive the economy.

The 11th Five-Year Plan

The assumptions underlying these competing perspectives produce differing assessments of the 11th Five-Year Plan. Both perspectives maintain that Soviet economic difficulties will increase during the 1980s. Contrasting evaluations of the Plan's prospects depend on differing estimates of the severity of these difficulties, the extent and impact of resource stringencies, and the ambitiousness of the planned targets.

The baseline projection in the Bond-Levine paper asserts that the 11th Five-Year Plan is at least conditionally realistic. This projection assumes that the condition of the Soviet economy did not qualitatively change in the late 1970s. Productivity trends are expected to return to their pre-1979 patterns; improvements will be obtained as the result of a renewal of the capital stock. Optimistic projections for agricultural production are derived in large part from an expectation of favorable weather. Estimating the ambitiousness of the plan's overall targets is a statistically complex process, but the plan can be characterized as fairly modest in its goals. Indeed, investment targets might be deliberately low, reflecting the caution of planners who anticipate Western assistance which nevertheless must be omitted from the formally planned target pending completion of lending arrangements. Such assistance, if coupled with politically tolerable reallocations from the consumption sector of the economy, could permit overfulfillment of investment plans. The pressing demands of the many claimants for investment funds would then be satisfied, thereby spurring economic growth while easing social and political tensions. Achievement of fairly high levels of energy production would also facilitate the realization of the Plan's overall targets.

A number of participants at the conference questioned the soundness of the expectations underlying the Bond-Levine baseline projection. The low economic performance indices for the first quarter of 1981 reinforced these doubts. Particular problems were identified with regard to the overall measure of productivity, the pivotal factor in the fulfillment of the 11th Five-Year Plan. Some analysts, who attribute the recent downward trend in productivity primarily to factors other than adverse weather in agriculture, conclude that the 1968–78 productivity levels used in the Bond-Levine baseline projection for the plan are implausibly high. A rate tending downward from 1968–78 levels is viewed as a more plausible expectation. Doubts were also expressed with regard to the achievement of investment, energy, and agriculture targets.

Some economists questioned the realism of the planned investment targets, and noted that their realization may be impeded by domestic and international factors. Investment targets in the 11th Five-Year Plan are extremely taut, as Tikhonov admitted in his Congress speech. Given the size of the investment increment available for distribution, and the many claimants for these funds, it is considered unlikely that the government, having projected an already low rate of investment, can succeed in surpassing the planned investment targets. Such doubts are reinforced by the very real possibility that Soviet leaders, following the practice of the last thirty years, may sacrifice investments to promote consumer and defense-sector growth. Satisfaction of investment plans is further complicated by uncertainties in the international arena, particularly the Polish crisis. A Soviet invasion of Poland would poison East-West relations. Loan and credit agreements negotiated with the West would be cancelled, thereby depriving the Soviets of much-needed capital and technology and hindering the initiation of planned investments projects.

Even if the investment targets are met, the planned levels of investment appear inadequate to satisfy the demands of the various claimants in the economy. The enormous capital requirements of the proposed energy development programs impose an especially heavy burden. Some analysts have calculated that the proposed amount of capital investment in energy significantly reduces the amount of additional capital available for other industrial sectors. Even this level of capital investment in energy, however, will likely be insufficient to achieve the planned levels of development, particularly that of the newly announced crash program for expanded production of natural gas. In addition to these capital limitations, the plan is constrained by unrealistic technological requirements. The expected inability to produce a sufficient amount of rolled steel will impede deliveries of the pipeline necessary for the realization of this program. Given the long delays in applying compressor technology demonstrated by the Soviets in the past, the prospects for meeting the planned needs of this program are deemed to be poor. Barring the importation of technology, steel, and other materials from the West, the proposed gas development program appears unfeasible.

In contrast to the Bond-Levine baseline projection on agriculture, some observers characterize the prospects for the planned production increases in this sector as fairly grim. They note that agriculture during the 10th Five-Year Plan experienced the normal pattern of two good weather years, two bad years, and one average year. Therefore, hopeful expectations based on improved weather are unwarranted. Even if weather conditions were to improve, the consequent benefits should not be overestimated. As the Diamond paper explains, poor agricultural performance should not be attributed solely to climate and geography, but also to such structural problems as declining rates of inputs, low productivity, and overcentralized management. The 11th Five-Year Plan relies heavily on productivity increases to achieve its targets, but the failure of recent attempts to raise agricultural output and productivity offer little reason to expect that existing problems will be overcome. The dampening effect of these structural problems on production suggests that planned targets, notably those for meat and grain, are unrealistic. And even if these targets are met, some analysts project that agricultural production will only stabilize, without experiencing any real growth.

Despite stagnating per-capita agricultural production, the gradual rise of consumption has been maintained by a large and growing import program. During the early 1970s agricultural imports accounted for 18 percent of Soviet hard currency outlays; by 1980, that proportion had swelled—almost doubled —to 33 percent. In view of mounting hard currency constraints, some analysts anticipate that Soviet leaders will have increasing difficulty maintaining current levels of agricultural imports. In the absence of compensating domestic production increases, the social and political implications of such a situation may be significant.

Change and Succession in the 1980s

The perspectives which produce disagreement over the specifics of the 11th Five-Year Plan carry with them broader implications. Those analysts who question the feasibility of the plan focus on what they perceive to be qualitatively new and accumulating difficulties in the 1980s. Emphasizing these difficulties, they then ask what conditions would produce a systemic crisis in the Soviet Union.

Domestically, crises could occur within the party, the society, the leadership, or in center-periphery relations. One indication of a domestic systemic crisis would be an increase in social unrest beyond the effective control of the regime. For example, such a crisis could occur if the compact developed during the past two decades between the center and the native regional elites were violated. In the stringent conditions of the 1980s this could result from either cuts in regional investment or, conversely, increases in regional investment coupled with an influx of ethnic Russian bureaucrats into these regions. In foreign policy, a systemic crisis would be created by the widespread destabilization of the Soviet empire. The Soviet Union possesses political and military control of its empire, but it is an open question whether it can retain that control over Eastern Europe in the future, particularly in view of its limited economic influence.

A different perspective can be found among those analysts who deny the existence of a qualitatively new context. They assert that the current Soviet domestic situation will fall well short of becoming a systemic crisis because the regime retains the effectiveness and the capacity to control an unstable situation. Furthermore, a variety of policies could be adopted which would mitigate the effect of difficulties arising during the 1980s. For example, food subsidies could be cut, the six-day workweek restored, and preferential investment rates in Central Asia suspended in favor of the Ukraine and RSFSR—all without threatening the system's basic stability.

It is clear that fundamentally different estimates of the Soviet Union's present condition and future prospects divide Western analysis. Brezhnev's recent speeches, notably at the November

1979 and October 1980 Central Committee plenums, testify to the Soviet leadership's awareness of both the serious flaws in the functioning of the economy and the limitations imposed by mounting resource constraints. However, the incrementalist policies adopted at the 26th Congress suggest that the leadership, in contrast to some Western analysts, do not perceive a qualitative change in the problems they face. Beyond this general observation, Western observers disagree about the causes of this incrementalism and its near-term policy implications.

According to one interpretation, Brezhnev's perceived political dominance accounts for the incrementalist policies of the 26th Congress. Brezhnev is viewed as having strengthened his political position in the last five years. No changes were made by the 26th Congress in the membership of the Politburo precisely because Brezhnev had already made the necessary replacements before the Congress. This perception of Brezhnev as a powerful leader does not preclude the explanation that the gradualism of the downward trend of the economy during the entire post-Stalin period has habituated the leadership as a whole to temporizing and marginal policies. Thus, the leadership may not perceive economic changes to be dramatic, nor believe that the current economic difficulties—seen to resemble those of the past—require costly radical reforms. When analyzed in its own terms, then, the lack of policy initiatives can be understood as a deliberate and, from the leadership's perspective, an appropriate response; it does not testify to indecisiveness or paralysis in the face of perceived crisis.

Unless his health fails, this line of argument goes, Brezhnev will not be removed from power soon, nor will there be a change in the leadership's mindset or the existing incrementalism. Available alternatives have already been considered by the leadership during the past fifteen years, and their political palatability has not increased recently. Furthermore, it is believed that a leadership in its last years of power is preoccupied with retaining that power and thus seeks to avoid politically destabilizing changes.

The alternative interpretation, while granting that the leaders' advanced ages may have foreshortened their time-horizons and reduced their willingness to endure the sacrifices required by significant policy changes, nevertheless insists that the present leadership may be willing to adopt policies broader in scope than those of the past, though still within the confines of the existing system. Advocates of this interpretation acknowledge the absence of major initiatives at the Congress (aside from the new emphasis on gas production) but caution against judging the formation of policy solely on the basis of what happens at the Congress. As they point out, the history of the post-Stalin party congresses suggests that it often requires twelve to eighteen months after a congress for major policy initiatives to be revealed. This delay can be explained by the general secretary's need to consolidate his power within the leadership in order to secure support for his program. According to this argument, Brezhnev, confronted by Kosygin's reformist challenge, had not fully consolidated his position before the 26th Congress. The Congress is believed to have provided him with a forum to reinforce the preeminence of his conservative coalition.

What type of policies might be expected from this coalition? Most analysts argue that, given the current political context, the most likely initiatives would remain within the structural boundaries of the current system. There is little reason to expect that a Brezhnev generation which to date has not attempted any drastic restructuring of the economic and political system will now—in its last days of power—undertake such fundamental measures. The most that can be expected, it is argued, are large-scale projects which operate within short time-horizons and retain the traditional emphasis on a dramatic mobilization of massive inputs, while posing no challenge to the essential features of the system.

Both of these interpretations conclude that fundamental change is unlikely under the present leadership. There is also general agreement, however, that the approaching succession will introduce a new element of uncertainty. The depth and scope of the impending change in leadership should increase the vitality and volatility of Soviet politics. Evidence exists that a new political balance of power may be emerging within the leadership. Central Committee recruitment patterns have recently changed: the number of full members selected from the central party apparatus and the governmental bureaucracy has increased at the expense of these elites' regional counterparts. It is therefore possible that the underlying rules of political power formation, which ultimately will determine the succession, may be transformed. The political consequences of this change are unclear at the moment. Indeed, there is much disagreement about the criteria by which a successor is chosen, the actual conduct of the succession, and the likelihood that it will produce significant reforms.

Who will emerge from the succession as Brezhnev's replacement? Debate at the conference was sparked by the assessment in Jerry Hough's paper that Gorbachev, Grishin, and Andropov are the most likely candidates. This rejection of the prevailing assumption of Kirilenko's status as the probable short-term successor encountered several challenges during the discussions. It was noted that the Hough paper devotes a great deal of attention to the educational background of potential candidates as a determinant of the actual successor. For example, Hough mentions Gorbachev's legal training at prestigious Moscow University as evidence of his strength as a candidate. Some discussants commented that, given the absence of a direct relationship between higher education and recruitment for Politburo posts—particularly the general secretary's position—educational background should not be overemphasized. Furthermore, the practical relevance of education as a major determinant of political mobility is uncertain. It was suggested that educational background exercises a diminishing influence as an individual's career advances, and that factors such as experience and patronage become more important. Evaluated in these terms, Gorbachev's prospects significantly diminish; at present, he lacks the experience and political connections deemed necessary for a general secretary.

Kirilenko's prospects—and thus the case for conventional wisdom—are substantially enhanced by both his position in the Secretariat and his broadly based patronage network. The importance of prior membership in the Secretariat as a prerequisite for the general secretary's position—a relationship derived from study of previous successions—seriously reduces Grishin's prospects. Andropov's candidacy is jeopardized by his long-standing association with the security apparatus. The terror of the Stalin years remains a sufficiently vivid experience for much of the elite to prevent the appointment of a KGB chief as general secretary.

Discussion at the Conference focused not only on the name of the specific successor, but also on the process by which the succession will be conducted. Office and patronage were identified as the two critical sources of power during the succession. It is possible that the political prominence of the general secretary's office will be reduced, and that other leadership positions will also be subject to redefinition because, above all, the succession is a politically dynamic process. It is probable that the succession will develop in two stages. In the first stage of this scenario a member of the current leadership generation will succeed Brezhnev, but it is unlikely that a coup—such as that which ousted Khrushchev—would occur. During the second stage of the succession a new generation of leaders will attain power. Some participants suggested that this second stage could be accompanied by a diffusion of power within the leadership lasting well into the 1980s. This possibility is increased by the fact that none of the current candidates possesses a patronage base sufficiently broad to aggrandize power rapidly and decisively. However, other commentators noted that the opportunities for power aggrandizement presented by the many personnel changes which will inevitably occur during the succession might conceivably enable a powerful individual to consolidate his position rather quickly.

The conduct of the succession will significantly influence the types of policies which will be enacted during the 1980s. Examining this relationship, some analysts observe that since the successor is chosen not by the Soviet elite as a whole, but by the currently ruling Politburo, it is unlikely that the present leaders would select someone who disagrees with prevailing orthodoxies. Thus no immediate fundamental changes in policy should be anticipated; the mechanism of personnel change reinforces the incrementalism which already is so prominent in Soviet politics. Leadership selection by cooptation also may minimize the adoption of major policy innovations during the succession. Those individuals who reach the upper ranks of the leadership have done so by advancing within a relatively conformist environment which requires obedience to the bureaucratic rules of the game. This process encourages the promotion of those individuals perceived to share the attitudes of the existing, established elites. It is noteworthy that this type of career pattern is quite typical of those members of the elite now in their fifties who constitute the primary source of replacements for the present leadership.

Whereas some analysts detect pressures in the succession encouraging conservatism, others perceive opportunities for significant policy reforms. Many in the new generation of elites are believed to be frustrated with the inability of the current regime to solve existing problems. If these individuals acquire political power, they may attempt to redirect current policies in a reformist direction. Proponents of this argument suggest that the current hindrances to political innovation may be unique to the final years of the Brezhnev era and will be eliminated as a consequence of the succession. In response to this argument, those who minimize the prospects for meaningful change note that, in addition to the conformist pressures within the political process itself, reformist tendencies among the new leaders may be dampened by the conservative influence of ideology—a perhaps diminishing but by no means entirely irrelevant consideration.

The Nature of Soviet Reformism

Much of the disagreement regarding the future course of Soviet politics can be attributed to the uncertainty surrounding the succession process itself. Yet, as discussion at the conference showed, an even more important reason underlies these disagreements. There exist basic differences in the ways in which analysts comprehend the notion of reform. Differing understandings of this concept are integrally linked with diverging evaluations of the urgency of reform and the effectiveness of various reform programs.

Some analysts contend that the concept of reform should be limited to *structural* changes, thereby excluding consideration of *policy* measures. Defenders of this proposal emphasize that attempts to effect systemic change produce results very different from those obtained from incremental changes in existing policies. The question of the priority assigned to military expenditures, for instance, involves a policy issue concerning the reallocation of resources; it need have no effect on systemic features such as central planning. This argument concludes that to include both structural and policy changes within the concept of reform encourages both insufficiently discriminating analysis and unnecessary confusion.

The emphasis on structural change is related to the perception of a qualitative shift in the recent downturn of the economy. From this perspective, current economic problems are seen as systemic and incremental policies to correct them, which by their nature do not change vital structures, are seen as inadequate. For example, attempts to install self-financing (discussed in the Nimitz paper) are considered likely to fail because the non-bureaucratic mechanism necessary for its proper functioning is incompatible with the Soviet Union's "bureau economy." Current attempts to establish territorial-production complexes and reorganize ministries are believed to be merely a reshuffling of the enormous Soviet bureaucracy, whose operation is regarded as the fundamental systemic problem which must be combated by structural reforms.

According to this view, structural reforms require a redefinition of the link between success indicators and plan fulfillment, the derationing of producers' goods, and the correction of the current pricing system. This argument insists that only structural reforms of such scope will prove effective and that the implementation of frequent incremental reforms only exacerbates the poor performance of the economy by diverting managers' attention from the production process.

According to an alternative definition, incremental changes must also be included within the concept of reform. This formulation stems from the view that the cumulative effect of reforms which lie well within the purview of existing core values may substantially improve the performance of the Soviet economy. Furthermore, it is contended that those reforms having a small but positive impact are politically feasible, while reforms of a more sweeping nature are less likely to be undertaken by the Soviet leadership. Because of their potential economic effectiveness and political feasibility, then, it is considered important to study incremental changes, rather than disregarding them, in order to determine whether and how they can ease the problems confronting the Soviet Union during the 1980s.

This alternative interpretation is related to the position that the Soviet economy has not experienced a qualitative change. It does not consider the downturn in economic performance to be sufficiently drastic to necessitate the types of structural changes which would be required to raise the economy to a new growth pattern. Rather, only incremental reforms need be applied, to bring the economy closer to its existing technology frontier.

From this perspective, the series of reforms implemented during the past decade have produced some, albeit limited, improvement of the economic system. A representative incremental reform adopted at the 26th Congress involved increased support for private plots. While not breaking with past policies, this reform permits the allocation of additional land beyond existing limits to those farmers contracting to sell to the collective farm (*kolkhoz*) the feed-grain crops produced on their plots. To the extent that it improves the incentive system, this measure can raise agricultural production.

Finally, proponents of this position argue that it is precisely the currently difficult economic situation which makes incremental reform not only more necessary but also more feasible. Thus, the anticipated continuation of the downturn in the economy during the 1980s may in fact facilitate implementation of such reforms. For example, the relative scarcity of labor might finally alter the psychology which favors investment in new plants instead of in the modernization of old ones. The resulting increase in allocations to plant modernization, which would come to be recognized by planners and managers as a quicker and cheaper way to increase production capacity, would significantly ease pressures on investment funds in the 1980s.

While the precise content of future domestic policies is uncertain, it is clear that policy incrementalism need not be a permanent feature of Soviet politics in the 1980s. The dynamics of the succession might inject a new vitality into what has been during the Brezhnev era a rather conservative political system. It is also uncertain whether the present accommodationist style of Soviet politics simply reflects the personal preferences and political dominance of Leonid Brezhnev, who led the Soviet Union during a period of stability and relative economic well-being, or whether it reflects a generally accepted feature of the political process which can be expected to outlive Brezhnev. If the Brezhnev succession becomes an extended process, its existing political relationships could be redefined, and fundamental policies could be changed.

It is by no means a foregone conclusion that the Soviet Union will experience a precipitous economic decline or other systemic crisis during the 1980s, or that the new set of leaders will initiate sweeping policy innovations. Impressive conformist pressures, both attitudinal and institutional, pervade the Soviet system. Their effect, according to some Western scholars, reduces the political feasibility of a wide-ranging systemic transformation. Proponents of this view emphasize that the continuation of incremental policy changes will remain a likely possibility during and after the succession. The very real prospects of such persisting incrementalism require, then, that serious attention be devoted to the political economics of muddling through.

Foreign Policy

Soviet Foreign Policy at the 26th Congress

Discussions at the Rand-Columbia Conference exposed fundamental disagreements regarding both Soviet foreign policy's current configuration and its future prospects. Examination of the Brezhnev era's foreign policy in terms of the leadership's motivations and expectations yielded an image of significant achievements and frustrated ambitions. A similarly complex evaluation emerged from the analysis of foreign-policy pronouncements of the 26th Congress. Some observers characterized current Soviet foreign policy as incomplete and temporizing, while others considered this description to be premature or exaggerated.

The argument defending the appropriateness of the foreign policy adopted at the 26th Congress asserts that changes in the essential features of Soviet foreign policy are impending, but not yet present; thus the Soviet leaders perceive no immediate reason for departing from the modified détente policy outlined in Brezhnev's Report. The Report therefore should be understood not as mere propaganda or a nostalgic appeal to past formulae, but as an entirely appropriate response based on the very real possibility of conducting a two-track relationship with the West.

According to this analysis, the Soviet leaders believe that while détente with the United States has soured, other global trends favourable to the Soviet Union have further developed: Soviet influence in the third world has increased, especially since 1975; détente with Western Europe continues, while divisions within NATO deepen; the destabilization of the Persian Gulf region has significantly reduced American influence there. Above all, the Soviet Union remains territorially secure and strategically competitive. Trends in the military balance of power have not been reversed; the Soviet position continues to improve both centrally (that is, in terms of the East-West balance of power) and regionally. While the Soviet leaders are sensitive to possible reversals of these achievements and trends, they are by no means historical pessimists; they perceive exisiting problems to be the price which inevitably must be paid in order to underwrite a more assertive foreign policy.

This argument also claims that although increasing tensions with the United States have made Soviet policy-makers less optimistic about the correlation of forces in the world, they are by no means panic-stricken or resigned to an irreversible deterioration of their relations with the United States. While Soviet leaders are disquieted by the very real prospect of a remilitarized, reassertive American foreign policy, they have not prejudged the Reagan administration or abandoned their efforts to dissuade it from adopting a confrontationist posture. Soviet elites do not believe that the Reagan administration has yet defined its foreign policy; they are thus for the moment content to wait and see which policies will actually be adopted and how they will be implemented. This view contends that even if the

United States enacts a more assertive policy it will have to bear the attendant socioeconomic costs and domestic political backlash which might restrict its scope, if not also its tenure. Soviet elites are not yet persuaded that the United States can sustain the program proposed by the Reagan administration. When analyzing current Soviet-American relations, therefore, proponents of this position stress that it is important not to portray potential changes as accomplished facts.

If the Soviet leaders' perceptions are analyzed from this point of view, it is argued, there is no justification for the conclusion that the foreign policy of the 26th Congress is inadequate or indecisive. The Congress' inaction on the Polish crisis is seen to reveal the Soviet leaders' recognition of the complexity of the situation and the magnitude of the costs which would be incurred by invasion. Détente with Western Europe provides Soviet foreign policy with the opportunity to increase tensions within NATO and isolate the United States in its efforts to formulate a more militant and assertive response to the Soviet Union. At the same time, the Soviet leaders hope that détente with the West Europeans may oblige the Americans to soften their position and restore some elements of détente for the sake of preserving the alliance. Current Soviet foreign policy on détente has been devised in order to pursue both goals. According to this interpretation, the results of the 26th Congress therefore reveal not a Soviet foreign policy in disarray, but a sensible, carefully formulated response to a changing global context. The Soviet leadership's effort to keep its foreign-policy options open should not be mistaken for indecision or paralysis.

According to this view, current Soviet foreign policy is also justified by the domestic political benefits it can provide. The two-track détente policy, in the estimate of this position, has been designed to preserve access to Western technology and credits which can facilitate Soviet efforts to extract the Siberian resources which can then be traded for Western consumer goods. The Soviet leaders thereby hope to sustain their conservative domestic program and still provide regular increases in the level of consumer satisfaction while foregoing structural economic reforms.

As with domestic policies, disagreements about Soviet foreign policy can be traced to contrasting time-perspectives. Those who take issue with the preceding position insist that the "neodétente" strategy adopted by the 26th Congress neglects the fundamental foreign-policy problems confronting the USSR in the long run. The policy of differentiated détente is portrayed as essentially passive because it minimizes the Soviet Union's ability to blunt the military buildup promised by the Reagan administration. Exclusive détente with Western Europe risks sacrificing control over the incentives which might persuade the United States to return to a more balanced relationship with the Soviet Union. This argument further claims that much of current Soviet foreign policy is conducted according to a temporary, damage-limitation strategy which lacks the vision and decisiveness which the current situation requires. These shortcomings of Soviet foreign policy are seen to be especially visible in the Congress' failure to formulate an effective policy which might resolve the Polish crisis.

A number of participants asserted that the Soviet leaders have lost the policy initiative in Poland, and that there is no indication that their persistent retreats will be reversed, or that their present losses will be contained and stabilized. The process of worker-initiated reformism is not only "rolling," but also, in the Soviet leaders' view, dangerously open-ended. Most alarming is the disorder within the Polish Workers' Party itself, both at the grassroots level and within its central apparatus. To date, the Soviet Union has been unable to arrest, much less reverse, the reformist tide.

Poland, however, is not the only situation cited as an example of Soviet foreign-policy indecision. In contrast to those who assert the persisting relevance and viability of present Soviet policies, some analysts contend that differentiated détente is no longer adequate or appropriate because American foreign policy has undergone a qualitative and decisive change in its essential orientation. Whereas some observers argue that a broad gap separates the Reagan administration's rhetoric from the reality of U.S. purposes and capabilities, others insist that a fundamental shift has occurred in its perceptions, and that a corresponding reassertion of genuine resolve is evident in American foreign policy. According to this interpretation, a majority of the American public and of American policymakers now assume that the Soviet Union will not be inhibited by a "code of détente" and will exploit available opportunities in order to expand its influence and undermine America's geopolitical position. This changed perception of the Soviet Union has been accompanied by a decision to undertake a sweeping renewal of America's military capability.

Proponents of this position further contend that the reorientation of American policy effectively discredits the presuppositions of the Soviet Union's differentiated détente policy. Soviet leaders have not comprehended the implications of this change, and persist in the belief that the United States will not resolutely oppose Soviet international adventurism or other Soviet initiatives deemed inimical to American interests. These presumptions are no longer valid; they have been discredited by the reemergence of American resolve. The reaffirmation of détente at the 26th Congress is thus interpreted as a signal of increasing Soviet foreign-policy disarray rather than as a testimony to the Soviet leaders' responsiveness to shifting international circumstances.

Soviet Foreign Policy in the 1980s

Will Soviet foreign policy be significantly altered during the succession? Adventurism abroad might be employed as a substitute for meaningful domestic reforms or as a means of demonstrating personal leadership effectiveness (and thus expanding what is referred to in the Breslauer paper as "leadership authority"). On the other hand, increased social and economic opportunity costs imposed by military expenditures will provide incentives to reduce the military budget. At the same time, these internal pressures for reduced arms expenditures will be crosscut by persisting international tensions. How these issues will be resolved will depend on who the actual successors are. Domestic problems might encourage the new leaders to restrain themselves internationally and consolidate their position domestically. However, given the Soviet Union's expanded international influence, such a "siege mentality" policy would encompass a geographic scope wider than in the past. The Soviet Union could be expected to make a determined effort to preserve ties with its newly acquired allies in Africa as well as to consolidate its influence throughout Eurasia. It is uncertain whether such a policy of domestic consolidation would encourage East-West trade or whether it might reinforce the long-standing pressures for autarky.

In addition to changes produced by the succession, there is general recognition that changes are most likely to occur in the domestic context of Soviet foreign policy, the status of the Soviet empire—especially Poland—and the content and conduct of U.S.-Soviet relations.

The effect of the trade-off between defense expenditures and civilian investment constitutes one of the crucial domestic constraints on Soviet foreign policy in the 1980s. Rates of investment growth for the 11th Five-Year Plan are already at extremely low levels, and little room remains for further cuts. Even these planned low levels can be viewed as inappropriate from the standpoint of supporting satisfactory long-term GNP growth. If the plan is underfulfilled—a very real possibility in the view of some economists—then the regime will be confronted with the difficult choice of reducing either consumption or military expenditures in order to compensate for the investment shortfall. The possible demonstration effects of the Polish crisis make the CPSU hesitant to place the entire burden of budgetary cuts on consumption and may make them seriously consider reducing defense allocations.

The domestic strategy projected by this scenario significantly differs from the one employed by the Soviet leadership during the 1970s. In 1975, when the 10th Five-Year Plan targets were being finalized, a decision was made to reduce the civilian investment increment in order to provide the resources necessary to maintain the regime's commitment to both the social welfare of its population and its program of military expansion and international activism. If extended to the 1980s, such a reduction in civilian investment would have a more severe impact than in the past. It has been estimated that an increase in the growth of the defense budget from the present 4.5 percent yearly rate to 7 percent would consume between 66 and 80 percent of the entire increment of industrial investment planned for 1981–85. Conversely, if the defense budget is frozen at the 1980 level, then the available increment of industrial investment would be doubled. In view of the demand for investment capital in the civilian sector, the allocation of defense expenditures will have a major impact on the overall performance of the Soviet economy during the 1980s.

Eastern Europe poses especially difficult choices for the Soviet Union. Energy will become a decisive element in the determination of Soviet-East European relations during the 1980s. It is predicted that by 1985 Eastern Europe will require 35 million new tons of oil annually. If the USSR does not provide this increment—and several projections of reduced levels of Soviet oil production suggest that it won't—then the oil will have to be purchased from the international market at a price of at least $7.5 billion. These capital requirements place enormous hardships on the economies of Eastern Europe. Financing the projected level of energy imports would impose a new demand of 35 percent of the region's current total hard currency export earnings. Romania will be especially hard hit; how it will finance its energy needs for the next two years alone is difficult to foresee.

The financial burden on Eastern Europe will not be alleviated even if the Soviet Union can provide the necessary energy resources. If Soviet oil production continues to stagnate, then East European demand must be satisfied by natural gas exports. The Soviets have not yet made any formal commitments in this area, possibly because satisfying all of Eastern Europe's energy needs would consume almost one-quarter of the entire Soviet natural-gas production increment anticipated for the 11th Five-Year Plan period. Furthermore, this natural gas would be sold by the Soviet Union at nonsubsidized prices, thereby imposing a significant drain on East European financial resources.

The satisfaction of Eastern Europe's energy requirements during the 1980s clearly depends on its ability to pay for increased supplies. In his Report, Brezhnev offered cooperative Soviet-East European ventures as a possible solution. These projects would entail the sending of pipe, compressor stations, and technicians by the East European countries to assist in the development of Soviet energy resources, the output of which would then be shared on a proportional basis. Although this program may ultimately produce more energy, the Eastern Europeans would still have to borrow from the West in order to finance the provision of required inputs. In view of their already restrictive debt-service ratios, the new debt requirements of such a strategy would prohibit the requisite levels of borrowing by many of the East European countries.

The Soviet Union's problems in Eastern Europe are epitomized by the Polish crisis. The political situation in Poland continues to deteriorate and may be further destabilized by the outcome of the Polish Party Congress in July. There exists a real possibility that the Polish party whose authority continues to disintegrate, may even be transformed into a "de-Leninized" social democratic party. This situation would provide the first example of such a transformation of a ruling Communist party. Few at the conference expected the Soviet Union to tolerate such an extensive degeneration of the Polish party's authority. Given Poland's importance within the Soviet empire, the Soviet Union would be likely to invade in order to arrest the course of events and restore the party's political dominance.

Some analysts suggest that invasion has been delayed so far because the Soviet leaders believe that the more the situation in Poland deteriorates, the easier it will be to legitimate armed suppression as a necessary defense of socialism. Others suspect that invasion has not occurred because the Soviet leaders doubt that ideological cohesion within the bloc would be significantly increased or that the authority of the Polish party would be substantially enhanced as a result. Furthermore, it is projected that a Soviet invasion of Poland would evoke organized resistance not only from the Polish people but also from their army. There was general agreement at the Rand-Columbia Conference that the Soviets probably would invade Poland, but that they would wait until after the July Congress. Invasion and occupation might require as many as one million soldiers to reassert Soviet control over Poland. This type of commitment is unprecedented in the USSR's postwar use of force, and would impose a massive strain on Soviet resources and manpower.

The Soviet leaders might attempt to recover from the consequences of invasion in one of two ways. On the one hand, they may accept the costs of invasion—increased East-West tensions in the short run and the burden of suppressing a hostile Polish population—and hope for a repetition of their experience in the aftermath of the 1968 invasion of Czechoslovakia, when East-West tensions eventually subsided and party discipline was reimposed. On the other hand, the Soviet leaders may conduct a more belligerent, militant, intractable policy, and harden their attitude toward the West. Whatever impact the invasion would have on East-West relations, there would probably be little immediate consequent ferment in the rest of Eastern Europe, except among the intelligentsia. It is uncertain, however, whether broader-based negative reactions extending into the working class could be contained in the long run.

Relations with the United States constitute another critical variable in the determination of Soviet foreign policy during the 1980s. U.S.-Soviet relations can be markedly affected by international events which are beyond the direct control of either country, but the effects of such external circumstances should not be exaggerated. Some observers believe that increasing uncertainty in the Soviet Union's domestic situation provides the United States with an opportunity to influence Soviet foreign policy. For example, trade and credit agreements—a potentially important source of relief for Soviet economic stringencies—are believed to provide a basis for influencing Soviet international behavior. Those skeptical of this position argue that Soviet leaders, instead of moderating their foreign policy because of internal constraints and American pressures, are likely to react with a greater assertiveness.

Another perspective maintains that the direction of American policy and its impact on Soviet calculations will vary according to its underlying intentions. If the United States attempts to challenge and redefine the role and position of the Soviet Union in international relations, then it will adopt a policy of "global rollback." If, on the other hand, the United States concentrates on influencing the way in which the Soviet Union behaves internationally—without attempting to redefine the actual role of the Soviet Union—then it will conduct a policy of "regulated competition."

What would be the Soviet response to a more consistent, less ambivalent American global counterstrategy? Some analysts accept Solzhenitsyn's contention that the Soviet leaders, when confronted by resolute external opposition, prefer to recalculate their policies and retract adventuristic initiatives rather than maintain an assertive posture. This reasoning implies that, by acting forcefully on potential points of conflict early enough to influence Soviet risk calculations, the United States could avoid tests of strength and reduce the dangers of escalation. Assuming an imbalance of power in the Soviet Union's favor, this argument further suggests that a resolute policy toward the Soviets can promote American interests and minimize, or even reverse, previous setbacks.

Other analysts contend that the USSR would respond to a confrontationist American policy with a dual strategy incorporating elements of "selective détente" and "selective assertiveness." A selective détente strategy would seek to broaden the differences between the United States and Western Europe, preserve Soviet-European détente, and isolate the United States. It differs from current Soviet foreign policy in that it would not attempt to manipulate the residual détente with Western Europe as a potential means of moderating American behavior. This strategy, however, resembles current Soviet foreign policy in that it would still be marked by an essential preoccupation with the United States. A policy of selective assertiveness would not seek a direct global challenge to the United States but it would refuse to retreat in the key areas of the U.S.-Soviet competition. No confrontation would occur in El Salvador, for example, but continued Soviet resolve could be anticipated in areas such as the Persian Gulf region, Eastern Europe, and Northeast Asia.

The successes achieved by such a Soviet response would be in part determined by how the United States conducts its own foreign policy. Some analysts believe that the United States could blunt a Soviet selective détente strategy if American policy-makers demonstrated a greater concern for their European allies' interests than they have in the recent past. They argue that much of the current West European neutralism and pacifism which facilitates the Soviet selective détente approach results from a lack of confidence in both the constancy of U.S. behavior and the ability of the United States to conduct a measured policy toward the Soviet Union. The belief that American foreign policy can measurably influence Soviet policy calculations also applies to the second Soviet option, selective assertiveness. Advocates of this possibility reason that the risks of U.S.-Soviet confrontation attending a Soviet strategy of selective assertiveness can be minimized by an American policy like the one developed during the Cuban missile crisis: while giving priority to power considerations, this approach would leave the Soviet Union an option by which it could reduce its offensive posture without losing face.

The Military Balance

Can arms control negotiations make a positive contribution to the reduction of East-West tensions and restore the military balance of power between the United States and the Soviet Union? Some analysts voice unequivocal opposition to current arms control programs, arguing that the United States cannot realistically expect them to ease its security problems significantly. The Soviet leadership lacks the incentives to facilitate the reduction of the American security burden by participating in meaningful arms control talks. Nor should the United States support such negotiations simply for political reasons at the present time. Support for arms control encourages "arms control pietism" in the West, according to these analysts, and generates the mistaken belief that negotiations by themselves promote security. Conducting negotiations according to these premises permits a completely unreciprocated Soviet codetermination of Western security policy.

This position, however, is not universally accepted. Other analysts argue that arms control still provides a useful mechanism for regulating the U.S.-Soviet competition. They agree that the military balance must be restored, but claim that the resulting economic burden can be reduced, and the risks of uncontrolled escalation minimized, by carefully negotiated arms control agreements. For example, negotiations can reduce the fractionation problems encountered in the regulation of strategic weaponry. Given such potential benefits, this line of reasoning concludes, arms control should remain an integral part of the U.S.-Soviet relationship.

These differences regarding the utility of arms control negotiations are indicative of equally profound differences regarding the status of the overall East-West military balance. There exists a basic consensus in the West that the Soviet leaders have been committed to a persistent expansion of their country's military power during the Brezhnev era. There is substantially less agreement, however, not only about the motivations behind this buildup, but also about its implications.

Analysts who stress the monotonic rise in Soviet defense expenditures during the past two decades conclude that the enormous and prolonged Soviet defense effort has produced a corresponding modification of Soviet military capabilities. As a result, the USSR enters the 1980s with its military power not only intact, but also significantly enhanced. Some Western observers contend that the Soviet Union has achieved "essential superiority" in the East-West military competition—superiority not only in the quantity and quality of its forces, but also in the relationship between force capability (a function of size, deployment, doctrine, and ability) and the purposes these forces are designed to serve in particular geopolitical contexts. The Soviet Union enjoys essential superiority throughout Eurasia; only the rough parity with the United States in the intercontinental strategic domain mitigates the Soviet Union's military preeminence. Some analysts further project that the Soviet Union possesses the ability to fight and win a "general war" —that is, it could survive a strategic nuclear exchange with its political system intact, its society capable of recovery, and its economy able to produce the resources necessary for a renewed projection of military power.

The question of Soviet essential superiority remains a contentious issue. Some analysts argue that the practical significance of the Soviet military buildup has been exaggerated. They stress that the methodological complexities involved in calculating the Soviet defense burden can produce imprecise results which may unjustifiably inflate the size of the actual increase in the USSR's military power. This argument also questions whether an improved strategic position confers upon the Soviet Union a usable advantage in any military theater. Proponents of this view maintain that the practical effect of the Soviet military buildup has yet to be satisfactorily demonstrated. The Soviet invasion of Afghanistan and the possible invasion of Poland, for example, do not decisively prove that the Soviets adhere to a predictable pattern of aggression, or that they would have behaved very differently if faced by similar problems a decade ago, when their military position was considerably less well developed.

Other analysts, while granting that this argument contains a large element of truth, emphasize that changes in the Soviet strategic position nevertheless do influence the leaders' foreign policy calculations. The crucial question in this debate concerns how Soviet military advantages influence actual Soviet behavior. Two types of answers are offered. The first claims that the Soviet Union need not engage in direct tests of strength with the West in order to exploit its enhanced power position. Instead, it can be expected to conduct aggressive diplomatic programs designed to improve its position and expand its influence. According to this interpretation, the likely thrust of Soviet foreign policy in the 1980s will be to slow, deflect, and if possible prevent American efforts to reverse existing trends in the international environment which are deemed favorable to Soviet interests. The USSR will neither retreat before the United States nor adopt a confrontational posture. Instead, it will respond to assertive American policies by demonstrating its willingness to compete on an equal basis regardless of the costs. At the same time, the Soviets will conduct a major international political campaign designed to pressure the Americans into a less militant posture. The Soviet Union thus will attempt to preserve its military gains while simultaneously presenting itself as the champion of international equilibrium.

The second answer claims that the enhanced Soviet military capability has increased the leadership's propensity to conduct a high-risk foreign policy, thereby encouraging the prospects of direct East-West confrontation. This conclusion is derived from an interpretation of the decision to cut the civilian investment increment during 1976–80, as part of a deliberate Soviet plan to trade economic growth for expanded military power. Convinced that the current imbalance of military power between East and West will not be reversed or arrested in the near future, the Soviet leadership is now believed to be more willing than in the past to take foreign-policy risks in order to exploit or create new opportunities for expanding its influence.

Other analysts respond that there is no necessary relationship between increased military expenditures and a greater propensity to take risks. Soviet risk calculations are influenced more by the opportunities and costs presented by the international environment than by the interplay of domestic factors determining the composition of the defense budget. These analysts see the increased possibility of East-West confrontation more as an indirect consequence of the Soviet Union's expanded global presence than as a direct consequence of a conscious Soviet decision. Soviet vested interests today encompass a geographic and strategic scope wider than in the past. The USSR can be expected to defend these interests to the extent permitted by the prevailing military balance of power. For example, if challenged by an American strategy of global rollback, the Soviet Union will offer determined resistance in order to consolidate and, where possible, expand its influence. However, there need be no concomitant increase in Soviet risk propensities.

Many observers suggest that proper analysis of Soviet risk behavior requires a broader understanding of how the Soviet Union perceives its adversaries, particularly the United States. A common interpretation proposes that the Soviets envision the world as a battlefield with one central antagonist, the United States. The Soviet leaders conduct their bilateral relations with the United States guided by the belief that there exists an essential, uncompromisable incompatability of interests between the two nations. Soviet leaders assume that their country's influence can increase only to the extent that Western —particularly American—influence declines. Rather than seeking equality, they desire to supplant the West. Soviet foreign policy is therefore portrayed as intractable and motivated by an "attacking essence."

Other analysts note that intractability need not imply aggressiveness. Differences of interpretation arise from contrasting images of the political dynamics which define Soviet foreign policy. If one assumes that changes in Soviet military capability are the product of an action-reaction competition with the West, then there is no need to impute nefarious intent to the Soviet leaders. The Soviet military buildup appears in this light to be an inevitable, but perhaps controllable, aspect of the broader East-West relationship. However, if one assumes that the decision to reduce civilian investment during the 10th Five-Year Plan in favor of the military testifies to the leadership's willingness to achieve foreign-policy gains at the price of economic performance, then the military buildup, at least in the latter part of the 1970s, can be attributed to a deliberate choice by the leadership. An examination of the institutional and political context of the Soviet defense budgetary process yields still another interpretation of the Soviet military build-up. According to this view, the level of Soviet military expenditures is decided by a bureaucratic process which encourages not discontinuity and incoherence in policy, but incrementalism and consistency. This interpretation also diminishes the explanatory value of the action-reaction dynamic. An examination of the operations of the military sector's adminstrative and planning organizations, according to this view, reveals that much of the Soviet buildup derives from the inertia of domestic politics rather than from the competition of international powers.

Postscript: The Grain Embargo

The second session of the conference convened on the day the removal of the American grain embargo was announced. This action was interpreted by many at the conference as an unnecessary sacrifice of U.S. political-economic leverage. Renewed grain sales leave the impression that the United States is rewarding the Soviets for not invading Poland even though they remain in Afghanistan, whose occupation prompted the original decision to impose the embargo. At a time when American rhetoric insists upon a more steadfast posture toward the Soviet Union, actual policy reveals continuing vacillation.

The embargo's removal reinforces the position of those who argue that Soviet leaders are not yet reconciled to the inevitability of a long period of confrontation with a reassertive United States. It is true that the decision to remove the grain embargo can be explained solely in terms of American domestic politics, but it is uncertain whether the Soviet leaders accept such an explanation. Although there may be little impact on the actual amount of grain available to the Soviet Union as a result of the embargo's cancellation, its implications are both important and ominous. The United States has reduced its moral authority in NATO and will find it more difficult to convince its European allies to take a firmer stand in their trade policies with the Soviet Union. The grain embargo's removal creates further doubts abroad—especially within the USSR—concerning both American resolve and ability to implement a more assertive policy designed to counter what has become an increasingly activist Soviet foreign policy.

Conclusion

If a party congress is viewed as the forum for major policy initiatives in response to the dominant problems of the day, then the 26th Congress can only be judged a nonevent. The Congress offered few new responses to the domestic issues posed by a faltering economy and emerging social tensions. It cast little light on the eventual outcome of the impending succession. Nor were solutions offered for the foreign challenges presented by the deterioration of relations with the United States and the crisis in Poland.

Why was the Congress a nonevent? What significance should be assigned to this outcome? The answers to these questions are by no means clear. What is clear from the proceedings of the Rand-Columbia Conference, however, is that differing responses are rooted in prior assumptions about the likelihood that the Soviet Union is approaching a crossroads in the 1980s. Disagreement stems from different views of the problems confronting the Soviet Union.

Expectations that the Soviet Union is approaching a crossroads in its history orient one response. The situation anticipated during the 1980s appears analogous to that of the 1920s. Although the specific problems differ, this analogy is based on the view that the challenges posed are of comparable proportion. Whereas during the 1920s, when the Soviet Union felt isolated and encircled, the critical foreign-policy issue was the survival of the state itself, during the 1980s a central issue is expected to be the management of the empire. Added problems are created by the increasingly close linkage betwen defense spending and overall economic well-being. If in the 1920s a primary domestic issue was manifest in the industrialization debates, the Soviet domestic agenda of the 1980s will, according to this view, be dominated in large part by the need to affect a fundamental shift from an extensive to an intensive economic growth pattern. The expressed urgency of this shift arises from the perception of a qualitative change in Soviet economic performance beginning in 1979 and 1980. Extending the analogy, this view projects that the severity of problems will create pressures which may induce fundamental systemic changes as sweeping as those of the 1920s.

According to this view, the outcome of the 26th Congress itself raises serious doubts about the system's capacity to carry out those changes required by these grave challenges. The absence at the Congress of major policy initiatives is believed to reflect precisely that systemic paralysis which has permitted problems to accumulate, thus bringing the Soviet Union to a crossroads. In the 1980s this deeply rooted malaise may be replaced by a new vitality as a consequence of the succession. In this sense too, these scholars liken the present situation to that of the 1920s, when a confluence of serious domestic and international challenges with a major succession provided the opportunity for a fundamental redirection of the Soviet system.

The alternative response grants that changes are occurring in the context of Soviet policies, but does not believe that the Soviet Union has reached a crossroads necessitating major changes in the existing system. Foreign-policy setbacks have occurred, but are seen to be balanced by equally significant achievements. It is further argued that Soviet leaders lacked answers at the time of the Congress to some critical foreign-policy questions—foremost among them the future course of events in Poland—and therefore justifiably adopted a carefully crafted, wait-and-see approach. Domestic problems, while recognized, are not believed to be critical. No qualitative change is seen to be occurring in the Soviet Union's economic performance; economic problems can be managed, and their social and political consequences contained, within the existing system. Given this view of the domestic and international situation, the decisions of the 26th Congress appear to be appropriate responses to uncertain but far from grave conditions.

Perceiving no domestic or foreign problems comparable to those of the 1920s, advocates of this position insist that the historical analogy is unfounded. While uncertainty always surrounds a period of succession, it is argued that the objective conditions do not sustain the conclusion that the Soviet Union lies at a crossroads. There is little reason to expect, then, that the new leaders, any more than their predecessors, will feel obliged to undertake a basic restructuring of the system.

Considering the uncertainties which presently define Soviet politics, it is not now possible to determine whether the Soviet Union in fact has arrived at a crossroads. Nonetheless, as we have seen, two quite distinct positions have emerged among Western analysts of the contemporary situation, the cutting edge being precisely the existence of such a crossroads. The outcome of the leadership succession, the performance of the economy, and the conduct of Soviet foreign policy—particularly the management of the East European empire—will resolve the uncertainty which marked the 26th Congress. These developments will also provide the evidence to settle the debate which currently divides Western analysts. Thus, while the Soviet Union may or may not reach a crossroads during the 1980s, a crossroads in Soviet studies is surely to be expected.

Index

Note: Page numbers in bold type refer to chapters or large sections; page numbers in italic type refer to tables and figures

Afghanistan, invasion of 11, 15–16, 158; attitude of Western Europe to 16, 96
agriculture 31, **108–19**; conservative approach to, by Brezhnev (1965–76) 68–9; 11th Five-Year plan, goals of 110–19, 196–7, 203; Fruit and Vegetable Ministry 97–8; grain requirements 118–19, 120; harvest failures 88; inputs in agriculture (1976–80) 110, *111*; organization and management of 114, 115–16; output performance (1976–80) *109*; output projections using SOVMOD IV 99–*100*, 101–2; planned inputs/outputs (1981–5) 112, *113*, *115*; private sector, encouragement of 117–18, 120; product targets and performances in 9th-11th Five-Year plans *94*, *95*, *96*; 26th Party Congress, Brezhnev's speech on 72, 77, 78
Aleksandrov-Agentov, A. M. *53*
Aliev, G. A. *41*
Andropov, Iu. V. 40, *41*, 65; as potential transitional leader 45, 200
Arkhipov, I. 42
Armenia: employment of Central Committee members *50*; Party Members and Central Committee representation of *49*
Azerbaidzhan 63; employment of Central Committee members *50*; Party Members and Central Committee representation of *49*

Baibakov, N. K. 129
Bannikov, V. L., as head of atomic program 63
Belorussia: employment of Central Committee members *50*; Party Members and Central Committee representation of *49*
Bogoliubov, K. M. *53*
Brezhnev, Leonid I. 65; on Central Committee *53*; on 11th Five-Year plan 97; and energy policy 130; and foreign policy 156–9, 165; on Poland 179–80; in Politburo 40, *41*, 42; reformism and conservatism under (1965–76) 65, 65–71; speech to 26th Party Congress 72–4, 81–5, 86; and stabilization of Soviet Union 24–5; on technological innovations 144

Bulgaria 180

capital productivity 90
Central Committee, changes in composition of 46–56, 61–2, 64, 80–1; age distribution of *62*; employment of members, types of *46*, *47*; foreign-policy specialists on 52–4; KGB representation on 54–5; provisional representation, decline in 52; Republican Party Bureaus, occupations of members *48*, *49*; turnover among top officials 57, 61; of Union Republics *49–51*, 52–3, *58*; women representation on 55–6
Chernenko, K. U. 40, *41*, 42, 45, *53*
China, relationships with 8, 11, 183–4; American relations with 14, 160, 166
coal: growth projection, using SOVMPD IV *101*; output targets (1985) *123*; product targets and performances in 9th-11th Five-Year plan *94*, *101*; strategy, eclipse of 122–4, 131–3
Conference on Security and Cooperation in Europe (CSCE) 163
conservatism 65–6; under Brezhnev and Kosygin (1965–76) 67–71
consumer welfare, and 11th Five-Year plan 95
Czechoslovakia 180, 185; intervention in 163

defense: growth in expenditure 95–6; military balance with the West 213–17; projections using SOVMOD IV *100*, 101, 103–6
Demichev, P. N. *41*
Demidenko, V. P. 64
détente, with United States of America 8, 12, 159–61, 162–3, 168, 169, 207–8, 212; collapse of 12–15, 82, 163–4, 205
détente, with Western Europe 162–3, 207, 212; and benefits to Soviet Union 17–18, 168
Dolgikh, V. I. *53*
domestic policy 193–204, 218; and change and succession in 1980's 197–202; and 11th Five-Year plan 194–7; in late 1970's 193–4; reformism, nature of 202–4; *see also* internal environment
Dymshits, V. E. 130

economic situation: decreases in economic growth 87–9; and 11th Five-Year plan 195–7, 197–8, 203–4; and effects on political system 28–38; and ties with the West 75, 79, 175; *see also* agriculture, industry etc.
11th Five-Year Plan *see* Five-Year plan
energy 31; Brezhnev's speech to 26th Party Congress on development of 72–3, 76, 83–4; decision making on 129–33; growth projections using SOVMOD IV 100–*1*; investment resources, competition for 126–8, 196; new strategy, implications of 133–5; policies **121–35**; product targets and performances of 9th-11th Five-Year plans *94*; prominence of, at 26th Party Congress 122,*123*; substitution and conservation 125–6; *see also* coal, gas, oil
Estonia: employment of Central Committee members *50*; Party Members and Central Committee representation *49*
Europe, Eastern 163, **178–90**; deteriorating economics of 183; economic reform in 189–90; energy requirements in 1980's 209–10; and influence on Soviet internal environment 36–7, 209–11; *see also* Poland
Europe, Western; and attitude to Afghanistan invasion 16; and maintenance of détente, benefits to Soviet Union 17–18, 170–2, 173; and attitude to Russian intervention of East Europe 185
expansionism 169

Five-Year Plans (11th, 1981–5) 73–4, 78, **87–107**; alternative projections, using SOVMOD IV 99–106; domestic policy 194–7; general characteristics of 91–2; key issues 97–9; main indicators of plan 92–6; targets and performance of 9th-11th plans 92, *93–4*
foreign policy: expansionism of 169; of the 1970's 10–11; in the 1980's 208–13, 219; reformist approach to, by Brezhnev (1965–76) 69; and 26th Party Congress **156–76**, 204–8; *see also* United States of America
foreign trade 96, 102
Fruit and Vegetable Ministry 97–8

gas: exports of 134; growth projections using SOVMOD IV *101*, 102; new strategy for 121–2, 124–5, 133, 196; output targets (1985) *123*; product targets and performances in 9th-11th Five-Year plan *94, 101*; Siberia, development of 73, 85

Georgia: employment of Central Committee members *50*; Party Members and Central Committee representation of *49*, 53
German Democratic Republic (GDR) 180
GNP (gross national product) 88, 89, 93; growth projections using SOVMOD IV *100*, 101
Gorbachev, M. S. 40,*41*, 42,*53*; as potential leader 43–4, 200
Gostev, B. I. *53*
Grechko, A. 40
Grishin, V. V. 40, *41*, 45, 63, 200
Gromyko, A. A. 40, *41*, 159
growth investment, decline of 96

heavy industry, development of, in 11th Five-Year plan 73–4, 78
Hungary 185

industrial output: for 11th Five-Year plan 93–4, 196; projections of using SOVMOD IV *100, 101*; *see also* technological innovations
Instruments and Means of Automation, Ministry of (Minpribor) 149; and experiment on self-financing 149, *151*
internal environment **7–38**; economic situation, and effects on political system 28–38; Europe, Eastern, and influence on 36–7; leadership of USSR 24–8, *see also* leadership; Poland, effect of possible invasion on 22–3; stability of (1965–76) 8; weaknesses and strengths, assets and liabilities of 9–10; *see also* domestic policy
international environment **7–24**; foreign policy for the 1970's 10–11, *see also* foreign policy; Persian Gulf, involvement in 18, 172, 205; Poland, problems with 18–23, *see also* Poland; United States of America and détente 8, 12–15, *see also* détente, United States of America; Western Europe and détente 17–18, *see also* Europe, Western
investment: decline in growth of 95, 195–6; growth projections using SOVMOD IV *100*
Iran 158; possible involvement in 18
Iran-Iraq war 18

Kania, Stanislaw (head of PUWP) 178
Kapitonov, I. V. *53*, 63
Karlov, V. A. *53*
Katushev, K. 44
Kazakhstan: employment of Central Committee members *50*; Party Members and Central Committee representation of *49*

KGB, representation on Central Committee 54–5
Kirgizia: employment of Central Committee members *51*; Party Members and Central Committee representation of *49*
Kirilenko, A. P. 40, *41*, 42, *53*, 63, 200
Kiselev, T. Ia. *41*
Kosygin, Alexei 40, 59; and coal-oriented energy policy 129, 132, 135; reformist approaches to domestic economics (1965–76) 65, 67–71
Kriuchkov, V. A. 54
Kruchina, N. E. *53*
Kulakov, F. 40, 41
Kunaev, D. A. 40, *41*
Kuusinen, O. 45, 64
Kuznetsov, V. V. *41*, 53

labor: productivity, and 11th Five-Year plan 88–9, 94, 95; resources of 34, 152
Latvia: employment of Central Committee members *51*; Party Members and Central Committee representation of *49*
leadership, in Soviet Union 24–8, 35–6; Central Committee 38, 45–56, 57, *see also* Central Committee; change and succession of in 1980's 197–202; Council of Ministers 39, *60*; elite composition, changes in **39–62**; Politburo 38, 39–46, 57; postwar generation, rise of 56–62; turnover, among top officials 57
light industry 74, 77, 78; growth projection using SOVMOD IV *101*; Kosygin and reformist approaches to 70–1
Lithuania: employment of Central Committee members *51*; Party Members and Central Committee representation of *49*

management, reform of 98–9
Mazurov, K. 40, 41
Moldavia: employment of Central Committee members *51*; Party Members and Central Committee representation of *49*

NATO alliance 167, 172, 205
Non-Black-Earth zone development program 68, 72

oil: Eastern Europe, requirements of 209–10; exports of 134; growth projections using SOVMOD IV 100–*1*, 102, 103; output targets (1985) *123*; product targets and performances in 9th-11th Five-Year plans *94*; Siberia, and development of 73, 85, 131

Pel'she, A. Ia. 40, *41*
Persian Gulf 172, 205; involvement in 18
Petrovichev, N. A. *53*
Podgorny, N. 40
Poland 9, 11, 18–23, 156, 178, 179; invasion of, dangers of 20–3, 176, 206–7; Solidarity movement in 19, 187; Soviet response to developments in 62, 180–2, 186–8, 195, 210–11
Poliansky, D. 47
Politburo 38; budgetary policy of (1965–76) 67; changes in composition of 39–46, 80–1; members of in 1981 *41*, 57
Ponomoarev, B. N. *41*, *53*

Rakhmanin, O. B. *53*
Rashidov, Sh. R. *41*
reformism 37–8, 65–6; under Brezhnev and Kosygin (1965–76) 67–71; definitions of 66; in 11th Five-Year plan 98–9; nature of 202–4; and technological innovations *see* technological innovations
Republican Party Bureaus: occupations of members of *48*, 49, 55–6; turnover among officials 58
Riabov, I. 42
Romania 180
Romanov, G. V. 40, *41*
RSFSR: age distribution of officials 59, *61*; employment of Central Committee members *51*; KGB representation on 55; Party Members and Central Committee representation of *49*; turnover of, among Regional officials 59
Rusakov, K. V. *53*

Sakhmiuk, I. I. *53*, 64
SALT negotiations 14, 17, 21, 157, 162–3, 171, 172
Savinkin, N. I. *53*
Self-financing, and extension to state sector of industry 147–50, *151*
Shchekino experiment 68
Shcherbitsky, V. V. 40, *41*, 45
Shevardnadze, E. A. *41*
Siberia: development of 65, 68, 73, 85; and oil and gas strategy 124, 131
Solomentsev, M. S. *41*
SOVMOD IV (Wharton Econometric Model of the Soviet Union) 87, 99–106; alternative projections of 11th Five-Year plan 99–106; baseline projections 99–102; defense-growth projections 103–6; low-productivity projections *100*, 102–3
standard of living, and growth in mass consumption 31–2
Stepanov, V. T. 64

Suslov, M. A. 40, *41*, *53*

Tadzhikistan: employment of Central Committee members *51*; Party Members and Central Committee representation of 49

technological innovations 31, 74, 75, **140–53**; new investments, declining effectiveness of 145, *146*, 147, 196; obstacles to 141–7; producer incentives 145; reform measures 147–53; self-financing in state sector 148–50, *151*

Theater Nuclear Forces (TNF) in Europe 14, 16–17, 21, 172

Tiazhel'nikov, E. M. *53*, 64

Tikhonov, Nikolai A. 40, *41*, 42, 59; and 11th Five-Year plan 97; speech to 26th Party Congress 78–9, 80, 81–5, 87, 96

Tolstikov, V. 47

Trapeznikov, S. P. *53*

Tsukanov, G. E. *53*

Turkmenia: employment of Central Committee members *51*; Party Members and Central Committee representation of 49

Ukraine: employment of Central Committee members *51*; Party Members and Central Committee representation of 49

United States of America, relationships with 23, 158–9, 162–3, 166–7, 168, 170–1, 172, 205–6, 211–13; and attitude to Afghanistan invasion 15–16; collapse of détente, 12–15, 158, 163–4; détente 8, 159–61, 162–3, 168, 169, 207–8, 212; grain embargo 217; military balance 213–17; SALT negotiations 14 *see also* SALT; strategic parity 8, 12

Ustinov, D. F. 40, *41*, 42; as head of rocket program 63

Uzbekistan: employment of Central Committee members *51*; Party Members and Central Committee representation of 49

Wharton Econometric Model of the Soviet Union *see* SOVMOD IV

Zagladin, V. V. *53*
Zimbabwe 158
Zimianin, M. V. *53*